D0201817

LABOR AND EMPLOYMENT
RELATIONS ASSOCIATION SERIES

PUBLIC JOBS AND POLITICAL AGENDAS

The Public Sector in an Era of Economic Stress

Edited By
Daniel J. B. Mitchell

First Edition
ISBN 978-0-913447-05-5
Price: $29.95

LABOR AND EMPLOYMENT RELATIONS ASSOCIATION SERIES
Proceedings of the Annual Meeting (published electronically beginning in 2009)
Annual Research Volume (published in the summer/fall)
LERA Online Membership Directory (updated daily, member/subscriber access only)
LERA Newsletter (published electronically 3-4 times a year)
Perspectives on Work (published once a year in the summer/fall)
Perspectives on Work Online Companion (published twice a year as a supplement)

Information regarding membership, subscriptions, meetings, publications, and general affairs of the LERA can be found at the Association website at www.leraweb.org. Members can make changes to their member records, including contact information, affiliations and preferences, by accessing the online directory at the website or by contacting the LERA national office.

LABOR AND EMPLOYMENT RELATIONS ASSOCIATION
University of Illinois at Urbana-Champaign
School of Labor and Employment Relations
121 Labor and Employment Relations Building
504 East Armory Ave., MC-504
Champaign, IL 61820
Telephone: 217/333-0072   Fax: 217/265-5130
Websites: www.leraweb.org   www.employmentpolicy.net
E-mail: leraoffice@illinois.edu

CONTENTS

Introduction 1
Daniel J.B. Mitchell

Chapter 1—Effects of Deep Recession on Public Sector Pay,
Benefits, and Employment 13
David Lewin

Chapter 2—Local Government Restructuring in a Time of
Fiscal Stress 41
Mildred E. Warner

Chapter 3—Public Sector Employment in OECD Countries Post-
Economic Crisis 59
Sabina Dewan

Chapter 4—Cash-Strapped Governments: Privatization as a
Response to the Crisis of the Great Recession 79
Ellen Dannin

Chapter 5—The Great Recession's Impact on African American
Public Sector Employment 105
William M. Rodgers III

Chapter 6—Trends in the Relative Compensation of State and
Local Employees 133
Keith A. Bender and John S. Heywood

Chapter 7—The Fiscal Crisis, Public Pension and Labor and
Employment Relations 167
Ilana Boivie and Christian E. Weller

Chapter 8—California's Public Sector Adapts to the Great
Recession 195
Daniel J.B. Mitchell

Chapter 9—Public Service Cost Containment in Trinidad and
Tobago: Assessing the Impact of Contract Employment 237
Charlene M.L. Roach and Gloria Davis-Cooper

About the Contributors 257

Introduction

Daniel J.B. Mitchell

University of California, Los Angeles

In many respects, concerns and issues in managing employment are the same in the public and private sectors. There are traditional personnel responsibilities: recruitment, evaluation, incentives, discipline, retention, and compensation. But while these are common elements to both sectors, there are also substantial differences. Not surprisingly, a period such as the Great Recession and its aftermath—with the obvious strains it put on public sector budgets—tends to highlight differences. Readers may recall a quote attributed to financier Warren Buffett that "only when the tide goes out do you discover who's been swimming naked." Some state and local governments that had engaged in precarious fiscal practices indeed faced increasing public attention as their tax revenues receded. But that is not the whole story.

The reasons public sector workers and human resource practices are under scrutiny go beyond the impact of a recession putting the spotlight on already strained budgets. There are important public/private differences that account for the special attention visited upon the public sector starting with the Great Recession. The first of these differences was the timing of the response to the recession and its aftermath on revenues. The second difference involves employee compensation and the contrasts between public and private practices in that area. Intertwined with these two factors is politics.

Employment Response

As Figure 1 shows, there were major differences in the employment response between the private sector and state and local sector when the Great Recession occurred. The former sector exhibited a much sharper and more immediate drop in employment than the latter. Indeed, the state and local sector for a time gained jobs even after the start of the Great Recession in late 2007 (as dated by the National Bureau of Economic Research).

Generally, as depicted in Figure 2, public employment has historically been less variable than private employment in response to business cycles. In that regard, the Great Recession was no exception. The decision process in government is more cumbersome since it involves legislative decisions, which often occur with a lag. Tax revenue may respond to the cycle with a lag since taxes on personal income and profits are collected after

FIGURE 1
Private Nonfarm vs. State and Local Payroll Employment (December 2007 = 100)

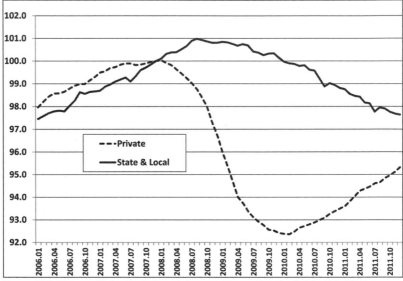

Source: U.S. Bureau of Labor Statistics website www.bls.gov (downloaded April 9, 2012).

FIGURE 2
Annual Percentage Change in Nonfarm Payroll Employment,
State and Local vs. Private

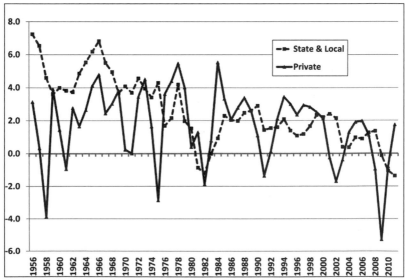

Source: U.S. Bureau of Labor Statistics website www.bls.gov (downloaded February 7, 2012).

the fact and are based on past income. Governments may also find ways—or simply be forced by their slow responses—to borrow to support current services. The decision lag in government means that the adjustment period is lengthened as accumulated debt is initially worked off even after economic recovery begins. As Figure 1 illustrates, private sector employment began to grow by early 2010. In contrast, after government employment peaked, the public sector exhibited a steady job decline through 2011, which reflected extended budget crises.

The consequences of the response differences between public and private employment were twofold. First, the public perception that government employment seemed more protected than private, particularly in the early stages of the economic downturn. Second, the ongoing crisis in public sector fiscal affairs (which was reflected in the protracted government employment decline) kept the issues of budget imbalances and state and local fiscal crises in the headlines.

Pay Practices

Table 1 compares pay and benefits of private sector and state and local employees. Generally, private sector workers receive lower pay and lower employer expenditures on benefits than workers in the public sector. Workers in private employment may receive no health insurance at all, whereas regular workers in public employment typically receive health insurance and are likely to have a generous plan compared to workers who have some form of health insurance in private employment. There is a similar contrast with regard to pensions. In particular, public workers most often have defined benefit (traditional) pension plans under which retirement income is determined by a formula based on age, service, and pay history. Private sector workers, if they have any employer-based pension, are more likely to have a defined contribution plan in which investment risk for target retirement income is borne by the employee.

Of course, the data shown in Table 1 are not standardized for occupation, education, or size of employer, which are the kinds of statistical adjustments economists (and personnel directors) would want to make. However, especially in the context of a recession-induced budget crunch in public employment, average unadjusted pay and benefit magnitudes may matter more for public perceptions than carefully controlled comparisons.

Public perceptions, however, do not occur in a vacuum. There is a political context. That context was aggravated by a pension funding crisis. Beginning in the 1980s, public pension funds were more likely to be invested in the stock market, making their returns more sensitive to the ups and downs of that market. As Figure 3 shows, the financial crisis of 2008 substantially reduced the market value of pension portfolios relative to their annual payouts. Moreover, the stock market gains of the 1990s had led to more generous promises of future pension payouts. Thus, unfunded liabilities appeared or grew as the value of pension portfolios dropped.

TABLE 1
Hourly Compensation of Private Workers Compared
to State and Local Workers, September 2011

	Private		State and local	
	Amount	Share	Amount	Share
Total compensation	$28.24	100.0%	$40.76	100.0%
Wages and salaries	$19.91	70.5%	$25.57	65.2%
Benefits*	$8.33	29.5%	$14.19	34.8%
Health insurance	$2.15	7.6%	$4.74	11.6%
Pension				
Defined benefit	$0.45	1.6%	$3.10	7.6%
Defined contribution	$0.56	2.0%	$0.33	0.8%

*Benefits include payments for leaves, supplements, insurance other than health, and legally required benefits not shown separately.
Source: U.S. Bureau of Labor Statistics (2011), Tables 4 and 5.

FIGURE 3
Ratio of Market Assets to Total Expenditures of
State and Local Pension Plans, 1957–2009

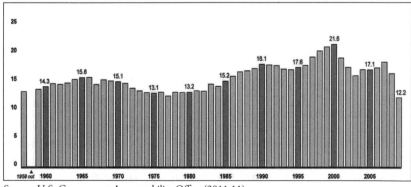

Source: U.S. Government Accountability Office (2011:11).

Politics

Particularly when focusing on state and local government, the kinds of jobs that come quickly to mind are basic services such as police, fire, and education. However, over the years and especially since the New Deal of the 1930s and the Great Society of the 1960s, state and local government has become intertwined with the federal government in the delivery of social welfare programs. Such programs may receive substantial funding from the federal government, but they are administered locally. For example, the New Deal ushered in unemployment insurance, a joint state–federal program. The same Social Security Act of 1935 that created the modern unemployment insurance system also provided federal support for state and local welfare programs. Medicaid, another joint federal–state–local program, was implemented in the 1960s.

It is a commonplace observation that the United States has seen widening polarization between the two major political parties along a liberal–conservative divide. At one time, conservatives might have favored local government over federal. But with the increased linkage of the two, a person who does not like social welfare programs may be hostile to all levels of government, not just federal. There is the old saying that a job not worth doing is not worth doing well. So, even the most efficient state and local governments—and those employees carrying out public functions—are likely to be disdained if one does not like what they are doing. And anything that smacks of inefficiency, irresponsibility, or even corruption will be an obvious target.

In fiscal year 2009, 22% of state and local expenditure fell into the social welfare category (public welfare, hospitals, health, social insurance administration, and veterans' services). Twenty-two percent of state and local revenue came from the federal government. Much of the expenditure of state and local governments goes to outside contractors who provide goods and services or to transfer payments. But about 37% of such expenditure goes to public employee pay and benefits (Barnett 2011). It is hard to separate social welfare from state and local governments and the employees of those governments, given these magnitudes.

Public and private employees are marked by substantial representation differences. As Table 2 shows, the private sector has become largely deunionized. The public sector, in contrast, has unionization rates similar to those achieved in the private sector by organized labor in the heyday of unionism back in the 1940s and 1950s. Union workers in the public sector, as in the private, are more highly paid than nonunion workers (again not adjusting for occupation or other characteristics). Seen along

TABLE 2
Union Representation in 2011

	Private	State Government	Local Government
Unionization rate	7.6% (6.9%)	35.0% (31.5%)	46.6% (43.2%)
Weekly earnings of full-time wage and salary workers			
Union	$875 ($878)	$946 ($956)	$967 ($973)
Nonunion	$716	$785	$743

Note: Figures in parentheses refer to actual union members as opposed to workers represented by unions who may or may not be actual members.
Source: U.S. Bureau of Labor Statistics (2012), Tables 3 and 4.

the conservative–liberal divide, however, unions in the public sector are more than collective bargaining agents. They are advocates of the programs their members administer (which conservatives often dislike) and opponents of outsourcing public functions to the private sector (which conservatives like). In terms of funding political activities, unions are much more likely to fund Democrats than Republicans. Unfortunately, there are no data sources that aggregate political contributions across state and local government. At the federal level in 2007–2008, however, more than 96% of union contributions in House of Representatives races went to Democrats. In U.S. Senate races, 93% of union contributions went to Democrats. In contrast, business interests are more likely to split contributions between Republicans and Democrats. Indeed, corporate and trade association contributions to members of the House and Senate were divided 50/50 in 2007–2008 (U.S. Bureau of the Census 2012:264). Put bluntly, weakening public sector unions equates to defunding Democrats.

In some states, such as Wisconsin and Ohio, there were overt moves by Republican governors and legislators to reduce the strength of public sector unions, ostensibly based on budgetary rationales. In states where the political balance did not allow such strategies, the funding problems of public pension plans became a proxy for such battles. The Great Recession's negative impact on the portfolio value of public pension plans combined with past excesses in pension practices and the fact that defined benefit pensions were becoming rare in private employment made the plans a logical surrogate.

The Chapters in This Book

With the exception of Chapter 9 (on Trinidad and Tobago), the Great Recession and its consequences linger in the background throughout this volume—and sometimes the foreground.

Chapters 1 and 2, by David Lewin and Mildred E. Warner, respectively, are overviews of the impact of the economic downturn on state and local government. Chapter 3, by Sabina Dewan, provides an international overview. These three broad chapters are followed by two chapters looking at the consequences of the downturn and of the resulting fiscal pressures. In Chapter 4, Ellen Dannin looks at pressures for privatization. William M. Rodgers III in Chapter 5 examines the differential impact on black and white public workers.

Two chapters then focus on pay issues. In Chapter 6, Keith A. Bender and John S. Heywood examine the issue of comparing public and private compensation. In Chapter 7, Ilana Boivie and Christian E. Weller focus on pensions and pension funding.

The final two chapters are case studies. In Chapter 8, I report how California, the most populous state in the United States, adjusted to the Great Recession. In the final chapter, Charlene M.L. Roach and Gloria Davis-Cooper look at the use of contract employees rather than civil servants for providing public services.

Overviews

In his chapter on the Great Recession and its impact on the public sector, Lewin first notes the large size of government employment. Not counting private contractors and their employees, government directly employs roughly one sixth of the U.S. workforce, and most of those workers are in the state and local sector. He notes that employment adjustment to the economic downturn in government was slower in the public than in the private sector. Pay adjustments in state and local government also were slower to respond. Apart from these macrolevel effects, there were a variety of eventual responses about restructuring of retirement plans and health care plans, with different states taking different approaches. Lewin notes the challenges to prevailing union–management relations that developed.

Warner reports in her chapter that one of the factors delaying the state and local response to the Great Recession was the availability of federal stimulus funds. Once these funds disappeared, however, adjustments had to be made. One difference she notes between public and private employers is that while revenues flowing to each are procyclical, the demand for many public services is countercyclical and rises during recessions. Apart from cutbacks even in the face of such demand, local governments have looked for efficiencies by pooling service delivery to achieve economies of scale. In some cases, local businesses and residents have assumed previous governmental roles through such devices as business improvement districts. In effect, the participants under these arrangements tax themselves for incremental services. Such arrangements existed before the Great

Recession, but the economic downturn stimulated a quest for new forms of service delivery.

The internationally oriented chapter by Dewan is macrofocused. She looks at all levels of government and includes central governments that have long been the locus of macroeconomic policy. Initially, she notes, many countries expanded their public sectors and public jobs to provide a fiscal stimulus as a counterweight to the unfolding economic crisis. However, after the initial move toward stimulus, many countries—worried about rising budget deficits and debts—reversed course. They embarked on austerity policies and public job cuts. A number of the countries Dewan cites are in the euro zone. It may be that this reversal of policy was a consequence of their earlier decision in joining the zone to abandon their national currencies.

As analysts cautioned before the euro zone came into effect, countries without monetary policies have limited fiscal discretion as a result. They become similar to U.S. state and local governments that must move toward austerity during hard times (Mitchell 1998). But although some countries had little choice about cutting back their public sectors, others with discretion (i.e., countries such as the United Kingdom, which retained national monetary systems) also cut back when voters chose conservative governments. Accordingly, some of the policy options described by Dewan appear to have been ideologically driven.

Privatization

Dannin notes in her chapter that the Great Recession led to another pre-existing arrangement receiving more attention: privatization. In a sense, the "make or buy" decision in the public sector is analogous to decisions that private employers regularly make. However, in the private sector, the decision-making process is conducted not within an ideological framework but on the basis of relative costs and quality control. In the public sector, advocates of outsourcing often do not base their decisions on a strict cost–benefit analysis. Rather, they simply prefer that the private sector be used to perform public functions and take it on faith that the outcomes of private provision will be better. Dannin also points out that resentment against public workers was used by post–Great Recession advocates of outsourcing to promote their agendas.

Demographics

Another consequence of the Great Recession, which Rodgers examines in his chapter, is a differential impact on black public worker's job losses compared to those of white public workers, with the former now having a higher probability of being laid off. In the private sector, the probability of job loss for blacks was also higher than for whites. However, prior to the Great Recession, blacks in public employment had a job loss probability equal to whites. What seems to have occurred, therefore, was an erosion of institutions in public employment that had previously equalized the rates.

Pay and Pensions

Bender and Heywood begin their chapter with the observation that there has long been a belief that public sector compensation should be comparable to private. In practice, determining comparability poses challenges because of occupational and other differences between the sectors. Like other authors, after standardizing for key differences in the public sector, they found no evidence of average overpayment in total compensation. They do note, however, the tendency of the popular news media to make comparisons without standardization. They also note that public sector pay from the lowest paid to the highest tends to exhibit more compression than is found in the private sector. The wage–benefit mix in the public sector is tilted more toward benefits, but much of that differential is because many private employers do not offer particular benefits (i.e., they spend nothing rather than just less on those benefits).

The public sector benefit that has gotten the most attention is pensions, the topic of Boivie and Weller's chapter. In that chapter, the authors note that alternatives to defined benefit pensions, such as defined contribution and cash balance plans, are more portable than traditional pensions, which have their primary payoff for career employees. Thus, private sector alternatives might be more attractive to other classes of workers. However, the mobility-retarding aspect of traditional pensions might be an advantage for public employers who do not want to lose key employees. At the same time, the incentives under defined benefit plans produce departures at retirement age, which can also be an advantage to public employers seeking new talent. Boivie and Weller examine the alternative approaches that public jurisdictions have used to reduce the costs of underfunded plans. They found evidence that most public employers have kept at least some key elements of the defined benefit structure in revised plans they have implemented; the authors also found evidence that public workers prefer the defined benefit approach.

Case Studies

California, the most populous state in the United States, also—and not surprisingly—has the largest public pension plan, CalPERS, and other large state and local pension systems. However, California's immediate fiscal problem involves the general fund budget which, as I report in Chapter 8, was in a precarious position before the Great Recession. The state's heavy reliance on direct democracy processes complicates its adjustment process. Pressures for fiscal prudence were weak during a long period from World War II through the end of the Cold War in which military expenditure fueled economic expansion; in an important sense, the state has not adjusted to the end of that era. Expectations of services exceed revenues. The Great Recession led to large deficits, budget cuts, and temporary tax increases. But the process was painful and even included an episode in which some state bills and tax refunds were paid in IOUs.

The use of contract workers (i.e., workers outside the regular civil service system) in Trinidad and Tobago was not a Great Recession story. As Roach and Davis-Cooper describe in their chapter, the development of that practice does, however, have some common elements with post–Great Recession public sector events in the United States. On its face, contract employment is a way of acquiring workforce skills that may be unavailable within the regular civil service. It may save money under some circumstances or have other benefits. On the other hand, it may have the downside of upsetting morale of regular workers. In that respect, it is similar to outsourcing and privatization. What the consequences may be of such practices is an empirical matter, and the decisions involved require an analytical approach and evaluation after the fact. However, in actual practice Roach and Davis-Cooper found the policy toward contract employment to be a mix of ideology and politics. In that respect, the Trinidad and Tobago story has strong analogies to many state and local decisions in the United States that were undertaken during and after the Great Recession.

A Still Unfolding Story

The issues described in this volume's chapters remained in flux as this book was being completed. The U.S. economy was in a recovery phase, albeit a recovery at a rather lackluster pace. Because of the lags in adjustment in state and local governments, the public sector was coping with prior circumstances even as the private sector resumed an economic expansion. At the international level, some European elections in the aftermath of the Great Recession have suggested that there is public frustration with austerity policies.

The Great Recession occurred in an era of political polarization, which the sharp downturn exacerbated. As a result, resolving the issues related to public sector employment was complicated by an infusion of ideology. Working out the problems that remain unresolved is likely to be marked by continued partisan struggles in state and local affairs, and in similar conflicts around the world.

References

Barnett, Jeffrey L. 2011 (Oct.). *State and Local Government Finances Summary: 2009.* U.S. Bureau of the Census. <http://www2.census.gov/govs/estimate/09_summary_report.pdf>.

Mitchell, Daniel J.B. 1998 (Jun.). "Eur-Only as Sovereign as Your Money: California's Lessons for the European Union." *UCLA Anderson Forecast for the Nation and California.* <http://www.anderson.ucla.edu/documents/areas/fac/hrob/Mitchell_Eur-Only.pdf.>

U.S. Bureau of the Census. 2012. *Statistical Abstract of the United States: 2012.* Washington, DC: U.S. Government Printing Office. <http://www.census.gov/prod/2011pubs/12statab/election.pdf>.

U.S. Bureau of Labor Statistics. 2011 (Dec. 7). "Employer Cost for Employee Compensation: September 2011." News release USDL-11-1718. <http://www.bls.gov/news.release/archives/ecec_12072011.pdf>.

U.S. Bureau of Labor Statistics. 2012 (Jan. 27). "Union Membership (Annual)." News release USDL-12-0094. <http://www.bls.gov/news.release/pdf/union2.pdf>.

U.S. Government Accountability Office. 2011 (Mar.). *State and Local Government Pension Plans: Economic Downturn Spurs Efforts to Address Costs and Sustainability.* GAO-12-322. <http://www.gao.gov/assets/590/589043.pdf>.

CHAPTER 1

Effects of Deep Recession on Public Sector Pay, Benefits, and Employment

DAVID LEWIN
University of California, Los Angeles

Introduction

What have been the effects of deep recession on pay, benefits, and employment in the state and local public sector of the United States? This chapter begins with a brief consideration of macrolevel pay, benefit, and employment trends in government during the first decade of the 21st century. That decade began with a relatively modest recession (2001), which was followed by recovery and relatively rapid growth (2001–2007) and then by deep recession (2007–2009).[1] Analytical emphasis will be placed on the relationship between public sector and private sector employee compensation—that is, pay and benefits—during this decade.

Next, the chapter turns to a microlevel focus on state governments that emphasizes recent actions taken by these governments to revise public employee compensation, especially fringe benefits and retirement and health care plans—actions that were motivated by deep recession and its aftermath. An especially notable feature of this analysis is to show how state-level decisions regarding public employee compensation apply not just to the employees of the state governments but also to the employees (and officials) of local governments in these states. Local government employment is typically much larger than state government employment.

The main lessons learned from these analyses are then identified and discussed, including lessons about public perceptions of public employee compensation, the likely effects of state-level reforms on public employee compensation, the power of state governments in effecting such reforms, and the role and limited influence of public employee unions on these reform efforts. Conclusions are presented in the final section of the chapter.

The Macro Picture

Employment

Government is a major industry in the United States, directly employing more than one sixth of the nonfarm workforce and indirectly affecting a substantial portion of private sector employment. Among major

U.S. sectoral divisions, government is second only to the trade, transportation, and utilities sector in terms of total employment (about 22.5 million compared to about 24.5 million) and is larger than professional and business services, health care, and leisure and hospitality. The government sector employs about twice as many people as the number employed in manufacturing.

Of the more than 22 million individuals who work for U.S. governments, about one eighth are employed by the federal government, about 23% are employed by state governments, and the clear majority, about 64%, are employed by local governments (Table 1). In state and local governments, more than half of the workforce, approximately 53%, is employed in education. In state governments, educational employment basically means the employment of faculty and staff in public colleges and universities that provide post-secondary education. In local governments, educational employment mainly means the employment of teachers and staff in public schools (i.e., K–12) that provide primary and secondary education.

The employment effects of recession typically differ between the public and private sectors (Table 2). For example, during the relatively mild 2001 recession and the two immediately following years (to 2003),

TABLE 1
Government Employment by Level, Total, and
Percentage, United States, 2009 and 2010

	Total		Total	
	2009 (millions)	2010 (millions)	2009	2010
Total	22,555	22,482	100.0%	100.0%
Federal	2,832	2,968	12.6%	13.2%
Federal w/o postal service	2,129	2,312	9.5%	10.3%
Postal service	703	65	3.1%	2.9%
State	5,169	5,142	22.9%	22.9%
Education	2,360	2,377	10.5%	10.6%
Other	2,809	2,765	12.4%	12.3%
Local	14,554	14,372	64.5%	63.9%
Education	8,079	8,011	35.8%	35.6%
Other	6,475	6,361	28.7%	28.3%

Source: Computed from ftp://ftp.bls.gov/pub/suppl/empsit.ceseeb1.txt, Table B-1.

U.S. nonfarm private sector employment declined by about 2.3 million, or 2.1%, whereas government employment rose by about 465,000 or 2.2%. During the deep recession of 2007–2009 and the first year thereafter (2010), U.S. nonfarm private sector employment declined by about 6.9 million, or 6.1%, whereas government employment declined by about 27,000, or 0.1%. During both recession periods, moreover, private sector employment declined more or less continually, while government employment rose during the early portions of the recessions and fell later.[2] Hence, by two years after the end of the 2001 recession, government employment had risen to 16.6% of all nonfarm employment and by 2010 had risen to 17.3% of all nonfarm employment. During the first two thirds of 2011, however, nonfarm private sector employment increased by about 0.8%, while government employment declined by about 0.2%, thereby reducing government's share of total nonfarm employment to 16.7%.

These trends imply that private sector employment is considerably more sensitive to macroeconomic (i.e., business) cycles than public sector employment. They also imply, however, that if recovery from the deep recession of the late 2000s is sluggish and slow to develop, government's share of total nonfarm employment will decline further. This is because such sluggishness means that state and local governments will continue to have

TABLE 2
Employees on Nonfarm Payrolls, United States, 2000–2011

Year	Total employment (in 000s)	Govt. (in 000s)	Govt. as % of total
2000	131,785	20,790	15.76
2001	131,826	21,118	16.02
2002	130,341	21,513	16.51
2003	129,999	21,583	16.60
2004	131,435	21,621	16.45
2005	133,703	21,804	16.31
2006	136,086	21,974	16.15
2007	137,598	22,218	16.15
2008	136,790	22,509	16.46
2009	130,807	22,555	17.24
2010	129,818	22,482	17.32
Sep. 2011	131,334	21,985	16.74

Source: ftp://ftp.bls.gov/pub/suppl/empsit.ceseeb1.txt, Table B-1.

budget deficits and will therefore have to determine the extent to which revenues can be raised and costs reduced to combat the deficits. If private sector employment rises slowly, then revenue growth will be insufficient to cover state and local budget deficits and policy makers will concentrate on deficit reduction through cutting costs. Given that state and local government services are human-capital intensive, such cost cutting will most likely be achieved by limiting or reducing public sector employment.

Compensation

Turning to the effects of recession on public employee compensation, these may be gauged in part by examining the Employment Cost Index (ECI) for state and local government workers compiled by the U.S. Bureau of Labor Statistics (BLS).[3] During the relatively mild 2001 recession and the two subsequent years, this index rose by 5.7%, which was larger than the 3.4% increase that occurred during the subsequent (i.e., 2003–2007) economic recovery. During the deep recession of 2007–2009 and the first year thereafter (2010), this index rose by 4%. However, all of the increase—and in fact slightly more—was concentrated in the first year of deep recession. By two years later (i.e., 2010), the index had declined by 0.2%. During the first half of 2011, the index declined by another 2.5%.

These changes can be compared to those that occurred for private industry workers during the same periods (Table 3). During 2001–2003, the ECI for private industry workers increased by 5.1%, which was about 0.5% less than for state and local government workers. During the subsequent economic recovery, however, the ECI for private industry workers declined by 0.1%, which contrasts notably with the 3.4% ECI increase that occurred for state and local government workers. During 2008–2010, the ECI for private industry workers increased by 2.1%, or about half of the increase for state and local government workers. During the first half of 2011, the ECI for private industry workers declined by 1.4%, or about half of the decline for state and local government workers. In sum, by the end of the first decade of the 21st century, the ECI for U.S. state and local government workers stood at 104.3 and the ECI for private sector workers stood at 101.0. Nevertheless, the ECI for both groups of workers was lower at the end of 2010 than at the onset (in December 2007) of deep recession.

These trends again imply that the private sector is more sensitive to macroeconomic (i.e., business) cycles than the public sector. In this instance, such sensitivity takes the form of compensation adjustments, with private sector pay and benefits clearly falling during recession and rising during recovery, whereas public sector pay and benefits rise during both recovery and mild recession but fall during deep recession. If recovery from deep recession is sluggish and slow to develop, however, then public sector compensation will either rise less rapidly than private sector compensation or will decline. As noted earlier, with sluggish recovery from deep recession, state and local governments will face

TABLE 3
Employment Cost Index (ECI), Constant Dollars,
March 2001–June 2011 (December 2005 = 100)

Year	Private industry workers			
	Mar.	Jun.	Sep.	Dec.
2001	94.9	94.9	95.7	97.3
2002	97.1	97.5	97.5	97.9
2003	97.7	98.8	99.1	100.0
2004	99.7	99.5	100.3	100.5
2005	100.0	100.1	98.5	100.0
2006	99.3	98.6	99.4	100.6
2007	99.6	99.1	99.7	99.6
2008	98.9	97.2	97.7	102.0
2009	101.2	100.0	100.2	100.5
2010	100.5	100.8	101.1	101.0
2011	99.8	99.6	NA	NA
	State and local government workers			
2001	93.4	92.9	94.7	96.0
2002	95.4	95.2	96.7	97.6
2003	96.6	97.2	98.1	99.1
2004	98.2	97.4	98.9	99.3
2005	98.7	98.4	98.1	100.0
2006	98.9	97.9	100.1	101.5
2007	100.7	99.8	101.6	101.6
2008	100.3	98.4	100.1	104.5
2009	103.9	102.9	103.8	104.0
2010	103.5	103.6	104.4	104.3
2011	102.7	101.8		

Source: www.bls.gov/web/eci/ecconstnaics.pdf.

continued budget deficits that necessitate public policy decisions regarding revenue increases and/or cost reductions. A slowly growing private sector means that public sector revenue increases will be modest at best. In this circumstance, state and local government officials will pursue budget deficit reduction through cuts in public employee pay, benefits, or both.

Political Climate

While these aggregate employment and total compensation data constitute one way of telling a story about the effects of deep recession on the U.S. public sector, another way is to consider the political climate affecting the public sector, especially the differences between that climate during mild recession and deep recession. During 2001–2003, it was not uncommon for government employers to undertake hiring freezes and workforce reductions and to seek bargaining concessions from unionized employees. These initiatives were especially pursued during the latter part of that recession and the immediate post-recession period and in some ways closely resembled similar initiatives that occurred during prior recessions, such in the mid-1970s, early 1980s, and early 1990s.[4]

During the more recent deep recession, government employers, especially elected officials, have for the most part gone much further than previously to hold public employees responsible for governments' fiscal adversity. Operating under this premise, some elected officials have sought to limit or eliminate public employees' rights to unionize and bargain collectively with their government employers.[5] This dynamic has played out largely at the level of state government and has been especially notable in 2011, ostensibly a post-recession year. Governors and other elected officials in Wisconsin, Ohio, New Jersey, New Hampshire, Florida, and several other states have led this charge. In doing so, they claim that public employees are overcompensated compared to their private sector counterparts. How valid is this claim?

Public–Private Sector Pay Relationships

Available evidence indicates that on a total compensation basis, the claim is not valid. To illustrate, consider the data shown in Figure 1 comparing the total compensation of public and private sector employees for the United States as a whole and for eight U.S. states (Keefe 2011). Nationally, these data indicate that, controlling for education, public employee pay is about 11.5% lower than the pay of comparable private sector employees. This differential declines to about 3.7% when fringe benefits are taken into account, which suggests in turn that fringe benefits are about 7.8% higher in the public than in the private sector.[6] This national picture encompasses considerable variation by state in public–private sector pay and total compensation relationships, which is also illustrated in Figure 1.

FIGURE 1
Public Sector Hourly Wages and Hourly
Total Compensation Compared to Private Sector
Employees of Equal Education (Keefe 2011)

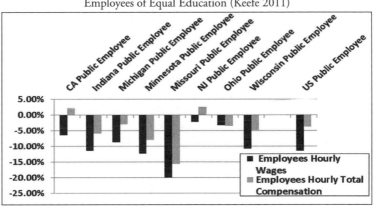

In a related study, Munnell and her colleagues (2011) point out that the ratio of public to private sector wages in the United States, which stood at about 103% during the mid-1990s, declined markedly to about 93% during the remainder of the 1990s, rose to about 96% by 2003, and declined to about 94% by 2010 (Munnell, Aubry, Hurwitz, and Quinby 2011). More to the point, Munnell and colleagues (2011) used Current Population Survey (CPS) data to estimate the U.S. public–private sector pay differential during 2006–2010, controlling for level of government employment (i.e., federal, state, and local), organizational size, region, and human capital and demographic variables such as education, work experience, race, gender, marital status, and immigration status. The main findings were that state and local government employees earn about 9.5% less than comparable private sector employees and that federal government employees earn about 14.5% more than comparable private sector employees. Because state and local government employment is about seven times greater than federal employment, aggregating these two empirical findings indicates that, on an overall basis, U.S. public employees earn roughly 6.5% less than their private sector counterparts.[7]

This study also found that public–private sector pay differentials varied considerably by job and pay level. When the basic wage equation was re-estimated by wage tercile, the results showed that public employees in the lowest third of the pay distribution were paid more than their private sector counterparts, those in the middle third were paid about the same, and those in the top third were paid about 20% less than their private sector counterparts. Hence, this study confirmed a finding first reported almost 40 years ago, which is that the job/occupational pay structure is considerably more egalitarian in public sector than in private sector organizations (Fogel and Lewin 1974).

Additional insight into public–private sector pay differentials is provided by focusing on knowledge workers, meaning those whose work requires specialized education, training, or skills. Analysis of CPS data indicates that knowledge workers constitute 32.3% of all private sector workers compared to 68.7% in state government and 67.5% in local government (Greenfield 2011).[8] In state and local government, workers with education below a college degree earn more than private sector workers with comparable education. By contrast, state and local government workers with college degrees earn less than their private sector counterparts, and this differential increases with higher levels of education.[9]

According to one recent estimate, knowledge workers in state government earn 20% less than knowledge workers in the private sector, and knowledge workers in local government earn 25% less than knowledge workers in the private sector (Greenfield 2011). These differentials are likely to increase in the wake of deep recession. Private sector demand for knowledge workers remains relatively strong. In contrast, state and local governments are restricting pay for public employees (including knowledge workers) through a combination of modest pay increases for some, pay freezes for others, and pay reductions for still others.[10]

Public–Private Sector Pension Benefits

The main nonwage benefits for both public sector and private sector employees pertain to retirement and health care. Traditionally in both sectors, pension plans were used to "finance" retirement benefits, and health insurance plans were used to finance benefits and mitigate risks associated with employee health. Also, most pension plan contributions traditionally were made by employers or jointly by employers and employees, and most health care insurance premiums were paid in whole or in large part by employers. During roughly the last quarter century, however, pension plans for private sector employees shifted from defined benefit to defined contribution plans (often so-called 401(k)s), and the costs of (premiums for) health care insurance plans increasingly shifted from employers to employees. While these developments in the private sector are well known, they did not spur similar shifts in the public sector, including during the relatively mild 2001 recession and subsequent recovery period.

These developments help to explain how and why various researchers find that public employee fringe benefits, notably retirement benefits (or pensions) and health care benefits (including for retirees), are considerably greater than comparable private employee fringe benefits. But they are not sufficiently greater to fully offset the pay disadvantage of public sector employees relative to the private sector. Hence, Munnell and her colleagues (2011) conclude that total compensation is about 4% less in the public than in the private sector—a conclusion that closely matches the conclusions reached by other researchers (Keefe 2011; Lewin et al. 2011; Bender and Heywood 2010).

Nonetheless, in the wake of the deep recession of the late 2000s, claims that state and local governments are in fiscal crisis have become widespread, and a great deal of attention has focused on the supposed role of public employee fringe benefits, especially retirement and health care benefits, in this crisis. For example, a much-publicized characterization of public employee pension plans is that they are $1 trillion underfunded. But rather than being due to overly generous pension arrangements, to the influence of unions on such arrangements, or to the behavior of public sector management and employees more broadly, the vast bulk of this underfunding is due to the sharp financial market decline that occurred during the deep recession of 2007–2009. As one public sector pension expert put it, "If [state and local government] pension funds had earned returns just equal to the interest rate on 30-year Treasury bonds in the three years since 2007, their assets would be more than $850 billion greater than they are today" (Baker 2011:1).

Only about $80 billion of this underfunding (or shortfall) resulted from the decisions of state and local governments to cut back their pension plan contributions during the 2007–2009 recession. Hence, any upswing in financial markets—about a 20% increase in the value of publicly traded equities occurred between mid-2009 and mid-2011—will reduce the underfunding of public employee pensions. Even without such a development, however, the aforementioned increase in the underfunding of state and local government employee pensions amounts to less than 0.2% of projected gross state product over the next 30 years for most states, and less than 0.5% of projected gross state product in states with the greatest underfunding. It is mainly for this reason that various pension specialists regard the current public sector pension shortfall as manageable and consider that "most state and local pension funds have been seriously misrepresented in public debates" (Baker 2011:15).

Also typically missing from such debates is recognition or acknowledgment of the fact that for many state and local government employees, pension funds substitute for federal Social Security as a source of retirement income. This is the case for nearly half of all public school teachers—the largest group of local government employees—and about two thirds of police and firefighters in local government (ICMA 2011). This point is especially germane in light of the fact that the average (annual) retirement benefit for public employees is estimated to be $22,600 (ICMA 2011; Boivie and Almeida 2009).

Public–Private Sector Health Benefits

Regarding health care, the rising costs of premiums for health insurance policies has presented challenges to public sector and private sector employees alike. The average family health insurance plan cost (i.e., premium) for private sector employees increased from $5,742 per year in 1999 to $13,770 per year in 2010, adjusted to 2009 dollars (Lewin et al. 2011). Comparable data for the public sector are not available; however, a study of teachers employed in the state of Illinois found that the average family health insurance plan cost increased from $5,758 per year in 1993 to $10,905 per year in 2008, again adjusted for 2009 dollars (Olson 2011). Such rates of cost (premium) increase are not sustainable over the longer run, which is why both private and public employers are undertaking various initiatives, such as increased employee co-payments, deductibles, and additional limitations on catastrophic illness payments, to control employer health care expenses. Such initiatives are also aimed at health care payments for retired workers, who represent an especially substantial portion of overall health care costs paid by older companies and governments.

The Compensation Trade-Off

State and local government employees typically contribute less than private sector employees to cover their respective health care costs, and they also receive a relatively higher proportion of their total compensation in the form of health insurance benefits, although in this regard there is considerable variation by state (Lewin et al. 2011). The same is true of pension benefits; that is, public sector employees receive a relatively higher proportion of their total compensation in pension benefits than do private sector employees (Bender and Heywood 2010). Consequently, there is a wage–benefits trade-off in government employment generally and in state and local government in particular, whereby public employees accept relatively lower pay in exchange for relatively higher benefits.

This trade-off is not a new phenomenon but rather one of long standing. What is new and motivated by deep recession, however, are the widespread calls by elected officials for state and local governments to change their employee retirement and health care policies, practices, and financing, and, in this respect, to follow private sector trends. It is the perceived public–private sector benefit disparity that appears to be the main driver of elected officials' claims that public employees are overcompensated and are therefore primarily responsible for governments' fiscal crisis.

Unionization and Collective Bargaining

Further to remedy this disparity and enable change, say many elected officials, public employees should also have their unionization and collective bargaining rights curbed or shorn. This particular claim is further supported by the continuing decline of private sector, but not public sector, employee unionization. Today in the United States, less than 7% of the private sector workforce is unionized, whereas about 35% of public sector workers are union members. Public employee unionization is especially prevalent in education (meaning largely among teachers) and to a lesser but still substantial extent in health care. Elected officials in state and local governments are therefore able (and obviously willing) to claim that the overcompensation of public employees is mainly attributable to union influence. That claim in turn has led such officials to initiate the afore-mentioned efforts to restrict and/or eliminate public employee unioniza-tion and collective bargaining rights.

In sum, the deep recession of the late 2000s has fundamentally shaped a political climate favoring the reduction of public employment, public employee compensation, especially benefits, and public employees' exer-cise of unionism and collective bargaining rights. These deep recession-induced effects have persisted and expanded during the post-recession period. They stand in sharp contrast to the relatively modest effects on the political climate associated with the mild recession of the early 2000s and with similar recessions, ranging from relatively deep to relatively mild, that occurred during the last quarter of the 20th century.

The Micro Picture

At a more microlevel, consider the findings from a survey of state and local government human resource executives and professionals conduct-ed in late 2009 by the Center for State and Local Government Excellence (2010).[11] This survey found that the current economic climate (i.e., deep recession) caused two thirds of the state and local governments repre-sented by the respondents to implement hiring freezes, about 60% to institute pay freezes, 40% to conduct layoffs, 30% to initiate furloughs, 20% to offer early retirement incentives, 10% to make pay cuts, and 5% to undertake employee buyouts.

Survey respondents reported that almost half of these governments post-poned employee retirement dates and about 11% accelerated employee retirement dates. A slight majority of state and local governments repre-sented by the respondents to this survey had made changes to employee health care plans. Among these governments, 70% increased employee contributions to the plans, 24% reduced health care benefits, and 10% decreased employer contributions to the plans. While a majority of these governments did not make changes to their employee retirement plans, among those that did about 18% instituted higher employee contributions to the plans and about 5% replaced a defined benefit plan with a defined contribution plan.

These findings can be compared to those reported by the National League of Cities, which conducted a survey in mid-2010 of the finance officers of 1,055 U.S. cities.[12] About 80% of the survey respondents indicated that their city governments "were instituting some kind of personnel-related cut" (Hoene and Pagano 2010:5). More specifically, respondents reported that 74% of the cities initiated hiring freezes, 54% froze or reduced employee salaries and wages, 35% conducted employee layoffs, 23% adopted new early retirement provisions, 22% effected employee furloughs, 17% reduced employee health care benefits, 15% revised their union contracts, and 7% reduced employee pension benefits. These findings are notable because the survey was limited to the local government level (i.e., cities), the respondents were finance officers rather than human resource officers of their local governments, and 44% of the respondents were employed by relatively small cities (populations between 10,000 and 49,999).

As indicated above, these two surveys were conducted in late 2009 and mid-2010. However, there is every reason to believe that the types of actions regarding state and local government employment and employee compensation reported by these survey respondents have broadened and deepened since then. For example, according to the International City and County Management Association (ICMA), "More state and local governments enacted significant modifications to improve the long-term sustainability of their retirement plans in 2010 than in any other year in recent history. In the past few years, nearly two thirds of states have made changes to benefit levels, contribution rate structures, or both; many local governments have made similar fixes to their plans" (ICMA 2011:1).

A detailed report of these changes was provided by the National Conference of State Legislatures (Snell 2010). This report found that in 2010 alone, 19 states enacted a wide variety of modifications to their public employee retirement and health care plans affecting both state and local government employees within their respective jurisdictions.

Changes in Retirement Plans: Illinois

To illustrate some of these changes, in late 2010 the state of Illinois adopted Public Act 96-0889, which specifies new financial contributions that the Chicago Board of Education is required to make to the Chicago Teachers' Retirement System through fiscal year 2013.[13] The same law also raised the retirement age to 67 for employees who became members on or after January 1, 2011, of the Chicago Teachers' Pension Fund and pension funds of the Chicago Metropolitan Water Reclamation District, Cook County government, Chicago municipal government, Cook County Forest Preserve, Chicago Park District, Judges' Retirement System, General Assembly Retirement System, State Employees' Retirement System, Illinois

Municipal Retirement Fund, Teachers' Retirement System, Chicago Laborers, and the State Universities' Retirement System. The only major exclusions from this law are the Chicago Transit Authority, Chicago fire and police departments, suburban fire and police departments, and certain employees covered by the sheriff's formula in the Illinois Municipal Retirement Fund.

Changes in Retirement Plans: Colorado

Also in late 2010, the state of Colorado enacted legislation (specifically, SB-146) that increased by 2.5% employee contributions to the Public Employment Retirement Association (PERA) for state employees, troopers, and judges, and decreased employer contributions by the same amount. A related Colorado law enacted in late 2010 reduced and otherwise limited PERA's commitment to make post-retirement cost of living adjustments. Further, this law raised the age and service requirements for state employees to retire and receive retirement benefits, placed a cap on salary increases to count toward calculation of highest average salary in determining retirement pay, and required PERA-covered state and local government employees to increase their contributions to PERA from funds that would otherwise be used for salary and wage increases.

Changes in Retirement Plans: Missouri

The state of Missouri was especially active in early 2010, as perhaps implied by the legislature's "First Extraordinary Session of 2010," changing numerous provisions of its public employee retirement plans in a law known as HB1. HB1 specified new contributory tiers for employees who become members of the Missouri Department of Transportation and Highway Patrol Employees' Retirement System (MPERS), the Missouri State Employees' Retirement System, or the retirement plan for judges. In particular, those hired after January 1, 2011, must make a pre-tax contribution of 4% of salary; previously, none of these plans required an employee contribution. Also under this law, most Missouri state employees are required to reach age 67 with at least ten years of service, rather than the previous 62 years of age with at least five years of service, to be eligible for normal retirement and benefits derived therefrom. Elected officials in the state of Missouri will henceforth be eligible for normal retirement at age 62 with one four-year term of office, in contrast to the prior age of 55.

Changes in Retirement Plans: New Jersey

In the state of New Jersey, Public Law 1 (SB 2) of 2010 incorporated numerous changes to public employee retirement systems. For example, new members of the Teachers' Pension and Annuity Fund (TPAF) and the Public Employees' Retirement System (PERS) will be eligible for coverage only if they work 35 or more hours per week (or 32 or more hours per week for political subdivision employees). While employees who work less than 35 hours per week may be eligible to enroll in the Defined Contribution Retirement Program (DCRP), the membership compensation threshold for such enrollment was increased to $5,000 from $1,500.

Another provision of this law increased the retirement calculation multiplier for new TPAF and PERS members from 1/55 to 1/60, the latter having been the pre-2001 multiplier in this state. Especially notable is the provision of Public Law 1 specifying that the maximum compensation for determining retirement contributions for new employees who become covered by the Police and Firemen's Retirement System (PFRS) and the State Police Retirement System (SPRS) is a base salary equivalent to the annual maximum wage contribution base for Social Security. Further, the maximum retirement allowance for a new member of TPAF or PERS will be calculated using the average annual compensation for the highest five years of service, rather than the previously specified highest three years of service, and for a new member of the PFRS or SPRS, the maximum retirement allowance will be calculated using the average annual compensation for the three highest years of service, rather than the previously specified final year of service.[14] These and other changes adopted by the New Jersey state legislature are estimated to result in about $1.6 billion of state and local government savings between fiscal year 2013 and fiscal year 2016.

Changes in Retirement Plans: Minnesota

The state of Minnesota enacted Chapter 359, Laws of 2010, which required increased employer and employee contributions to several state and local government retirement plans. As examples, for the State Patrol Retirement Plan (SPRP), the annual employer contribution was increased by 2% of salary and the annual employee contribution was increased by 3% of salary. For the Public Employee Retirement Association (PERA) General Employee Plan, both the employer and employee contributions were increased from 6% to 6.25% annually. For the PERA Police and Fire Plan, the employer contribution was increased from 14.1% to 14.4% annually and the employee contribution was increased from 9.4% to 9.6% annually. For the Teachers' Retirement Association (TRA), both the employing unit contribution rate and the member contribution rate began to be increased by 0.5% annually for four years on July 1, 2011.

This legislation also decreased compound interest on deferred retirement annuities provided by the Minnesota State Retirement System (MSRS), PERA, and TRA from 3% before age 55, 5% after age 54 for employees hired before 2006, and 2.5% for employees hired after 2006, to 2%, 1%, and 0%, respectively. In addition, the new legislation increased the vesting requirements for newly enrolled members of the various Minnesota state and local government retirement plans. For the MSRS General Plan and the SPRP and PERA General Employee Plans, the vesting period was increased from three to five years of credited service for employees hired after June 30, 2010. For the PERA Police and Fire Plan, the pre-legislation three-year cliff vesting provision was replaced by gradual vesting, moving from 50% with five years of service to 100% with ten years of service. Also of note, the legislation raised the early retirement annuity reduction from 1.2% to 2.4% annually for members of the SPRP and from 2.4% to 5% annually for members of the MSRS Correctional Plan.

Changes in Retirement Plans: Pennsylvania

In late 2010, the state of Pennsylvania enacted legislation (HB 2497) that made several changes to the Public School Employees' Retirement System (PSERS) and the State Employees' Retirement System (SERS). Main changes included the establishment of "collars" through fiscal year 2013–2014 on increases in public employers' annual contribution rates to PSERS and SERS, and changes in contributions for future employees who become members of PSERS on July 1, 2011, or thereafter, or of SERS on January 2, 2011, or thereafter. Regarding public employee contributions to retirement plans, the Pennsylvania legislation featured a novel provision whereby employees' annual contributions will increase by 0.5% if the actual rate of return to the PSERS or SERS retirement funds investment is 1% or more below the actuarially assumed rate of return and will correspondingly decrease by 0.5% if the actual rate of return is 1% above the actuarially assumed rate of return. In no instance, however, can the employee contribution rate drop below the regular contribution rate or increase by more than 2%.

Further, the legislation created a new PSERS member class that will make the same 7.5% annual retirement plan contribution as current employees make but have a 2% benefit accrual rate compared to the 2.5% benefit accrual rate for current employees. It also established an optional new class of PSERS membership that provides a 2.5% annual benefit accrual rate but requires covered employees to contribute 10.3% of their base pay to the retirement plan. Similar arrangements were established in SERS, which covers members of the Minnesota General Assembly, except that the employee contribution rate for new members is 6.5% rather than 7.5% annually and the contribution rate for optional membership in the new class is 9.3% rather than 10.3% annually.

Changes in Retirement Plans: Louisiana

The state of Louisiana enacted legislation in 2010 (Act 992) that made several changes to its four retirement systems: the State Employees' Retirement System (LASERS), the Teachers' Retirement System (TRSL), the School Employees' Retirement System (LSERS), and the State Police Pension and Retirement System (LSPRS). Some changes apply to employees who are currently covered by these plans. For example, the annual contribution rate for most members of the LASERS was increased from 7.5% to 8% of salary; for hazardous duty, member contributions were increased from 8% to 9.5% of salary. The annual contribution rate for employees covered under Louisiana's Judges' Plan was also increased, specifically from 11.5% to 13% of salary. Other changes applied largely to employees who become eligible for coverage under one of these retirement plans on January 1, 2011, or thereafter.

One such change specified that for teachers, hazardous duty personnel, and certain other categories of public employees, an employee's retirement pay will be based on that employee's average compensation during the five highest-paid consecutive years of employment rather than on the three highest-paid consecutive years of employment (the five-year retirement pay formula already applied to general state employees and LSERS members). Accompanying this provision of the law is a 15% anti-spiking cap applicable to all new members of the aforementioned retirement plans. Another change basically raises the age and service requirements for receiving retirement pay. In particular, teachers in Louisiana were previously able to retire and receive full retirement pay at age 60 with at least five years of service or at age 55 with at least 25 years of service. These retirement arrangements were eliminated and replaced by a requirement of age 60 with at least 10 years of service.

Changes in Retirement Plans: Michigan

The state of Michigan also enacted public employee pension reform legislation in 2010, with a major focus on the Michigan Public School Employees' Retirement System (MPSERS). Michigan Act 75 requires all school employees hired after July 1, 2010, to be enrolled in a hybrid defined benefit and defined contribution retirement system. This hybrid plan also increased age and service requirements for the defined benefit portion of this plan and for two other defined benefit plans that covered school employees at the time the new plan was enacted. In particular, the final average compensation for determining school employee retirement pay was increased from the final three years of service to the final five years of service. The minimum retirement age was set at 60 with at least ten years of service compared to the prior 55 years of age with at least ten years of service in one pre-existing retirement plan and 30 years of service with no minimum age in the other pre-existing retirement plan. Employee purchase of service credit to meet retirement plan service requirements was eliminated, as were cost of living adjustments to pension allowances. Finally, the new defined contribution benefit was set at a maximum employee contribution of 2% of salary with a 50% employer match or, in other words, a maximum employer contribution of 1% of an employee's salary.

In addition, Michigan Act 75 created an early retirement incentive plan for most state employees, including civil service, unclassified, legislative branch, and judicial branch employees. Beginning January 1, 2011, employees who elect early retirement forfeit their right to a lump sum payment of the value of their accumulated annual leave and sick leave. They will instead receive such payment in 60 monthly installments. Further, retirees who contract with the state to provide services must forfeit their retirement benefits while serving in this capacity.

Changes in Health Care Plans: New Jersey

Several of the states that have recently made changes to public employee retirement plans have also made changes to public employee health care plans. Again to illustrate, New Jersey Public Law 2 of 2010 alters the State Health Benefits Program (SHBP) and the School Employees' Health Benefits Program (SEHBP) with respect to eligibility, cost sharing, choice of plan, application of benefit changes, waiver of coverage, and multiple coverage under existing plans. Most notably, perhaps, the law requires that after the expiration of applicable collective bargaining agreements, "active employees of the state, local governments and boards of education will contribute 1.5% of base salary toward the cost of health care coverage under the SHBP and SEHBP" (Snell 2010:19). Further, employees of the state and local governments and boards of education who become members of state- or locally administered retirement systems on or after the law's effective date will be required in retirement to pay 1.5% of their pension benefit toward the cost of health care coverage under the SHBP and the SEHBP. Notable, too, is that this post-retirement contribution toward health care coverage is (or will be) in addition to any other amounts agreed to in negotiations between unionized public employees and their employers.

Changes in Health Care Plans: Michigan

In the state of Michigan, Act 75 requires all members of the Michigan Public Schools' Retirement System (MPSERS) to contribute 3% of annual compensation in an irrevocable trust to pay for health care benefits for retirees and their eligible dependents. Employees who earn less than $18,000 annually will contribute 1.5% of compensation to the trust during 2010–2011 but will contribute 3% annually thereafter. A related Michigan law, SB 1226, made additional changes to public employee health care coverage and costs, including eliminating an option that allowed retirees to elect health care insurance coverage other than that provided by the Civil Service Commission (CSC) while continuing to receive a state subsidy equal to that for insurance provided by the CSC. After January 1, 2011, retirees must pay the full cost of any alternative health care coverage.

Changes in Health Care Plans: Kentucky

Other states have also made changes to public employee health care plans irrespective of whether they made changes to public employee retirement plans. To illustrate, in 2010 the state of Kentucky passed Act 159, which replaces pay-as-you-go funding of retiree health benefits with a new advance funding arrangement that is estimated to save the state $560 million in subsidies. Effective July 1, 2010, most members of the Kentucky Teachers' Retirement System (KTRS) will contribute an additional 0.25% of salary annually to a medical insurance fund, with this contribution rate scheduled to increase to 3% annually during the next six years. Retired members will participate in this plan by paying either the Medicare Part B premium if they are eligible for Medicare or by paying the equivalent amount to the medical insurance fund if they are under age 65. For retirees under age 65, the initial payment levy was set at one third of the health care insurance premium but will rise to 100% of the premium by July 1, 2012. For all retirees, these contributions will be deducted from pension payments.

Changes in Health Care Plans: Connecticut and New Hampshire

In the state of Connecticut, a new State Employees Bargaining Agent Coalition Agreement, reached in 2009, required all new employees who are eligible for state-paid health insurance to contribute 3% of their annual compensation to offset the cost of retiree health benefits. Effective July 1, 2010, all health care–eligible employees with less than five years of state service as of that date were required to begin contributing 3% of compensation to the Retiree Health Fund until they either complete ten years of service or otherwise qualify for retiree health care coverage. In the state of New Hampshire, Chapter 104, Laws of 2010, requires state employees to have 20 years of service with the state in order to receive state paid medical and surgical benefits in retirement. Previously, there was no such length of service requirement for retirees.

Changes in Health Care Plans: Vermont

In the state of Vermont, Act 74 of 2010 changed state subsidies and requirements for retiree health care. For new hires and those with less than ten years of state service, there is no longer any subsidized health care coverage. For those with more than ten years of service, a single coverage subsidy ranging between 60% and 70% is provided. Further, while spousal health care coverage remains available to long-term public employees in Vermont, employees with more than 30 years of service will have to work another five years to be eligible for spousal coverage. Employees with between 25 and 29 years of service will have to work a total of 35 years to be eligible for spousal coverage, and employees with between 15 and 24 years of service will have to work ten more years to be eligible for spousal coverage. Finally, employees with 10 to 15 years of service will be eligible for spousal coverage after 25 years of service.

Changes in Health Care Plans: Rhode Island

In the state of Rhode Island, legislation was adopted in 2008 that was aimed at reducing the cost of health care coverage for state employees who retire early. In response, Rhode Island Council 94 of the American Federation of State, County, and Municipal Employees (AFSCME) sued to block enforcement of this legislation, arguing that it violated employee rights under the Rhode Island and U.S. constitutions. In April 2010, a U.S. district court judge upheld the state's reduction of health care benefits for early-retiring employees, ruling that no enforceable contract exists for retiree health benefits under the state's past practice, the collective bargaining agreement between AFSCME Council 94 and the state, other state statutes, or common law. Similar lawsuits have been filed by unionized public employees in other states but generally have received no more favorable judicial reception than that which occurred in Rhode Island.

Lessons Learned

These examples of recent U.S. state legislative initiatives to revise public employee retirement and health care arrangements could be multiplied severalfold, to say nothing about comparable initiatives undertaken by many U.S. local governments. Collectively, they tell a clear story of a deep recession–induced perception by elected officials that public employees are overcompensated, especially regarding nonwage benefits. They illustrate the belief that such overcompensation must be corrected.

But it is not just elected officials who believe that public employees are overcompensated. This belief is shared by much of the citizenry, including and perhaps especially by those who have become unemployed from private sector jobs. It is also perhaps especially believed by private sector employees whose retirement income has been thrown into doubt by the declining value of their defined contribution plans and by health care benefits that are rapidly rising in cost.

If these developments had been assuaged, if not fully reversed, by robust recovery from deep recession—recovery of the type that occurred following prior recessions—then public opinion about the overcompensation of government employees would likely also have been assuaged. But four years following the onset of the deep recession and more than two years following the official end of that recession, unemployment and underemployment remained very high by historical standards. In this circumstance, citizens' and elected officials' perceptions of overcompensated public employees are likely to persist, even strengthen.

Regarding the compensation of public employees per se, the recent legislative actions of state governments described herein will surely reduce the nonwage benefit advantage of public sector employees over private sector employees; they have already begun to do so. This development, in turn, presages a larger total compensation disadvantage of public sector relative to private sector employees. As noted earlier, this disadvantage, or gap, has been estimated at about 4%, composed of an 11.5% pay advantage for private sector employees and a 7.5% fringe benefit advantage for public sector employees. Assuming little or no difference in prospective pay changes between public sector and private sector employees, recent and continuing concerted efforts to reduce public employee benefits could increase the public sector total compensation disadvantage to 10% or more during the next several years. Such an expanded total compensation gap would likely be even greater among relatively highly educated public employees and among employees in the upper levels of public sector job/occupational structures.

This drive to reduce public employee benefits also testifies to the power of state governments and their elected officials. The large majority of public employees work for local governments and have their wages and salaries set by those governments, either through management determination or collective bargaining. But nonwage benefits for local government employees and, of course, for state government employees are largely determined at the level of state government. This arrangement is readily evident from a recounting of the recent initiatives undertaken by numerous state governments to rein in public employee pension and health care costs. Ironically, it is these same state governments and their elected officials (as well as local governments and their elected officials) who, over several decades, basically acted on the premise that, compared to private employees, public employees accepted relatively lower pay for relatively higher security of employment and security of retirement income.[15]

Defined benefit pension plans for public employees strongly reflected this underlying premise, and such plans continued in place during the economic recessions of the 1970s, 1980s, 1990s, and early 2000s. But the relatively deep recession of 2007–2009 and the continuing aftermath of that recession have upended this premise. It is state governments that have clearly taken the lead in changing public employee retirement plans for *virtually all employees and governments* within their respective boundaries. Put differently, the 50 state governments—rather than the thousands of municipal governments—are the locus of power and action regarding public employee pay, benefits, and (to a lesser extent) employment.

Because the unionization rate is so much greater among public sector than among private sector employees, it might be supposed that public sector unions are in a position to mitigate if not reverse the recent actions of state governments regarding public employee retirement and health care benefits and costs. But such is clearly not the case to date. Why is this?

One reason is simply that the large majority (roughly two thirds) of state and local government employees do not belong to unions. Thus, state and local government officials and managers can determine and implement employment and compensation policies and practices without having to negotiate with, or even consult, a large majority of their employees. Another reason is that when it comes to the main public employee benefits, such as retirement and health care, collective bargaining between unionized employees and management is not typically the decision-making venue.

Instead, retirement and health care plans, coverage, costs, and other components are determined through a political process that features multi-party or multi-constituency negotiations rather than more narrow collective bargaining between union officials and management. Certain public employee unions have a long history of influencing state legislatures and executive branch officials to adopt and/or enhance "favorable" retirement plans for their members.[16] More generally, however, public sector union representatives must compete with other constituencies when dealing and negotiating with these legislatures and executive branch officials. In the wake of the deep recession of the late 2000s, the union voice in such negotiations and legislative actions has been a relatively less powerful voice than previously.

The Michigan Example

An example from the state of Michigan supports this analysis (Center for Local, State, and Urban Policy 2011). In this state, there are 1,856 units of "general purpose" local governments. While only 27% of these governments have unionized employees, such unionization is far more prevalent in larger than in local governments.[17] This fact means that a clear majority of Michigan's local government employees are represented by unions. In a recent survey of elected and appointed officials of these local governments, 56% indicated that public employee unions "have been a liability" in terms of their impact on "jurisdictional fiscal health" (Center for Local, State, and Urban Policy 2011:3).[18] Of particular note, differences in this regard between Democrat and Republican officials were relatively small, with 48% of the former and 61% of the latter indicating that public employee unions have a negative effect on local governments' fiscal health.

These survey findings are helpful in explaining the bipartisan support for Michigan's recent initiatives (described earlier in this chapter) to reform public employee retirement and health care plans. A related survey finding, namely, that 65% of Democratic officials and 58% of Republican officials in these local governments indicated that relationships between their public employee unions and their jurisdictional administrations were good or excellent, suggests that adversarial union–management relationships do not underlie these reform efforts. Rather, the findings indicate that elected officials distinguish union–management relationships from what they judge to be the impacts of those relationships on local governments' fiscal health.

The Employee Quality Contradiction

Many of the current and impending initiatives to reform public employee retirement and health care plans focus on teachers and other school employees. This tendency is understandable because such employees constitute the majority of U.S. local government employees. The irony here is that there are many other well-publicized national, state, and local efforts to raise the quality of public school teaching by attracting more capable individuals to the teaching profession and by promoting them based on performance rather than on tenure.

One well-known way of increasing the quality of human capital in a sector, profession, or occupational/job specialty is to increase compensation.[19] For teachers (and certain other school employees), such increases may be in the form of base pay, merit pay adjustments, performance bonuses, and/or deferred compensation. Each of these types of increased compensation has been pursued by individual schools and school districts in the United States. Such initiatives, however, pale in comparison to the concerted post–deep recession efforts of many states to convert teacher pension plans from the defined benefit to the defined contribution type, reduce or eliminate cost-of-living-allowance provisions attached to such pension plans, reduce health care benefits, and increase the costs of health care coverage borne by teachers. Hence, these reform initiatives run counter to the objective of increasing teaching quality in U.S. public schools.[20]

Conclusion

The deep recession of the late 2000s and its aftermath have brought about what appears to be a concerted effort at the level of U.S. state governments to reform state and local public employee terms and conditions of employment. This development is based on widespread perceptions among the citizenry and elected officials that state and local governments are in fiscal crisis, that public employees are overcompensated (and also overprotected in terms of job security) relative to their private sector counterparts, and that public employee unions have substantially contributed to the crisis and the overcompensation.

The main focus of these reforms has not been on public employee pay or even employment but rather on public employee nonwage benefits. In this regard, the defined pension benefit plan that has long prevailed in the public sector (and that at one time was widely used in the private sector) is in the early stages of being shifted to a defined contribution benefit plan. This shift is evident from the initiatives of many state governments to require a defined contribution plan for new and prospective public employees and to alter some provisions of existing defined benefit plans for current public employees and retirees. It is also evident from the related initiatives to reduce public employee health care benefits and perhaps especially to increase the costs to public employees and retirees of such benefits.

These decisions regarding reforms of public employee retirement and health care benefits have been, and are being, reached largely through state government decisions. Typically, it is the governors in certain states who propose public employee retirement and health care benefit reforms, which are then typically enacted by state legislatures. State governments have long been the locus of action when it comes to the retirement and health care benefits not only of state government employees but of local government employees as well. Thus, the 50 state governments are far more important to contemporary reforms than the thousands of local governments that actually employ a majority of public sector employees. While the 50 state governments, meaning their governors and other elected officials, have not pursued the same reforms of public employee retirement and health care benefits, they have commonly sought to combat fiscal crisis in part through a policy of reducing public employee pension benefits and health care costs.

In some states (Wisconsin being the leading example), these reform efforts have been accompanied by others to curb or eliminate public employee unionism and collective bargaining. In one sense, such efforts can be analogized to similar, largely successful, efforts undertaken by private sector employers over the last quarter century or so. But in other states

(New York, Michigan, and California being leading examples), reform efforts have been pursued without accompanying curbs on or the elimination of public employee unionism and collective bargaining. Here, too, these efforts can be analogized to those of certain private sector employers that not only remain highly unionized but that have achieved sustained union–management cooperation and otherwise managed their employment relationships in ways that positively affect organizational performance.[21]

Both sets of examples indicate that when it comes to the reform of public employee pay, benefits, and employment, union power is playing a far more limited role than is often generally ascribed by the citizenry to the relatively high level of public employee unionism or specifically attributed to it by elected officials in many state (and local) governments. This reduction of public employee union power is, in turn, one of the main consequences of deep recession and its aftermath.

Endnotes

[1] Recessions are identified by the National Bureau of Economic Research (NBER). According to the NBER, the first recession of the 21st century began in March 2001 and ended in November 2001, and the second recession began in December 2007 and ended in June 2009. In this chapter, emphasis is placed on the second, or deep, recession and on the effects that occur after a recession has technically ended.

[2] See Hatch (2004) for an analysis of the delayed effects of the 2001–2003 recession on public sector employment, and Goodman and Mance (2011) for a similar analysis of the 2007–2009 recession. Also see Eddleman (2010).

[3] These data are inconstant dollars or, in other words, dollars adjusted for inflation. The ECI is set at 100 as of December 2005 (BLS 2011).

[4] See, for example, Lewin and McCormick (1981) and Lewin (1983).

[5] See Lewin et al. (2011).

[6] For more on such public–private sector compensation relationships, see Bender and Heywood (2010) and Lewin (2003).

[7] This finding is similar to that reported by Schmitt (2010), whose analysis of an extract of 2009 CPS data concluded that state and local government employees earn 6% less than comparable private sector employees when education and age are controlled, and about 4% less when gender, race, and region are also controlled. Without any such controls, state and local government employees earned 13% more than private sector employees in 2009.

[8] Knowledge workers constituted 49.8% of the federal government workforce as of March 2006 (Greenfield 2011).

[9] Additional education beyond a bachelor's degree is referred to in the CPS as postgraduate education.

[10] It is likely that published data on earnings from employment are more accurate, perhaps considerably so, for public than for private employees. This is because public sector employee earnings largely take the form of annual salaries and hourly wages, whereas private sector employee earnings not only take these forms but also various forms of incen-

tive compensation such as bonuses, profit-shares, gain shares, piece rates, and commissions, many of which are paid after the fact, meaning that they are distributed after (in some cases well after) a particular performance or financial period. The CPS and various other pay surveys do not necessarily capture such later payments. They also do not capture (or only partially capture) private sector employee earnings that stem from equity participation plans, such as stock ownership or grant and option plans, the gains from which are treated as capital gains for tax reporting and tax liability purposes. Such plans are widespread in the private sector but nonexistent in the public sector. Further, because private sector knowledge workers are more likely than other private sector workers to be covered by incentive compensation and equity participation plans, differentials between private sector knowledge workers' compensation and public sector workers' compensation may be substantially larger than those indicated by CPS (and other survey) data. On this point, see Lewin (2003), who estimated that incentive- and equity-based compensation constituted about 19% of private sector employee compensation compared to about 6% of public employee compensation.

[11] The center received 396 responses to its electronic survey, which was conducted among members of the International Public Managers Association for Human Resources (IPMA-HR) and the National Association of State Personnel Executives (NASPE) from November 18 to December 14, 2009. The survey response rate was not reported by the center but may have been low, given that the IPMA-HR is reported to have had 8,378 members and the NASPE is reported to have had 110 members at the time of the survey.

[12] The National League of Cities received 338 responses to its mail survey, for a response rate of 32%. The survey was conducted April–June 2010.

[13] For more on the examples presented in this section, see Snell (2010). The state of California is not included in these examples because its experience with deep recession is analyzed by Mitchell (Chapter 7, this volume).

[14] It is common practice in municipal police and fire departments for police officers and firefighters near retirement to be assigned substantial overtime work in their final year of service to maximize the earnings on which their retirement pay will be based. This practice is replicated for higher-ranking police and firefighters (i.e., sergeants, lieutenants, and captains) and is strongly reinforced by the close adherence to a promotion-from-within policy in municipal police and fire departments—a policy that also operates in other protective service departments, units, and agencies in state and local governments. Hence, New Jersey's Public Law 1 and similar laws recently adopted by other state legislatures are basically intended to reduce this "final year" effect on the retirement pay of police, firefighters, and other protective service employees. Whether and to what extent projected savings will actually materialize from a final three years of service versus a final year of service earnings basis for determining retirement pay for such employees, however, depends on how different final-year base pay and overtime pay are from the final three years' average base pay and overtime pay.

[15] Whether and to what extent public sector employees have a job security advantage over private sector employees remains the subject of considerable debate. On one hand, this advantage has been estimated to be about 6% on average (Biggs 2011). On the other hand, this advantage is said to be nonexistent once educational attainment is controlled (Munnell, Aubrey, Hurwitz, and Quinby 2011). Both sides of this debate would likely agree, however, that the nascent movement away from defined benefit toward defined contribution plans for public sector employees and the more robust initiatives to lower

public sector retiree health care benefits and increase public sector employee health care coverage contributions/costs will reduce and perhaps eliminate whatever job-security advantage public sector employees presently hold over private sector employees.

[16] Most prominent in this regard are police and firefighters' unions, which have regularly negotiated with state legislatures to retain and in some cases enrich the 20-years-and-out pension arrangement that prevails for police and firefighters employed by local governments. Under this arrangement, a police officer or firefighter may retire after 20 years of service and receive a full defined benefit pension, irrespective of age.

[17] Specifically, more than 90% of Michigan's smallest local jurisdictions (those with 1,500 or fewer residents) have no public employee unions, whereas 98% of Michigan's largest local jurisdictions (those with 30,000 or more residents) have at least one public employee union (Center for Local, State, and Urban Policy 2011). More generally, meaning in U.S. states as a whole, public employee unionization is positively correlated with community population size.

[18] Fully completed surveys were received from 1,272 local government jurisdictions, for a response rate of 68.5%. This mail survey, known as the Michigan Public Policy Survey (MPPS), was administered April 18 to June 10, 2011.

[19] In another example of irony, a pay increase for teachers authorized by a local or state government to increase teacher quality is typically regarded as a positive development, whereas a pay increase for teachers resulting from collective bargaining between teachers' unions and local school districts is typically regarded as a negative (cost-raising) development.

[20] To promote teachers based on performance rather than on tenure, changes in local and state government civil service provisions and requirements are typically required. Such changes, in turn, usually involve multi-party negotiations in which teachers' unions are but one of the parties.

[21] Leading private sector examples include Southwest Airlines, United Parcel Service, and Willamette Industries. Leading public sector examples include local school districts and unionized teachers in Cerritos, California; Hillsborough, Florida; Norfolk, Virginia; Plattsburg, New York; St. Francis, Minnesota; and Toledo, Ohio (Rubinstein and McCarthy 2012).

References

Baker, Dean. 2011 (Feb.). *The Origins and Severity of the Public Pension Crisis.* Washington, DC: Center for Economic Policy and Research. 16 pp.

Bender, Keith A., and John S. Heywood. 2010 (Apr.). *Out of Balance? Comparing Public and Private Sector Compensation over 20 Years.* Washington, DC: Center for State and Local Government Excellence and National Institute on Retirement Security. 27 pp.

Biggs, Andrew. 2011. *The Value of Public Sector Job Security.* Washington, DC: American Enterprise Institute. <http://blog.american.com/2011/07/the-value-of-public-sector-job-security>. [May 7, 2012].

Boivie, Ilana, and Beth Almeida. 2009 (Feb.). *Pensioneconomics: Measuring the Economic Impact of State and Local Pension Plans.* Washington, DC: National Institute on Retirement Security. 24 pp.

Center for Local, State, and Urban Policy. 2011 (Aug.). *Public Sector Unions in Michigan: Their Presence and Impact According to Local Government Leaders.* Michigan Public Policy Survey. Ann Arbor, MI: Gerald R. Ford School of Public Policy. 6 pp.

Center for State and Local Government Excellence. 2010 (Jan.). *Survey Findings: The Great Recession and the State and Local Government Workforce.* Washington, DC: Center for State and Local Government Excellence. 4 pp.

Eddleman, John P. 2010. "Payroll Employment Turns the Corner in 2010." *Monthly Labor Review*, Vol. 134, no. 5, pp. 23–32.

Fogel, Walter, and David Lewin. 1974. "Wage Determination in the Public Sector." *Industrial and Labor Relations Review*, Vol. 27, no. 3, pp. 410–31.

Goodman, Christopher J., and Steven M. Mance. 2011. "Employment Loss and the 2007–09 Recession: An Overview." *Monthly Labor Review*, Vol. 34, no. 4, pp. 3–12.

Greenfield, Stuart. 2011. *Public Sector Employment: The Current Situation.* Washington, DC: Center for State and Local Government Excellence. 6 pp. <http://Facultysenate. unlv.edu/budget_memos/Public_Sector.pdf>. [May 7, 2012].

Hatch, Julie. 2004. "Employment in the Public Sector: Two Recessions' Impact on Jobs." *Monthly Labor Review*, Vol. 127, no. 10, pp. 38–47.

Hoene, Christopher W., and Michael A. Pagano. 2010 (Oct.). *City Fiscal Conditions in 2010.* Washington, DC: National League of Cities. 8 pp. <http://icma.org/ en/icma/knowledge_network/documents/kn/Document/301687/City_Fiscal_ Conditions_2010>. [May 7, 2012].

International City/County Management Association (ICMA). 2011. *Facts on State and Local Government Pensions.* <http://www.nasra.org/resources/PublicPension FactSheet110125.pdf>. [May 7, 2012].

Keefe, Jeffrey. 2011. *Utilizing Integrated Public Use Microdata Series (IPUMS) of the March Current Population Survey (CPS).* Working Paper, Rutgers University School of Management and Labor Relations.

Lewin, David. 1983. "Public Sector Concession Bargaining: Lessons for the Private Sector." *Proceedings of the 35th Annual Meeting.* Madison, WI: Industrial Relations Research Association, pp. 383–93.

Lewin, David. 2003. "Incentive Compensation in the Public Sector: Evidence and Potential." *Journal of Labor Research*, Vol. 24, no. 4, pp. 598–619.

Lewin, David, and Mary McCormick. 1981. "Coalition Bargaining in Municipal Government: The New York City Experience." *Industrial and Labor Relations Review*, Vol. 34, no. 2, pp. 175–90.

Lewin, David, Thomas A. Kochan, Joel Cutcher-Gershenfeld, Theresa Ghilarducci, Harry Katz, Jeffrey Keefe, Daniel J.B. Mitchell, Craig Olson, Saul Rubenstein, and Christian Weller. 2011 (Mar.). *Getting It Right: Empirical Evidence and Policy Implications from Research on Public-Sector Unionism and Collective Bargaining.* Employment Policy Research Network and Labor and Employment Relations Association. 32 pp. <http:// www.employmentpolicy.org/topic/402/research/getting-it-right>. [May 7, 2012].

Munnell, Alicia H., Jean-Pierre Aubry, Josh Hurwitz, and Laura Quinby. 2011 (Sep.). *Issue Brief: Comparing Compensation: State–Local Versus Private Sector Workers.* Washington, DC: Center for State and Local Government Excellence. 15 pp.

Olson, Craig. 2011. *The Battle Over Public Sector Collective Bargaining in Wisconsin and Elsewhere.* Employment Policy Research Network. <http://www.employmentpolicy .org/topic/402/op-ed/battle-over-public-sector-collective-bargaining-wisconsin-and-elsewhere>. [May 7, 2012].

Rubenstein, Saul A., and John E. McCarthy. 2012. "Public School Reform Through Union-Management Collaboration." In David Lewin and Paul J. Gallon, eds. *Advances in Industrial and Labor Relations, Vol. 20*. London: Emerald (forthcoming).

Schmitt, John. 2010 (May). *The Wage Penalty for State and Local Government Employees*. Washington, DC: Center for Economic Policy and Research. 18 pp.

Snell, Ronald K. 2010 (Nov. 23). *Pension and Retirement Plan Enactments in 2010 State Legislatures*. Denver, CO: National Conference of State Legislatures. 23 pp.

U.S. Bureau of Labor Statistics (BLS). 2011 (Oct. 7). *Current Employment Statistics Highlights September 2011*. <http://bls.gov/web/empsi>. [May 7, 2012].

CHAPTER 2

Local Government Restructuring in a Time of Fiscal Stress

MILDRED E. WARNER
Cornell University

Introduction

The Great Recession of 2008–2010 has engendered a public sector recession for state and local government, which is worsening in 2011 and 2012 because federal stimulus (American Resource and Recovery Act) funds are no longer available to shield state and local governments from the downturn in revenues. Local governments are especially hard pressed. The majority of local government revenue comes from property taxes, and the Great Recession of 2008–2010 was stimulated primarily by problems in the residential and commercial property markets. As those markets adjust—home prices fall and foreclosures mount—property tax receipts to local governments decline.

It is typical for impact on local government revenues to lag one to three years after a recession. U.S. Census of Governments data show that local property tax collections declined in 2010, two and a half years after the housing market began its decline (Muro and Hoene 2009). The public sector recession creates severe pressure on local governments to look at their budget and service mix. Pressure will be felt most severely in the current period, 2010–2012 (Hoehne 2009).

A mere decade ago, the public sector—from the federal level down—was expanding, with budget surpluses and a strong economic outlook (Joyce and Pattison 2010). At this writing, we seem to face indefinite public sector deficits. But we must be careful not to extrapolate current trends too far into the future. The local government budget crisis is a *direct* result of the financial and housing market crisis and subsequent economic recession. When recovery comes, much of the local budget crisis will resolve with it. Federal stimulus support could have greatly reduced local government budget pressure in the short term, but Congress lacked the political will. States, facing fiscal crises of their own, have reduced their aid to local governments. This reduction leaves local governments with little room to maneuver in the current crisis, making a difficult situation worse.

There is a need for long-term structural change. Local governments have long sought federal approval to levy sales taxes on expanding sectors of the economy, such as services and Internet sales, but Congress has refused (Warner 2010). This refusal has exacerbated the current crisis. A modern local government sector needs tax revenue sources that reflect growth areas in the economy. It also needs to explore expanded opportunities for user fees since citizens exhibit increasing demand for services without willingness to pay higher taxes. The crisis calls for new approaches and a new conversation about what kind of local government citizens really want and are willing to finance. This chapter explores the local government response.

Understanding the Current Fiscal Situation

News reports paint a distressing picture of local government layoffs, furloughs, and service cuts as cities and counties attempt to address the fiscal crisis that emerged in the aftermath of the Great Recession. Comprehensive data looking across all local governments have been collected by the International City/County Management Association as part of their ongoing State of the Profession survey (ICMA 2010). In the 2009 survey, which provides the most recent comprehensive data available, 83% of the 2,214 cities and counties responding reported that they were moderately, significantly, or severely affected by the fiscal crisis. On average, respondents predicted an 8.25% shortfall in their budgets for 2010. For 53% of respondents, this shortfall was greater than that experienced in 2009.

Although no nationally representative survey is available at this writing, we can anticipate the crisis deepened in 2011. The ICMA respondents predicted an average 10% decrease in property tax receipts for 2010. Similar decreases were reported for sales taxes (10%), and even higher decreases were anticipated for state aid (16%) as the states face their own fiscal crises and respond by reducing aid to localities. Local government respondents also predicted a decline in user fees (14%) as residents attempt to reduce their expenditures in the face of uncertain economic fortunes and high unemployment.

State Aid

State aid is an important source of revenue for local governments. On average, state aid makes up almost 40% of local government revenue, although this varies dramatically by state (Warner 2001). In the period 2009–2010, state budgets were under serious pressure due to declining income and sales tax revenue. This decline led to cuts in state services, cuts in aid to local governments, and efforts to shift expenditure responsibility from the state to the local level.

Previously, centralization of fiscal responsibility from the local to the state level had been shown to be more important than state aid in reducing fiscal stress on local governments (Warner and Pratt 2005). On average, 57% of state and local expenditures are financed at the state level—but the level of state centralization varies widely, from a high of 79% in Hawaii to a low of 42% in Nebraska (U.S. Bureau of the Census 2007). Localities in states with lower levels of state fiscal centralization will face more fiscal stress.

Education

A service area that has seen much centralization over the past 30 years is education. Education equity lawsuits, which argue that local property taxes are an inequitable basis to finance public education, have led 23 states to devise schemes to centralize more of the fiscal burden at the state level (Baicker and Gordon 2006). The majority of the finance burden is still local, raised by local school districts. Local school districts are a special purpose government separate from local government in most states, while cities and counties (the focus of this chapter) typically are not responsible for primary and secondary education. However, education uses a large proportion of property tax revenues and thus factors into politicians' and residents' considerations regarding tax rates. As states face their own fiscal crises, cuts to state aid for schools will increase the pressure on local property taxes.

Service Demand

During economic downturns, demand for local government services rises. More residents need job training and welfare services. Police and fire costs rise—especially in neighborhoods vacated by foreclosure. Government needs to be able to play a countercyclical role—spending more in times of economic distress. However, the heavy reliance of local governments on the property tax makes it especially difficult for local government to play this countercyclical role. As the value of real estate falls, the tax base shrinks and local governments need to raise rates to keep revenues equal. Local action is constrained by tax and expenditure limitations, enacted by 29 states, which limit the level of local property tax increases (Mullins and Cox 1995; Resnick 2004). Thus for local governments in states with tax and expenditure limits, raising tax rates to maintain revenue levels in times of fiscal stress is difficult. This constraint puts local governments in tough circumstances. Service demands are rising at the same time as revenue sources are weakening; for many cities and counties, tax limitations prevent raising additional local taxes even if there were the local political will.

As of mid-2011, there were some signs that the fiscal crisis might be lessening—at least at the state level. Data released by the U.S. Census at the end of the second quarter of 2011 show state tax collections rising 11.4% compared to the same period a year ago. The 2011 data as of this writing showed income and sales tax revenues were up for all states except for New Hampshire, and growth in state tax revenues was up 8.4% on average nationwide for the 2011 fiscal year (Dadayan 2011). However, revenues were still 7.8% lower in the second quarter of 2011 than in the same period three years ago. As state budget climates improve, prospects for local government aid may rise as well.

Local Government Response

How are local governments responding to the fiscal challenge? The 2009 ICMA survey explored these questions and found the most common responses were to leave vacant positions unfilled (66% of respondents) and to defer capital projects (60%) (ICMA 2010). Other budget responses included targeted cuts in expenditures (52%), increased fees for services (46%), and reduced services (35%). Employment, as a major expense for local government, is also a key focus in budget cuts. Salaries were frozen by 43% of responding municipalities and positions eliminated in 40%. Staff layoffs (19%), furloughs (11%), and reduced salaries (7%) were less common. Thirteen percent of respondents reported they had revised union contracts to reduce pay or benefits.

Public Employees

There has been much popular debate in the media regarding pay and benefits of public sector employees in the aftermath of the financial crisis. The argument was that both pay and benefits are too high to be sustainable over the long term. Downsizing and privatization were seen as insufficient; the idea was to cut salaries and benefits of local employees as well. But what does the research show? Are public salaries higher? Are pension benefits too generous?

Popular media reports that claim public sector employees earn more on average than private sector employees fail to control for skill levels. A recent study of public versus private sector salaries in New Jersey found that, on average, public sector workers make 17% less than private sector workers (Keefe and Fine 2010). Controlling for level of education, skilled public sector workers with bachelor's and master's degrees make 35% less than their private sector counterparts (Keefe and Fine 2010). Only for workers with less than a high school degree are public sector salaries higher.

For decades, workers have taken employment in the public sector, despite its lower wages, in exchange for greater job security and benefits (health insurance, pensions). This trade-off is one of the mechanisms the public sector has used to attract high-quality talent in a competitive marketplace. With baby boomer retirements and the effort to shrink staff to save money, local governments in the long run risk losing critical expertise.

Prior to the Great Recession, private sector leaders identified a looming public sector labor shortage. They formed the Federal Partnership for Public Service (http://www.ourpublicservice.org) to address this challenge by designing new financial management systems, implementing new hiring practices, and building a new ethic for public service. The Great Recession has crowded out that debate, but the challenge remains.

The Pension Issue

Public sector pensions, like all pension funds, took a hit as a result of the Great Recession. Fortunately, public sector pensions were in better shape than most private sector pensions precisely because many state and local governments have rules regarding minimum contributions—even in times when interest rates were high. Although the average annual return in the three years ending in 2009 was just 3.5%, the average annual return over the 25-year period ending in 2009 was 9.25% (Snell 2011). Long-term investment payouts of 8% are considered reasonable.

Local government pensions are typically defined benefit schemes. There has been some push toward defined contribution schemes, but experts do not recommend such plans because they are likely to be more expensive (Picur and Weiss 2011). Picur and Weiss use data from the State of Illinois to show that the shift to defined contributions would increase the state's pension costs for new employees over the next 30 years relative to the traditional defined benefits scheme. The risk under a defined contribution scheme is also higher for employees. They may fall victim to unsound investments—all the more likely, given the inappropriate risk assessment the market has given to many financial assets in the recent past.

Wall Street analyst Meredith Whitney captured the public imagination when she predicted a "financial meltdown of state and local governments" on the TV show *60 Minutes* in December 2010, but her claims were contested by experts in the field:

> The facts, as reported by the National Association of State Retirement Administrators (NASRA)—based on the audited financial statements of the 93 largest public pension systems, covering 85 percent of the state and local retirement community—demonstrate that on average these systems are 80 percent funded. Most actuaries and experts consider this an appropriate level. (Esser 2011:1)

Public pensions, for the most part, are funded adequately and future payouts will be covered. The problem is that the financial crisis has eroded pension values and earnings in the short term and rules regarding government contributions have required increased contributions in the past few years. Government contributions are in fact countercyclical—lower in good times and higher in bad—which increases short-term fiscal stress on local governments. As a longer-term solution, state and local governments are adjusting benefits of new hires and raising employee contributions. In some cases, they are attempting to make adjustments for current workers, some of which raise legal questions that are likely to be resolved by the courts.

Layoffs and service reductions are two common strategies to address the short-term fiscal crisis. The National League of Cities, the U.S. Conference of Mayors, and the National Association of Counties partnered to conduct a smaller national survey in spring 2010 focused specifically on layoffs. The survey, which was sent to all cities with populations greater than 25,000 and all counties with populations greater than 100,000, received 270 responses (214 cities and 56 counties). Respondents reported cutting 8.6% of full-time-equivalent positions between the most recent and the next fiscal year (2009 to 2011). Applying this percentage to local government employment nationwide led the study authors to estimate 481,000 layoffs in the local government sector. Responding local governments reported that the layoffs would be largest in public works, public safety, and parks and recreation. The study called for federal action to prevent layoffs, arguing that every 100 public sector layoffs stimulate 30 additional private sector layoffs due to lost contracts (Pollack 2010).

But federal action has been limited. Public outrage over the decision to bail out Wall Street investors has been channeled into public disdain for government programs—at all levels. As the federal government continues a policy of cuts and as states suffer under fiscal stress, local governments cannot look to higher levels in the fiscal hierarchy for assistance. Local governments are largely left to their own devices. This makes responding to the crisis created by the Great Recession more difficult.

Options in the Face of Crisis

What are local governments' options? They can shed services, but only if the services are not mandated. They can freeze or downsize staff or salaries, but only to the extent that union contracts allow. They can increase user fees, but only to the extent that users can or will pay. The survey results previously profiled show that local governments are doing all of these things. But an underlying assumption in much of the political debate is that government can trim services, staff, and funding without having an impact on the broader economy or the community's quality of life.

Reality belies this assumption. Local government provides critical social and physical infrastructure that supports economic development and maintains quality of life for residents. Although many government services are invisible, such as water and sewer infrastructure, or taken for granted, such as paved and plowed roads or regular garbage pickup, residents notice when they disappear or degrade.

The United States was facing an infrastructure crisis before the recession hit. The American Society of Engineers had warned that most city water and sewer systems were fully depreciated and needed replacement (ASCE 2005). In addition, the Environmental Protection Agency and Congressional Budget Office had estimated the cost of water and wastewater infrastructure renewal would be $30 billion per year over two decades (CBO 2002; U.S. EPA 2003). In the past, the federal government has been an important financial partner helping local governments make these long-term investments in infrastructure. Although there was talk of an infrastructure bank before the 2008 presidential election, such investment talk was pushed off the table by the financial crisis. Now, cutting costs—not investing—dominates the political agenda. But the infrastructure investment needs are real; they will not go away just because the politics of the present seeks to ignore them.

One option often touted is privatization—contracting out service delivery or establishing public–private partnerships for infrastructure finance (Savas 2000). Private capital may be interested in public infrastructure investments because they offer a secure rate of return and steady demand and governments typically do not go bankrupt. But the local government concern is whether private investment or private management will lead to improved efficiency. Another option is internal process improvements, either through inter-municipal contracting to gain economies of scale or through other forms of internal government service improvement. The next section outlines the local government experience with contracting out and inter-municipal contracting. Unfortunately, there are no panaceas.

Understanding Privatization

For the past several decades, local governments have been encouraged to pursue privatization or contracting out as a means to increase efficiency, promote competition, reduce costs, and improve service responsiveness to citizens (Savas 1987). While local government managers generally support the idea of market provision, they are pragmatic actors who want their reforms to result in lower costs or improved service delivery. The International City/County Management Association tracks the forms of service delivery used by local governments in surveys every five years.

From 1992 to 2007 (the most recent year for which survey data are available), privatization levels have remained relatively flat, from 15% to 19% of service delivery (Hefetz, Warner, and Vigoda-Gadot 2012). The most common alternative to privatization is inter-municipal contracting, which in 2007 was at the same level as privatization. Together, privatization and inter-municipal contracting are the most common alternatives to direct public delivery.

Fiscal Stress

Some argue that in times of fiscal stress, crisis creates incentives for innovation. There may be some support for this point. A meta analysis of factors leading to local government privatization found that fiscal stress was a driver of privatization in U.S. studies conducted in the 1980s (when fiscal stress was higher) and ceased to be a driver in studies conducted in the 1990s and 2000s (Bel and Fageda 2007). My own research on U.S. privatization behavior from 1992–2002 did not find fiscal stress to be a driver (Warner and Hefetz 2002; Warner 2006). However, models of 2007 data do show fiscal stress to be a positive motivator for privatization (Hefetz, Warner, and Vigoda-Gadot 2012).

With the Great Recession, political ideology and rhetoric has turned again toward privatization as a means to achieve cost savings, despite the fact that research evidence provides no support for cost savings under privatization (Bel, Fageda, and Warner 2010). However, in the U.S. data, political ideology is not a significant driver of privatization at the local government level (Warner and Hebdon 2001; Warner and Hefetz 2002; Warner 2006; Hefetz, Warner, and Vigoda-Gadot 2012). Across all international studies of local government privatization, similar results are found: political ideology is not a driver of privatization (Bel and Fageda 2007).

This finding may seem ironic, but U.S. data clearly show that local government managers are pragmatists who are looking for innovations that truly reduce costs and preserve service quality (Hefetz, Warner, and Vigoda-Gadot 2012). When such outcomes occur under privatization, managers will privatize. When they do not, they will keep the work or bring it back in-house.

A case in point is provided by former Indianapolis mayor Steven Goldsmith, a privatization advocate who privatized little when his internal teams presented competitive bids that were lower cost than the private competition (Goldsmith 1997). As deputy mayor of New York City in 2011, he also discovered that bringing contracted work back in-house would save money because private contractors cost more than city employees (New York Times 2011).

Reverse Privatization

Reverse privatization, or contracting back in, has been a common feature of U.S. local government service delivery for the past decade. We have linked the ICMA survey data over time to measure the level of new outsourcing versus reverse privatization, averaged across all local governments and all services. From 1992 to 1997, new outsourcing was 18% of all service delivery and reverse privatization was 11% (Hefetz and Warner 2004). This period was a time when privatization was growing among local governments.

In the next period, 1997–2002, the proportions switched, and reverse privatization rose to 18% of all service delivery while new outsourcing dropped to 12% (Hefetz and Warner 2007). Outsourcing peaked among local governments in 1997, so the reversal to insourcing in the 1997–2002 period can be viewed as making adjustments to experimentation that had pushed privatization too far. In the most recent period, 2002–2007, the rates of new outsourcing and reverse privatization are equal—11% and 12%, respectively (Warner and Hefetz 2012), suggesting a continuing process of experimentation.

We find that insourcing is high in the same services areas where privatization is high. This result reflects the different needs and market conditions faced by local governments across the country. One cannot say categorically that certain services should be outsourced. The correct decision depends on local needs and market conditions. ICMA asked local city managers why they reversed privatization. The answers were first, problems with service quality; second, lack of cost savings; and third, internal process improvements that make contracting unnecessary (Hefetz and Warner 2007).

Cost Savings

Whether there are cost savings from privatization is key. One of the purported advantages of privatization is that it will lead to cost savings due to competitive pressures private providers face in a market place (Savas 1987, 2000). However, a meta regression analysis of all published studies of privatization in water delivery and solid waste collection (the two local government services with the most privatization experience worldwide) found *no* statistical support for lower costs under private production (Bel, Fageda, and Warner 2010). In the ICMA surveys (2002 and 2007), more than 50% of local managers reported lack of cost savings as the reason to contract back in-house any previously privatized services (Warner and Hefetz 2009). Why would lack of cost savings be so common?

There are both theoretical and empirical explanations. Theoretically, cost savings from private production derive from the competitive pressures of private markets. But there is little competition in local markets for most public services. A national survey of competition in 2007 found that on average there are fewer than two alternative providers for most local government services (Hefetz and Warner 2012). For natural monopolies such as water, there are on average fewer than one. Thus, competition typically is *not* present in local government service markets.

A second explanation involves the nature of incentives. Private owners are driven by profit and will seek to internalize the gains from cost savings and process improvements, especially if competition is minimal (Hart, Shleifer, and Vishny 1997). Absent strong monitoring and careful regulation, one could expect to see erosions in service quality if cost savings were emphasized as the primary goal. Indeed, the ICMA surveys confirm that managers in more than 60% of cases report reductions in service quality as the reason for reverse privatization or contracting back in (Hefetz and Warner 2007).

Improving Efficiency in the Public Sector

A third explanation focuses on the public sector itself. Over the past several decades, there has been substantial improvement in public sector efficiency. Innovations in the private sector have been adapted to the public sector and have yielded a set of new public management reforms that involve internal competition, team leadership, greater focus on customer satisfaction, decentralization to neighborhood-based delivery, and more flexibility to meet outcome goals rather than input requirements (Osborne and Gaebler 1992). These innovations have resulted in internal process improvements within government that make privatization unnecessary in many cases. More than one third of respondents to ICMA's 2007 survey reported that internal process improvements led them to bring previously privatized work back in-house (Warner and Hefetz 2009).

Cooperation—A Promising Alternative

Inter-municipal contracting is now as common a form of alternative service delivery as privatization. The most recent ICMA survey (2007) found that on average 16% of services were delivered with inter-governmental contracts compared to 17% delivered with for-profit contracts. Direct delivery remains the most common form of public sector service delivery, accounting for more than 53% of service delivery. The remaining 15% includes nonprofit delivery (5%) and mixed forms where multiple delivery modes are used in tandem (Warner 2011a).

Fragmentation

There is much fragmentation at the local government level in the United States. The Census reports 39,000 multipurpose local governments, and the vast majority are quite small. Fewer than 8,000 cities and counties have populations greater than 5,000 (U.S. Bureau of the Census 2007). Many local public services—such as water, garbage collection, and mass transit—are natural monopolies. However, under our fragmented local government system, many provision units are too small to fully exploit economies of scale. A potential source of cost savings is to expand the scale of service delivery to capture all economies of scale.

Economies of Scale

Privatization is one means to gain economies of scale. Another means is inter-municipal cooperation. The 2007 ICMA survey shows that while the desire to achieve cost savings is a driver for both privatization and cooperation, managers see achieving economies of scale as a primary motivation for engaging in cooperation (63% of respondents) (Warner 2011a). Other reasons for cooperation are to promote regional coordination (49%), to achieve technical efficiencies (30%), and to avoid service shedding (6%).

Studies of cooperation and privatization have found that governments engaging in more cooperation and privatization have lower expenditures per capita—suggesting some efficiency gains (Warner and Hefetz 2002; Warner 2006, Hefetz et al. 2012). For rural governments, contracting to a public market of cooperating governments offers more scope than contracting to for-profit providers. The higher cost and sparse settlement patterns in rural areas make them less attractive markets for private purveyors (Warner 2006, 2009).

But in the current context of deep fiscal stress, will savings from cooperation be enough? Holzer and Fry (2011) in a recent study of inter-municipal cooperation point out that the scope for economies of scale may not be large. Economies of scale for many government services are exhausted at around 20,000–25,000 population (Holzer and Fry 2011). So the potential for small, rural communities to benefit exists, but many suburban and urban communities are already at a size where economies of scale are reached. More often than not, cooperation leads to professionalization of service delivery—which can lead to higher-quality service but also to higher costs. This result is similar to those found in international reviews of the topic (Bel, Fageda, and Warner 2010; Holzer and Fry 2011).

Potential of Service Integration

Service integration through inter-municipal cooperation or cross-agency collaboration does offer potential for increasing service effectiveness, however. For example, parks and recreation departments are now cooperating with neighborhood schools to share athletic facilities (Spengler, Young, and Linton 2007). Charlotte/Mecklenburg, North Carolina, is engaged in joint capital planning with the school district and transit authority by co-locating schools, park-and-ride lots, and transit stations (Wells 2011). The city also collaborated with the school district to build a common library in the middle school, which served as a branch library for the neighborhood. In this way, both the city and the school district are able to better meet the needs of parents, commuters, students, and neighborhood residents—and save money. Fiscal stress requires innovative approaches that move beyond the service silos segregated by user and service area to integrated service delivery, which can save money and improve quality for citizens.

Rethinking Local Government

So where does this leave local government? At an October 2011 Big Ideas conference of leading city managers, City Manager Debra Figone of San Jose, California, and Frank Benest, former city manager of Palo Alto, stated that

> local government typically performs as a "vending machine." Citizens with certain responsibilities and obligations have become passive consumers of local government services. They put a quarter into the vending machine and expect a quarter (if not a dollar) worth of service. When the vending machine does not perform as desired, consumers kick it. ... The vending machine model of local government is broken. As local government leaders are forced to downsize services and staffing, restrain pay and roll back benefits, shutter buildings, and eliminate grants to non-profits and subsidies to businesses, we will need to engage in difficult conversations focused on redefining the expectations, roles and systems of local government. (Benest, Danaj, Figone, and Walesh 2011:3)

In an age of austerity, they argue, government should become more focused on its core businesses. Discussions at the Big Ideas conference questioned the long-standing assumption that police and fire services are core; managers suggested that while citizens view public safety and quality of life as important, they are not as concerned about whether these services are provided locally, regionally, or privately. Other local government researchers have also noted that local governments are willing to entertain new perspectives on what constitutes core services and how to deliver them (Scorsone and Pierhoples 2010; Ammons, Smith, and Stenberg 2011).

Managers at the conference were concerned about the high pension and labor contract costs of police and fire services, as well as the organizational rigidity they perceive as undermining innovation. They were concerned that high costs in these traditional areas crowd out funding for services that may be higher priorities for citizens. Those services may include parks and recreation and other social and human services that relate more directly to quality of life than to public safety.

The managers were interested in means to create more integration in service delivery—across agencies and across local governments in metropolitan regions. They were also interested in exploring how technology could be better integrated to ensure more-effective resident communication and possible co-production of services. The local government of the future was assumed to be leaner, more adaptable, and change oriented.

A Broader Definition

Shared services were viewed as one positive way out of the fiscal crisis. These shared services were not limited to contracting. Shared service models also included self-service (library patrons check out their own books) and co-production (sports clubs help raise money for public facilities and provide some of the maintenance as volunteers).

Another form of shared services discussed at the Big Ideas conference was partnering with neighborhood organizations to provide services. Many cities have decentralized their services to the neighborhoods. A next step could be inviting residents not only to identify but also to provide services directly, with government as facilitator rather than as provider. Managers also identified expanded opportunities to share expertise and equipment with other community organizations to reduce costs for everyone. They argued that local government should no longer think of itself as the primary player but as a partner with others—citizens, neighborhoods, and community organizations—to provide services.

Regionalization was viewed as a means to promote better service coordination, reduce overlaps, and promote improved technology (especially of police and fire where improved dispatch, technical organization, and equipment sharing could result in improved service at lower cost). These regional services could be handled by regional authorities who would have their own power to tax.

Network Approach

Each of these collaborative arrangements reflects a new "network" approach to governance. This approach offers more promise than simple outsourcing, and these are innovations that have people talking. They require new types of collaboration—across public, private, and community actors. While contracting was based on the assumption of benefits from competition, sharing services is based on the assumption of benefits from cooperation (Warner 2011a). These benefits may prove more stable than the old system of contracting based on competition. And they invite new sources of revenue from the residents themselves. In a world where enthusiasm for taxation is declining, there is increasing interest in strategies that encourage residents to directly support the public services they value.

Business Improvement Districts and Homeowner Associations

Examples include business improvement districts (BIDs), where property owners in a commercial district agree to tax themselves extra to fund improved services (street cleaning, street furniture, security, garbage collection, cultural events) to promote more commerce (Becker 2010). BIDs are now proliferating outside central commercial corridors to neighborhood business districts (Schaller and Modan 2005). Homeowner associations (HOAs) have become the most common means to provide infrastructure in new housing developments (Nelson 2005). These private interest governments (infrastructure clubs) now outnumber public multipurpose local government ten to one.

Cities like HOAs because they focus the cost of infrastructure on the new developments themselves—building the cost into the housing price and maintenance fee. While many of these developments hook up to broader city infrastructure systems, others remain separate. The concern is these HOAs may be too small to maintain their infrastructure over the long term (McCabe and Tao 2006).

Club Approaches

Each of these examples represents a club approach to local government service provision, where residents and businesses promote voluntary, private contributions to defray the costs of public goods provision. In an era where citizen enthusiasm for taxation is low, these club approaches offer an alternative that encourages increased citizen investment in their own communities. The concern is that these clubs will fragment the city, creating pockets of higher and lower service provision (Warner 2011b; Graham and Marvin 2001; Frug 1999). This outcome can undermine both equity and efficiency. But in a time of severe fiscal stress, city managers will be looking at all possible alternatives.

For these new networked systems of government to function in the broader public interest, they need a civic core. This not only requires government to be at the center coordinating the effort but also ensuring that core public values of accountability, access, and sustainability are secured (Clark and Bradshaw 2004). In contrast to the competitive strategies of the past few decades, where privatization promoted private sector interest in the potential of profit from public service contracts, these new collaborative approaches stimulate increased investment and involvement of citizens in the quality of life in their own communities. They also promote service integration across agencies and sectors that can reduce redundancies and promote system streamlining with the potential of better service to the public.

However, these approaches also require a more flexible attitude on the part of organized labor to recognize new partnerships that facilitate integration. In some cities, there are as many as 20 different collective bargaining units. As collaborative network governance approaches proliferate, unions will need to identify new strategies to ensure labor rights are preserved while service integration benefits are explored. Organized labor has a critical role to play, as sustained productivity gains require the knowledge and involvement of those who directly do the work. Without union involvement, these integrative approaches risk being a passing fad, with limited real prospects for enhancing services.

Conclusion

The Great Recession has created one of the most severe fiscal crises ever to face local governments. Local governments are dealing with difficult circumstances, with many facing declining property values and tax bases, declining state aid, strict tax and expenditure limitations, and rising public demand for services. Something will have to give. New models of cooperative service delivery across local governments, agencies, and citizens themselves offer the most promise to maintain service quality in the face of budget constraints. However, they also challenge traditional models of service delivery and labor management. The future holds much uncertainty.

Acknowledgments

Research for this chapter was supported in part by funding from the U.S. Department of Agriculture, National Institute for Food and Agriculture Grant No. 2011-68006-30793.

References

60 Minutes. December 19, 2010. "State Budgets: The Day of Reckoning." New York: CBS.

American Society of Civil Engineers (ASCE). 2005. *Infrastructure Report Card.* Washington, DC: ASCE. <http://www.asce.org/reportcard>. [June 20, 2011].

Ammons, David N., Karl W. Smith, and Carl W. Stenberg. 2011. "Local Governments in the Wake of the Great Recession: Are Big Changes Ahead?" Paper presented at Big Ideas: The Future of Local Government conference, Fort Collins, Colorado, October 14–16.

Baicker, K., and N. Gordon. 2006. "The Effect of State Education Finance Reform on Total Local Resources." *Journal of Public Economics*, Vol. 90, pp. 1519–35.

Becker, C. 2010. "Self-Determination, Accountability Mechanisms, and Quasi-Governmental Status of Business Improvement Districts in the United States." *Public Performance & Management Review*, Vol. 33, no. 3, pp. 413–35.

Bel, Germà, and Xavier Fageda. 2007. "Why Do Local Governments Privatize Public Services? A Survey of Empirical Studies." *Local Government Studies*, Vol. 33, pp. 517–34.

Bel, Germà, Xavier Fageda, and Mildred E. Warner. 2010. "Is Private Production of Public Services Cheaper Than Public Production? A Meta-Regression Analysis of Solid Waste and Water Services." *Journal of Policy Analysis and Management*, Vol. 29, no. 3, pp. 553–77.

Benest, Frank, Mark Danaj, Debra Figone, and Kim Walesh. 2011. "What's the Future of Local Government? A White Paper Intended to Provoke a Needed Conversation." Paper presented at Big Ideas: The Future of Local Government conference, Fort Collins, Colorado, October 14–16.

Clark, Woodrow W., and Ted Bradshaw. 2004. *Agile Energy Systems: Global Lessons from the California Energy Crisis.* San Diego: Elsevier.

Congressional Budget Office (CBO). 2002. *Future Investment in Drinking Water and Wastewater Infrastructure.* Washington, DC: CBO.

Dadayan, Lucy. 2011. "Strong, Broad Growth in State Tax Revenues Continued in the Second Quarter of 2011." Albany, NY: Nelson Rockefeller Institute of Government.

Esser, Jeffrey. 2011 (Feb.). "Lies, Damned Lies, and Statistics." *Government Finance Review*, p. 1.

Frug, G.E. 1999. *City Making: Building Communities Without Building Walls.* Princeton, NJ: Princeton University Press.

Goldsmith, Stephen. 1997. *The Twenty-First Century City: Resurrecting Urban America.* Washington, DC: Regnery.

Graham, S., and S. Marvin. 2001. *Splintering Urbanism: Networked Infrastructures, Technological Mobilities and the Urban Condition.* London: Routledge.

Hart, O.D., A. Shleifer, and R.W. Vishny. 1997. "The Proper Scope of Government: Theory and an Application to Prisons." *Quarterly Journal of Economics*, Vol. 112, pp. 1127–61.

Hefetz, Amir, and Mildred Warner. 2004. "Privatization and Its Reverse: Explaining the Dynamics of the Government Contracting Process." *Journal of Public Administration, Research and Theory*, Vol. 14, no. 2, pp. 171–90.

Hefetz, Amir, and Mildred E. Warner. 2007. "Beyond the Market vs. Planning Dichotomy: Understanding Privatisation and Its Reverse in U.S. Cities." *Local Government Studies*, Vol. 33, no. 4, pp. 555–72.

Hefetz, Amir, and Mildred E. Warner. 2012. "Contracting or Public Delivery? The Importance of Service, Market and Management Characteristics." *Journal of Public Administration Research and Theory*, Vol. 22, no. 2, pp. 289–317.

Hefetz, Amir, Mildred E. Warner, and Eran Vigoda-Gadot. 2012. "Privatization and Inter-Municipal Contracting: US Local Government Experience 1992–2007." *Environment and Planning C: Government and Policy* (forthcoming).

Hoene, Christopher W. 2009. *City Budget Shortfalls and Responses: 2010–2012.* Washington, DC: National League of Cities. <http://www.nlc.org/file%20library/find%20city%20 solutions/research%20innovation/finance/local-governments-cutting-jobs-services-rpt-jul10.pdf>. [June 30, 2012].

Holzer, M., and J.C. Fry. 2011. *Shared Services and Municipal Consolidation: A Critical Analysis.* Alexandria, VA: Public Technology Institute.

International City/County Management Association (ICMA). 2010. *ICMA State of the Profession Survey, 2009 Summary Statistics.* Washington, DC: ICMA.

Joyce, P.G., and S. Pattison. 2010. "Public Budgeting in 2020: Return to Equilibrium, or Continued Mismatch Between Demand and Resources?" *Public Administration Review*, Vol. 70, no. S-II, pp. S24–32.

Keefe, Jeffrey, and Janice Fine. 2010. *In the Public Interest? Safeguarding New Jersey's Public Investments: A Response to the New Jersey Privatization Task Force Report.* New Brunswick, NJ: Rutgers University.

McCabe, B.C., and J. Tao. 2006. "Private Governments and Private Services: Home-owners Associations in the City and Behind the Gate." *Review of Policy Research*, Vol. 23, no. 6, pp. 1143–57.

Mullins, Daniel R., and Kimberly A. Cox. 1995. *Tax and Expenditure Limits on Local Governments.* M194. Washington, DC: Advisory Council on Intergovernmental Relations.

Muro, Mark, and Christopher W. Hoene. 2009. *Fiscal Challenges Facing Cities: Implications for Recovery.* Washington, DC: National League of Cities. <http://www.nlc.org/ file%20library/find%20city%20solutions/research%20innovation/finance/fiscal-challenges-facing-cities-implications-recovery-rpt-nov09.pdf>. [May 19, 2012].

Nelson, R.H. 2005. *Private Neighborhoods and the Transformation of Local Government.* Washington, DC: Urban Institute.

New York Times. 2011 (Apr. 3). "Is Privatization a Bad Deal for Cities and States?" <http:// www.nytimes.com/roomfordebate/2011/04/03/is-privatization-a-bad-deal for-cities-and-states>. [November 1, 2011].

Osborne, D., and T. Gaebler. 1992. *Reinventing Government: How the Entrepreneurial Spirit Is Transforming Government.* Reading, MA: Addison-Wesley.

Picur, Ronald D., and Lance J. Weiss. 2011 (Feb.). "Addressing the Media Misconceptions about Public-Sector Pensions and Bankruptcy." *Government Finance Review*, pp. 18–27.

Pollack, Ethan. 2010. *Local Government Job Losses Hurt Entire Economy.* Washington, DC: Economic Policy Institute <http://www.epi.org/page/-/pdf/issuebrief279.pdf>. [June 20, 2011].

Resnick, Phyllis. 2004. *Fiscal Cap Style TELs in the States: An Inventory and Evaluation.* Washington, DC: Center for Tax Policy.

Savas, E.S. 1987. *Privatization: The Key to Better Government.* Chatham, NJ: Chatham House.

Savas, E.S. 2000. *Privatization and Public–Private Partnerships.* New York: Seven Bridges Press.

Schaller, S., and G. Modan. 2005. "Contesting Public Space and Citizenship: Implications for Neighborhood Business Improvement Districts." *Journal of Planning, Education and Research*, Vol. 24, no. 4, pp. 394–407.

Scorsone, Eric A., and Christina Pierhoples. 2010. "Fiscal Stress and Cutback Management in State and Local Governments: What Have We Learned and What Remains to Be Learned?" *State and Local Government Review*, Vol. 42, no. 2, pp. 176–87.

Snell, Leigh. 2011. "Setting the Record Straight About Public Pensions." *Government Finance Review*, Feb. 2011, pp. 8–16.

Spengler, John O., S.J. Young, and L.S. Linton. 2007. "Schools as a Community Resource for Physical Activity: Legal Considerations for Decision Makers." *American Journal of Health Promotion*, Vol. 21, no. 4S, pp. 390–96.

U.S. Bureau of the Census. 2007. *Census of Governments, Organization File.* Washington, DC: U.S. Bureau of the Census.

U.S. Environmental Protection Agency (U.S. EPA). 2003. *EPA Clean Water and Drinking Water Infrastructure Gap Analysis.* Washington, DC: U.S. EPA.

Warner, Mildred E. 2001. "State Policy Under Devolution: Redistribution and Centralization." *National Tax Journal*, Vol. 54 , no. 3, pp. 541–56.

Warner, Mildred. E. 2006. "Market-Based Governance and the Challenge for Rural Governments: US Trends." *Social Policy and Administration: An International Journal of Policy and Research*, Vol. 40, no. 6, pp. 612–31.

Warner, Mildred E. 2009. "Civic Government or Market-Based Governance? The Limits of Privatization for Rural Local Governments." *Agriculture and Human Values*, Vol. 26, no. 1, pp. 133–43.

Warner, Mildred E. 2010. "The Future of Local Government: 21st-Century Challenges." *Public Administration Review*, Vol. 70, no. S-II, pp. 145–47.

Warner, Mildred E. 2011a. "Competition or Cooperation in Urban Service Delivery?" *Annals of Public and Cooperative Economics*, Vol. 82, no. 4, pp. 421–35.

Warner, Mildred E. 2011b. "Club Goods and Local Government: Questions for Planners." *Journal of the American Planning Association*, Vol. 77, no. 2, pp. 155–66.

Warner, Mildred E., and Robert Hebdon. 2001. "Local Government Restructuring: Privatization and Its Alternatives." *Journal of Policy Analysis and Management*, Vol. 20, no. 2, pp. 315–36.

Warner, Mildred E., and Amir Hefetz. 2002. "Applying Market Solutions to Public Services: An Assessment of Efficiency, Equity and Voice." *Urban Affairs Review*, Vol. 38, no. 1, pp. 70–89.

Warner, Mildred E., and Amir Hefetz. 2009. "Cooperative Competition: Alternative Service Delivery, 2002–2007." In *The Municipal Year Book 2009.* Washington, DC: International City/County Management Association, pp. 11–20.

Warner, Mildred E., and Amir Hefetz. 2011. "In-Sourcing and Outsourcing: The Dynamics of Privatization among U.S. Municipalities 2002–2007." Paper presented at the biennial meeting of the Public Management Research Association, Syracuse, New York, June 2011.

Warner, Mildred E., and James E. Pratt. 2005. "Spatial Diversity in Local Government Revenue Effort Under Decentralization: A Neural Network Approach." *Environment and Planning C: Government and Policy*, Vol. 23, no. 5, pp. 657–77.

Wells, Jonathan. 2011. *Joint Use Task Force, Charlotte–Mecklenburg, NC: Planning Department.* <http://ww.charmeck.org/Planning/CapitalFacilities/JUTF/Presentations/2011_04_April_05_SchoolSitingIssues.pdf>. [Nov. 21, 2011].

CHAPTER 3

Public Sector Employment in OECD Countries Post-Economic Crisis

SABINA DEWAN

Center for American Progress

The recent global economic crisis, billed as one of the worst recessions since the Great Depression, has slowed growth, exacerbated unemployment, and thrust fiscal balance sheets into disarray as countries struggle to cope with the adverse impact of the contagion. National governments are confronted with the dual challenge of getting their populations back to work while trying to streamline governments in the face of fiscal challenges posed by the crisis. Meeting both these goals at the same time is a challenge in a weak economy.

With the onset of the economic crisis, several industrial economies adopted fiscal stimulus packages that helped stave off an even deeper recession. As part of these packages, some countries undertook active measures to transition the unemployed back to work by investing in public works and infrastructure schemes. Many of these schemes expanded public sector employment. In times of economic crisis, an expansion of public sector employment is a preferred active labor market policy that reduces dependence on passive measures such as unemployment insurance and other welfare benefits. Yet the stimulus packages that countries adopted also exacerbated fiscal deficits.

Confronted with rising deficits, many economies are now scaling back public sector employment as part of their fiscal consolidation plans. Public sector downsizing to restore public finances, however, comes with negative externalities that exacerbate unemployment, exert pressure on already weak aggregate demand, and fuel uncertainty during an economic downturn. Ultimately, expanding or downsizing public sector employment as a means of curbing high unemployment or as a way of controlling fiscal deficits detracts from the fact that the breadth and the scope of the public sector's functions should determine its level of employment. The level of public sector employment should be contingent on the functions that the public sector serves, not an end to itself.

Size of Government

The political left and right have long debated the optimal "size" of the public sector. Size can refer to the breadth of government functions, the number of public sector employees, or a combination of the two. The political right has traditionally argued for less government intervention and fewer government workers, while the political left has called for a wider scope of government functions, which requires more government employees. The ideological divide notwithstanding, this chapter is premised on the notion that government—not big government or small government, but effective government—has a critical role to play in ensuring the well-being of its citizens.

While the breadth of the government's activities certainly has a bearing on how many people it employs, in an era where public sector employment is used as a strategy to cope with high unemployment or rising fiscal deficits, the size of government becomes increasingly disassociated from the government's functions. This weakening of the link between a government's scope of activities and its number of employees is problematic.

Optimal Size vs. Job Creation

Employing more workers without a concomitant expansion of government's responsibilities can fuel inefficiencies in which the sharing of work can contribute to lower productivity per worker. It may be that this loss of efficiency is deemed to be a worthwhile trade-off. Giving more workers the opportunity to earn wages as opposed to being unemployed offers the advantages of reducing the welfare bill, keeping workers in the labor force, and offering greater potential for harnessing worker productivity in the long run because a shorter duration of unemployment improves re-employment and wage prospects in contrast to prolonged unemployment for a year or more. Still, whether it is considered worthwhile or not, the trade-off must be acknowledged.

On the other hand, cutting workers to curb deficits not only can raise the welfare bill but also can exert pressure and lead to shortfalls in the delivery of essential government services. Those in favor of trimming the public sector argue that government expenditure, especially on the wages and benefits of public sector employees, is currently too high. Furthermore, as many countries struggle with rising unemployment, the stability of employment in the public sector relative to other sectors of the economy has come under increased scrutiny.

In looking at data from the Organisation for Economic Co-operation and Development (OECD), it is true that, on average, OECD governments have expanded their footprint over the past 50 years. General government outlays of OECD countries claimed less than a 30% share of gross domestic product in 1961; today, the average exceeds 45% (OECD 2011a). But data suggest that the increase in public spending in OECD countries has more to do with increases in social security, other income transfers, and in some countries such as the United States, rising health care costs, than with rising public sector employment or the increases in the wage bill. On average, between 2000 and 2008—years for which data are available—government employment as a share of the labor force remained stable at 15% across the OECD.

It is therefore important to examine how general government outlays can be adjusted to strike a better fiscal balance, but public sector employment should not be the first victim. It is not prudent to cut public sector employment in the face of high levels of unemployment during an economic downturn. Indiscriminately chopping public sector employment can exacerbate already rising and persistent unemployment, undermining the very economic growth that is essential to balance fiscal deficits.

Outsourcing and Decentralization

Alternatively, governments can outsource or contract out essential services, but this may not achieve the desired goal of reducing government expenditures. The extent to which a country's governance structure is decentralized also has a bearing on its size—both the scope and its number of employees. In some cases, countries cut federal or central government workforces only to delegate responsibilities to state and local levels that then hire more workers. Greater levels of decentralization can actually lead to overall increases in public sector employment. Both decentralization and outsourcing make it particularly hard to discern the causal relationship between the scope of a government's functions and its number of employees.

Pros and Cons of Public Jobs Expansions and Reductions

This chapter does not address what functions a government ought to undertake, its outsourcing, or its level of decentralization. It does not engage in conjecture about what the optimal level of public sector employment should be. Rather, it weighs the pros and cons of either expanding or downsizing public sector employment as a means of curbing unemployment and/or tackling fiscal deficits during an economic downturn.

In the analysis presented in this chapter, the size of the public sector in countries that are members of the OECD is examined. The chapter then explores how OECD countries incorporated schemes to expand public sector employment as part of their fiscal stimulus packages at the onset of the economic crisis. Yet as the downturn continued to persist, countries downsized public sector employment to curb rising deficits and debt. This chapter discusses the rationale behind these measures.

The unprecedented turnaround from public job expansion to contraction illustrates the difficulties in addressing persistent and rising unemployment while curbing growing fiscal deficits and debt at the same time. Persistent effects of the crisis are forcing a trade-off between employment (especially public sector employment) and fiscal consolidation. The analysis concludes by making the case that, ultimately, carefully managed, timely, and temporary projects to expand the public sector during a downturn are preferred over passive labor market policies. Conversely, downsizing the public sector during an economic crisis can exacerbate unemployment, further weaken aggregate demand, and perpetuate the negative effects of the contagion.

The Public Sector as an Employer

The public sector serves many important functions from military defense and law enforcement to the provision of varying levels of social welfare services. In serving these functions, the public sector has itself become a significant source of employment in many countries. Public sector employment accounts for an approximately 28% share of total employment in countries around the world (Lanfranchi and Perrin 1997). Using a narrower definition, public employment as a share of the labor force averaged 15% in 2008 across the OECD countries for which there are data.

Finding harmonized cross-country data on public sector employment is difficult primarily because definitions of what constitutes public sector employment can vary drastically across countries (World Bank 2011). Some countries count teachers, health workers, and paramilitary personnel as public sector employment, while others do not. Some countries take local government employees into account, while others refer to central or federal government employees only. Still others aggregate the two. Another question is whether employees of state-owned enterprises (enterprises that are majority owned by government) are included as part of the definition (World Bank 2011). These definitional challenges are in many ways symptomatic of the ongoing debate on federalism and decentralization and of the polemic between the political left and right on big government versus small government and the functions a government ought to serve.

According to the International Labour Organization, "Total public sector employment covers all employment of general government sector as defined in System of National Accounts 1993 plus employment of publicly owned enterprises and companies, resident and operating at central, state (or regional) and local levels of government. It covers all persons employed directly by those institutions, without regard for the particular type of employment contract" (ILO 2011). According to the OECD,

The scope of the public sector [is] measured on the basis of employees paid from public funds, either directly by government or on the basis of budget allocations from central government to services, departments or agencies. Therefore, all employees who work in institutions which are directly under the control of government or other public authorities are included in the public sector. The public sector covers all levels of government and these levels can vary from country to country. Therefore, it can include some or all federal, regional and municipal levels. (2002:4).

Figure 1 illustrates general government employment and employment in public corporations as a share of the labor force for OECD countries for the years 2000 and 2008. Employment in general government as a share of the labor force remained roughly the same between 2000 and 2008. The Slovak Republic, Turkey, Luxembourg, Estonia, and Greece saw slight increases of more than 1%, while Mexico, Germany, and Italy saw slight decreases over the same period. In 2008, general government employment ranged from almost 30% in Norway to just below 7% in Japan.

Employment in public corporations claims a greater than 5% share of the labor force in Greece (12.8%), Poland (11.7%), the Netherlands (8.8%), the Slovak Republic (8.6%), Slovenia (7.9%), and the Czech Republic (6.6%). All OECD countries for which data are available saw employment in public corporations either remain the same or decline between 2000 and 2008, with the exceptions of the Netherlands, Greece, Canada, and New Zealand, all of which saw very small gains. This is most likely the result of trends toward increasing privatization, particularly in countries that were formerly part of the Soviet Union.

Figure 2 illustrates general government compensation of employees as a share of GDP for the years 2000 and 2009. The wage bill ranges from a high of 19.5% of GDP in Denmark to a low of 6.1% of GDP in Japan in 2009. Despite the range, the wage bill for the public sector is nonetheless significant in OECD economies. Even though public sector employment remained stable between 2000 and 2008 across most OECD countries, public sector compensation nonetheless saw a rise in most OECD nations.

Employment in the public sector and the concomitant employee compensation are significant in economies across the OECD. In countries that have a sizeable informal sector that encompasses economic activity outside the purview of government taxation and regulation that is not accounted for in labor force statistics, public sector employment accounts

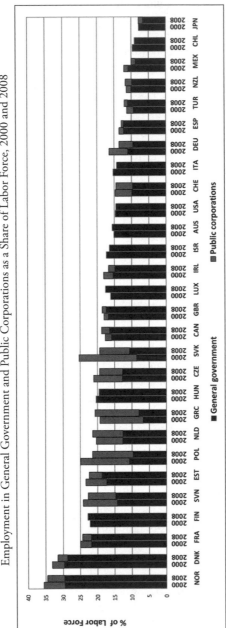

FIGURE 1

Employment in General Government and Public Corporations as a Share of Labor Force, 2000 and 2008

Source: OECD 2011a.
Note: The OECD obtained its data from the International Labour Organization (ILO), LABORSTA database. Data for Turkey are from the Ministry of Finance and the Turkish Statistical Institute. Data for Japan for employment are from the Establishment and Enterprise Census. Please see source for additional footnotes.

FIGURE 2

Government Compensation of Employees as a Share of GDP, 2000 and 2009

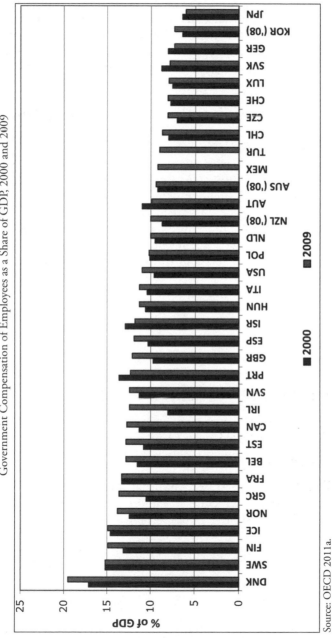

Source: OECD 2011a.

for a significant share of formal sector employment only. This tends to be true for developing and transition economies. In developed countries where the informal sector is smaller, public sector employment constitutes a significant share of the overall labor force. It is not surprising, then, that an expansion or contraction of public sector employment is considered as part of the economic strategy for coping with an economic crisis, especially in more developed economies.

Public Sector Employment Post-Economic Crisis: Expansion of Public Jobs

Scholars argue that the recent economic downturn, relative to recessions in the past, was particularly suited for public sector responses that were more comprehensive. They identify several preconditions that fueled the resurgence of Keynesian policy responses around the world.

Rapid globalization of the 1990s helped shape a world economy whose financial institutions were more interconnected than ever before. This interdependence, along with the development of increasingly complex financial instruments, created a sophisticated system in which individual financial institutions or governments could not get an accurate view of asset values or the risks they were being exposed to. Laissez-faire economic policies gained tremendous traction after Western stagflation through most of the 1970s. Keynesian policy took a backseat to neoclassical monetarism with its calls for "cuts in government spending on social services, privatization, new public management, liberalized financial markets, tax concession to the rich, and the free play of the market forces in the economy" (Aikins 2009:408).

In the 1990s, this allowed for the creation of more market-based regulatory instruments in place of legal ones, with fewer institutional safeguards and control mechanisms (Aikins 2009). The result was a global diffusion of regulatory capitalism (Busch, Jorgens, and Tews 2005), where having a liberal financial system made it easier to import external economic distress. But the collapse of the Japanese housing bubble in the late 1980s may also have served as an important reflection point for governments in determining their policy responses to this recession. The United States and British governments, for instance, were quick to turn to quantitative easing to avoid the slow growth and deflation that characterized the decade following the Japanese crash (Gamble 2010).

Return to Keynesian Remedies

The recent economic crisis dealt a serious and enduring blow to economic growth, especially in developed countries, that reduced aggregate demand for output and consequently for labor. The shock waves emanating from the financial crisis highlighted the weaknesses of unfettered markets, prompting a return to Keynesian policies to break the recessionary cycle and stem rising unemployment (Keynes 1936). Historical experience and a closely knit global economic landscape without a concomitant mechanism to correct for imbalances and gaps in regulation, as well as the speed with which the contagion spread across the globe, created room for public sector intervention that was unprecedented in many ways. Although Keynesian theory advocates broad stimulus measures (the outcome of which would likely create employment), Hyman Minsky called for a direct focus on job creation in the public sector as a way of coping with rising unemployment during a downturn (Minsky 1965).

With the exceptions of Austria, Germany, Israel, and Poland, every OECD country saw its unemployment rise between 2007 and 2010 with the onset of the economic crisis (Figure 3). Having reached the limits of monetary policy with interest rates close to zero and with rising unemployment levels, several OECD countries introduced sizeable discretionary fiscal stimulus packages to stabilize and reinvigorate their economies. Based on an unweighted average of OECD countries that carried out a stimulus, a typical stimulus package amounted to more than 2.5% of GDP over 2008–2010 (OECD 2009a). Australia, Canada, South Korea, New Zealand, and the United States introduced packages amounting to 4% of 2008 GDP or higher. At 5.5% of 2008 GDP, the United States had the largest stimulus package (OECD 2009a).

Expansion of Public Sector Jobs

A number of governments also took these Keynesian-style investments to subsidize demand a step further, pairing them with an expansion of public sector employment to curtail job losses. In the United States, for example, the first eight months following the crisis saw state and local governments add 110,000 jobs, even as the private sector shed 6.9 million jobs (Boyd 2009). These additions happened to coincide with the constitutionally prescribed decennial U.S. Census of Population. More often, they came in the form of emergency large-scale, labor-intensive public works programs that temporarily increased public sector employment in the initial phase of the crisis.

Infrastructure Investment

Most OECD countries undertook investments in infrastructure as part of their stimulus packages. Some invested public money in "shovel-ready" public projects with the hope that it would lead to the hiring of workers by contractors in charge of the infrastructure projects. Others, such as

FIGURE 3

Harmonized Unemployment Rates Across OECD Countries, 2007 and 2010

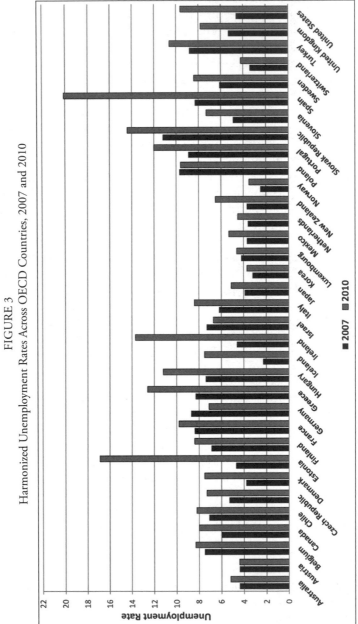

Source: OECD StatExtracts (http://stats.oecd.org).

Spain—the country that experienced the sharpest rise in unemployment in OECD countries since the crisis began (OECD 2011b)—undertook public works projects with the aim of specifically leveraging the public sector's ability to absorb unemployed workers and raise employment rates (Guellec and Wunsch-Vincent 2009). As the public sector shed jobs at a dizzying pace, these schemes provided a brief respite and a glimmer of hope in slowing down the rise in unemployment by leveraging the public sector's role as an employer.

Employer of Last Resort

In keeping with Keynesian theory, the purpose of these infrastructure investments was to stimulate the economy. Job creation was not the goal of these investments. The concept of prioritizing public sector job creation was put forth by Hyman Minsky, who in 1965 proposed utilizing the government as an "employer of last resort" (ELR). Underpinning the ELR strategy is the notion that the government can generate public sector jobs to match the unemployed with their respective capabilities and qualifications. This method would make jobs available to all without means testing for participation. Hiring by the public sector in labor-intensive services would at once generate employment and lead to readily visible public benefits.

According to Minsky, the government playing the role of an employer offers many advantages, particularly if an expansion of public sector employment is firmly rooted in active labor market programs such as infrastructure projects. Unlike the private sector, the government is not driven by profitability (Papdimitrou 2009). The government can therefore create demand for all workers who are table and willing to work for a set wage and benefits (Papdimitrou 2009). This maintenance of demand keeps people engaged in the labor force and prevents growth of "discouraged workers" outside the labor force. (A discouraged worker is one who wants a job and is currently available to work but has given up the search for employment, believing that a search would be futile because of a lack of available employment opportunities.)

Working for the Public Sector vs. Public Transfer Payments

Public sector employment also serves as an important alternative to transfer schemes that become increasingly controversial as an economic crisis endures. There is a long-standing debate over whether labor market policies such as unemployment insurance and other social transfers distort the labor market by creating dependence on the state and providing an incentive for people to stay out of work. Furthermore, the longer people remain unemployed, the harder it is for them to find work and the greater the long-term wage effects. As economic growth slows during times of economic duress, and as unemployment insurance and other welfare claims rise, these passive measures come under even greater scrutiny. Conversely, active measures, such as deliberate expansion of public sector employment to allow people to be employed, create incentives to work and are looked upon more favorably.

The public sector can create a "market for labor," buying the unemployed at a fixed wage and then selling labor back at a higher wage as private sector demand resumes. This approach creates a more flexible labor market (Papdimitrou 2009) as individuals continue to participate in the labor market. A shorter duration of unemployment also means fewer adverse impacts on future prospects and wages. Public sector employment can be utilized as an automatic stabilizer that generates employment during a downturn and shrinks demand for labor during an economic expansion.

The Politics of Public Job Creation

An expansion of public sector employment also serves a political purpose. Declining economic growth, mounting job losses, and prolonged unemployment inevitably fuel public discontent. Such discontent generates a space for opposition groups to direct public dissatisfaction toward the government in office. Expanding public sector employment against this backdrop creates jobs while providing visible political cover to governments.

Despite these advantages, critics argue that the public sector's role as an employer can impose certain costs. Depending on public sector employment as an automatic stabilizer can be problematic—once the jobs have been added, eliminating them is difficult for many of the same reasons it was advantageous to have them in the first place. The political space available to governments to cut jobs at a time when unemployment is high is very limited. Relocating workers displaced from the public sector can prove difficult because the workers may not have the skills required by the private sector (Diaz 2006). While it may seem that the government can generate an infinitely elastic demand for labor, this strategy comes with a loss of efficiency. Hiring more workers inevitably reduces productivity per worker unless the hiring comes with a concomitant expansion of the scope of the government's activities.

Active Labor Market Programs

Public sector expansion that is firmly rooted in active labor market programs such as public works/infrastructure projects that are timely, targeted, and temporary can help circumvent some of these costs in the wake of an economic crisis. Although public works programs in OECD countries are costly compared to those in developing parts of the world

(Auer, Efendioglu, and Leschke 2005), expanding public sector employment for active programs such as infrastructure projects offers certain advantages. In addition to the infrastructure itself, these measures create direct jobs in the near term in which workers are deployed for a finite period of time, making it easier to use this as a countercyclical measure. Workers understand that once the project is complete, they will no longer be on the public payroll. Such programs are especially suited for less-skilled segments of the population and can serve as an alternative to passive transfer schemes. The more people employed, the fewer unemployment checks the government has to cut. Finally, the availability of sound and reliable infrastructure can have a positive impact on private sector operations as well.

Public Sector Employment Post-Economic Crisis: Contraction of Public Employment

Although fiscal stimulus measures helped stave off an even deeper recession, they did contribute to the growing fiscal deficits in the OECD region. Fiscal deficits are both inevitable and necessary to nurse an economy back to health during an economic downturn, but there is consensus that a balanced budget is desirable in the long term (Dewan and Ettlinger 2009). Still, the rising deficits in many OECD countries not only pose an economic challenge, they pose a more immediate political challenge.

Greater economic growth that leads to more revenues, more jobs, and therefore less expenditure on people who are unemployed, can help reduce the deficit. Yet forecasts suggest that while economic growth may help with the deficit somewhat, it will not be enough to stabilize or reduce the mounting debt-to-GDP ratios in many OECD countries. Most OECD economies will have to undertake substantial steps toward fiscal consolidation (OECD 2011c).

Governments confronted with intense pressures to do something about rising deficit and debt levels are looking to reductions in expenditures to a greater extent than to measures to raise more revenue (OECD 2011c). A confluence of several factors, including a demographic shift and declining labor force participation rates, raises questions about the sustainability of expensive entitlement programs. Although government employment remained roughly the same between 2000 and 2008 (Figures 1 and 2), public sector compensation rose in several OECD countries, fueling the arguable misperception that government employees are "overfed bureaucrats" and big government is a bloated bureaucracy that absorbs too many taxpayer dollars to function (Smith 2010). Finally, tax increases tend to be politically contentious—tilting governments toward spending cuts rather than toward raising revenue.

Selected Job Cutbacks

As a result, several OECD economies are now significantly scaling back public sector employment to cut expenditures as part of their fiscal consolidation efforts. According to the OECD Fiscal Consolidation Survey of 2010, 15 of 30 OECD countries will undertake staff reductions in public sector employment as a means of fiscal consolidation (OECD 2011c). There should be 330,000 fewer employees in the public sector in the United Kingdom by 2014 and approximately 25,000 fewer in Ireland. The Czech Republic plans to scale back 10% of its public workforce, with the exception of teachers. Table 1 illustrates staff reduction targets for select OECD countries.

Job Cutbacks as a Financial and Political Tool

Public sector employment and wages constitute a substantial portion of public expenditure. Staff reductions are therefore seen as a direct measure to cut spending and improve the fiscal balance. Just as public sector hiring provides a visible indication that governments are working to curb rising unemployment, reducing public sector staff is a visible signal, especially to financial markets, that the government is serious about improving the fiscal balance (OECD 2011c). The ongoing debate between the political left and right has also fueled the perception that the public sector is an overstaffed, bloated bureaucracy, which makes it more

TABLE 1
Selected Public Sector Job Reductions

Country	Reductions
Austria	3,000 federal officials by 2014
France	97,000 public sector jobs by replacing only 1 out of 2 retiring state employees
Germany	10,000 federal public sector jobs by 2014
Greece	20% of retiring employees replaced; fewer public short-term contract employees
Ireland	24,750 public sector jobs by 2014
Portugal	Recruitment freeze of civil servants (no replacements)
Slovenia	1% of public sector employees from 2010 through 2011
Spain	10% replacement of vacant positions between 2011 and 2013
United Kingdom	330,000 public sector jobs by 2014

susceptible to cuts in government employment. And, as people become increasingly discontent and impatient about the challenges they confront with the economic crisis, they see public services as inefficient and ineffective and are troubled by the relative stability of public sector jobs while other sectors are susceptible to shocks. This makes the cutting of public sector jobs a popular strategy, although cuts are always unpopular among those that actually stand to lose their jobs.

Negative Externalities of Job Cuts

Several negative externalities arise from public sector downsizing, especially during an economic crisis like the current one that makes the downsizing less lucrative. At this writing, the speed with which governments are rushing to cut public sector employment is unprecedented, but the potentially adverse impacts of such rapid downsizing on the labor market and the macroeconomy are largely left out of the debate on fiscal consolidation.

Economic shocks and the concomitant decline in aggregate demand forced layoffs in the private sector. Three years into the crisis (as of this writing), the recovery remains fragile, and continued economic volatility is fueling uncertainty; the private sector continues to refrain from hiring. Public sector downsizing not only adds to the existing number of unemployed workers at a time when the private sector is not hiring enough, but it also introduces more competition for existing jobs in an already crowded marketplace. The increase in the supply coupled with the decrease in the demand for labor puts downward pressure on wages, further depressing consumption and fueling the vicious cycle.

Increased competition also means that some workers will be unemployed longer. Long-term unemployment, commonly defined as unemployment that lasts for a year or longer, makes it even harder for individuals to find work because they become demoralized and/or stigmatized in the eyes of potential employers. This effect diminishes long-term wage and career prospects of workers who are unemployed for prolonged periods of time.

Offsets to the Initial Budget Savings

While public sector downsizing reduces the government's wage bill, the severance payments and unemployment benefits it has to pay to the separated workers add to its expenses. Relocating workers displaced from the public sector can also be difficult since government workers may not have the skills required by the private sector. Any retraining and assistance in deploying workers in new jobs then adds to the costs of downsizing. As two-income households become single-income households, necessary retrenchments have a negative bearing on the health of the family and the education of the children over the long term. Workers may leave particular towns to move to other areas with seemingly better opportunities, adding to the economic deterioration of their hometowns and overcrowding in the receiving towns. Taking people off government payrolls when jobs are scarce also increases the burden on taxpayers, as more workers and their families have to rely on taxpayer-funded social welfare programs to make ends meet. As such, seemingly positive financial returns do not always translate into economic returns:

> The financial returns result from a reduction in public sector expenditures, particularly the public sector wage bill. When the present value of this reduction is higher than the upfront cost in terms of severance payments, safety nets, and the like, downsizing has positive financial returns. Economic returns, in contrast, result from a better allocation of labor across sectors. (Diaz 2006:224)

Yet a better allocation of labor across sectors is not possible when the private sector is not hiring because of weak aggregate demand and uncertainty.

Longer-Term Impacts

Where employment cuts in the public sector take place also has consequences for a nation's long-term growth and competitiveness trajectory. Among OECD nations, the United Kingdom undertook the most drastic cuts in public sector employment. The Office for National Statistics reported that the UK's coalition government oversaw a reduction of 143,000 in the number of state employees between 2010 and the first quarter of 2011 (Curtis 2011). Several of the victims of the cuts were teachers and public administrators. These cuts are seen to compromise the education of the UK's young people, which will make the country less competitive in the long run. As a series of negative economic data emerges, including a downward revision of the International Monetary Fund's growth projections for the UK, public sector downsizing is coming under increasing criticism, and the poor economic returns are becoming more apparent.

Drastic cuts in public sector employment as part of the European Union's austerity agenda have provoked street riots and protests in other parts of Europe. Critics question whether such front loading of austerity to reduce fiscal deficits is more damaging than helpful to economic growth and competitiveness.

Conclusion

The public sector's purpose is to provide necessary services to facilitate the health, security, and general welfare of its people. Which services the government ought to provide, its level of involvement in serving its people, and whether it can serve as a substitute for private measures are questions that evoke active debate. These issues characterize a major ideological fault line between the political left and right worldwide. Ultimately, however, the government's level of employment should be determined by the parameters set by the answers to these questions—whatever the answers may be.

Public sector employment claims a significant share of the labor force in all OECD countries. The sector's behavior as an employer has a significant impact on labor markets in general, including wage levels, and supply and demand for certain occupations such as teachers or health care workers (OECD 2009b), and on labor market tightness. It is tempting, then, to overlook the normative approach to public sector employment and instead actively manipulate it to influence labor market outcomes, especially during an economic downturn.

In the initial phase of the economic crisis, most OECD countries expanded public sector employment. They either hired more workers for temporary projects or adopted public works schemes and infrastructure projects that expanded the government's payrolls as part of their stimulus packages. An active expansion of public sector employment, when well timed, temporary, and targeted, helps reduce people's reliance on passive benefits such as unemployment insurance. It can serve as a powerful mechanism to cope with persistent unemployment during an economic downturn. The same is not true of public sector downsizing, however.

As the crisis continues and countries are faced with rising fiscal deficits and debt, several OECD nations are downsizing public sector employment to cut spending as part of their fiscal consolidation plans. Yet job creation in the private sector has been insufficient to absorb new entrants into the labor market, let alone those who have been laid off from government jobs. As long as fragile growth, weak aggregate demand, and uncertainty persist, this trend is likely to continue for some time—putting the goal of reducing unemployment at odds with curbing the fiscal deficit through cuts in public sector employment.

While cutting government personnel may provide immediate budget deficit reductions if severance and other benefit claims are less than the payroll reduction, the downsizing can cause significant economic losses from rising unemployment, discouragement, loss of productive potential, and other adverse multipliers that are harder to quantify.

Under such circumstances, public sector employment determines the functions of government rather than the government's functions determining the level of public sector employment. In the long run, this alternative role of government makes it difficult to determine what an efficient and effective level of public sector employment ought to be. Data on public sector employment levels should provide information on the scope of government's activities and vice versa. Public sector employment levels are not meant to serve as indicators for the health of the economy during a downturn. It is one thing to cope with reductions in government tax receipts by exploring additional sources of revenue and ways to extract greater efficiency in delivering services; it is another to slash the government's most important input—its labor.

References

Aikins, Stephen K. 2009. "Political Economy of Government Intervention in the Free Market System." *Administrative Theory & Praxis* Vol. 31, no. 3, pp. 405-6.

Auer, Peter, Umit Efendioglu, and Janine Leschke. 2005. *Active Labor Market Policies Around the World*. Geneva: International Labour Organization.

Boyd, Donald J. 2009 (Aug. 20). *State/Local Employment Up Slightly Since the State of the Recession, But Cuts Are Now Underway*. The Nelson A. Rockefeller Institute of Government.

Busch, P., H. Jorgens, and K. Tews. 2005. "The Global Diffusion of Regulatory Instruments: The Making of a New International Environmental Regime." *Annals of the American Academy of Political and Social Science*, Vol. 558, 146–67.

Curtis, Polly. 2011 (Jun. 15). "Education Bears Brunt of Public Sector Job Losses." *The Guardian*. <http://www.guardian.co.uk/business/2011/jun/15/education-bears-brunt-of-public-sector-job-losses>. [May 27, 2012].

Dewan, Sabina, and Michael Ettlinger. 2009 (Oct.). *Comparing Public Spending and Priorities Across OECD Countries*. Washington, DC: *Center for American Progress*.

Diaz, Juan José. 2006. "Public Sector Downsizing." In Aline Coudouel and Stefano Paternostro, eds., *Analyzing the Distributional Impact of Reforms: A Practitioner's Guide to Pension, Health, Labor Markets, Public Sector Downsizing, Taxation, Decentralization, and Macroeconomic Modeling, Vol. 2*. Washington, DC: The World Bank.

Gamble, Andrew. 2010. "The Political Consequences of the Crash." *Political Studies Review*, Vol. 8, no. 1, pp. 3–14.

Guellec, Dominique, and Sacha Wunsch-Vincent. 2009. *Policy Responses to the Economic Crisis: Investing for Long-Term Growth*. Paris: OECD.

International Labour Organization (ILO). 2011. *Public Sector Employment*. LABORSTA Internet Database. <http://laborsta.ilo.org/applv8/data/sectore.html>. [July 19, 2011].

Keynes, John Maynard. 1936. *The General Theory of Employment, Interest and Money*. New York: Harcourt Brace Jovanovich.

Lanfranchi, Nicole, and Hélène Perrin. 1997. *Measuring Public Employment in OECD Countries: Methods and Results.* Paris: OECD.

Minsky, Hyman. 1965. "The Role of Employment Policy." In Margaret S. Gordon, ed., *Poverty in America.* San Francisco: Chandler.

Organisation for Economic Co-operation and Development (OECD). 2002 (Mar. 27). *Statistical Questionnaire on Public Sector Pay and Employment.* Paris: OECD.

Organisation for Economic Co-operation and Development (OECD). 2009a (Mar.). "The Effectiveness and Scope of Fiscal Stimulus." In *OECD Interim Economic Outlook.* Interim Report. Paris: OECD.

Organisation for Economic Co-operation and Development (OECD). 2009b. *Government at a Glance 2009.* Paris: OECD.

Organisation for Economic Co-operation and Development (OECD). 2011a. *Government at a Glance 2011.* Paris: OECD.

Organisation for Economic Co-operation and Development (OECD). 2011b. "How Does Spain Compare?" In *Employment Outlook 2009.* Paris: OECD.

Organisation for Economic Co-operation and Development (OECD). 2011c. "Restoring Public Finances." In *OECD Journal on Budgeting.* Paris: OECD.

Papdimitrou, Dimitri B. 2009. "During and After the Crisis: Why Is an Employer of Last Resort Policy Needed?" Paper presented at *Employment Guarantee Policies: Responding to the Current Economic Crisis and Contributing to Long-Term Development.* Levy Economics Institute of Bard College. Blithewood, Annandale-on-Hudson, New York, June 22, 2009.

Smith, Lauren. *Correcting Myths About Federal Pay: Conservatives Compare Apples to Oranges.* 2010. Washington, DC: Center for American Progress.

World Bank. 2011. *Cross-National Data on Government Employment & Wages.* <http://web.worldbank.org/WBSITE/EXTERNAL/TOPICS/EXTPUBLICSECTORAND GOVERNANCE/EXTADMINISTRATIVEANDCIVILSERVICEREFORM/0,, contentMDK:20132629~menuPK:286372~pagePK:148956~piPK:216618~theSit ePK:286367,00.html>. [February 14, 2011].

CHAPTER 4

Cash-Strapped Governments: Privatization as a Response to the Crisis of the Great Recession

ELLEN DANNIN
Pennsylvania State University

Introduction

Privatization—contracting out federal, state, or local government jobs—received relatively little attention until after the 2010 elections. Since then, privatization has become headline news as state after state announced plans to balance their budgets by contracting out or auctioning off public infrastructure—water and waste systems, highways, parking meters, parking garages, ports, and airports—and government services as diverse as prisons, liquor sales, government data, computer systems, information technology, education, and the administration of welfare and unemployment benefits. Privatization often appeared bundled with changes to government workers' benefits, pay, civil service protections, collective bargaining rights, and union representation. Suddenly, public sector employment issues became a hotly contested battleground that drew thousands of protesters to state capitals.

While dramatic events, such as the demonstrations and sit-ins in Madison, Wisconsin, received wide news coverage, privatization and issues that were coupled with it played out as a team sport between bitter rivals rather than as a thoughtful exploration of how best to provide essential services and survive the Great Recession. As a result, even well-informed people lacked information that would help them understand decisions concerning the process of privatizing public services and assets and its effects. First, among the important themes related to privatization have been opposition to taxes and generalized anger about public employee pensions, pay, and benefits; unions; and collective bargaining. Second, public employees were depicted as incompetent, and privatization was presented as the way to provide superior services at lower cost.

The focus here is on state and local privatization, but many issues are common to privatization at federal, state, and local government levels and across occupations and industries. Even when limited to events during the Great Recession, the story of privatization can be fully analyzed only at far greater length than is possible in a single chapter.

Motivations for and Issues Related to Privatization During the Great Recession

The decision whether federal, state, or local governments provide a service or product or buy it from a private vendor has persisted throughout the existence of the United States. Factors in deciding how to provide a service often include cost, ideological views, the need for special expertise, meeting a short-term need, and the goal of providing better or more efficient services or infrastructure (Bender and Heywood 2010). Research by Mildred Warner and her co-authors over many years provides a baseline understanding about levels of work contracted into and out of the public sector, and insights into those decisions. That research, which focuses on local services, has shown that the decision to hire contractors or use public employees to provide services has been made primarily by professional managers and based on a mix of pragmatic and other motivations. In contrast, the primary motivation for bringing privatized services back in-house has been unsatisfactory performance by private contractors (Bel, Fageda, and Warner 2010; Bel, Hebdon, and Warner 2007; Hefetz and Warner 2004).

During the Great Recession, however, privatization decisions have been affected by new issues, such as opposition to taxes; anger over public employee pensions, pay, and benefits; and attacks on union representation and collective bargaining.

Opposition to Taxes

As the Great Recession dragged on, opposition to taxes became an increasingly important force affecting the services and infrastructure that government at all levels could fund. Anti-tax sentiment became an important force after the highly partisan 2010 elections. Tax increases to shore up government budgets were taken off the table, while tax cuts were promoted as the only way to stimulate the economy. The most dramatic effect of anti-tax views was the standoff it created as the clock ran down on a vote to increase the debt ceiling. With state and local budget shortfalls and no possibility of raising additional revenues through tax increases, the only options many states considered were cutting services and privatizing, both of which meant cutting public employee jobs or pay, or both.

Anti-tax sentiments have mostly been directed against income taxes (Anti-Defamation League, n.d.). However, fear of a backlash against tax increases has prevented increases in other taxes, such as the gas tax:

The federal gas tax, which funds our transportation infrastructure . . . no longer meets our needs because (1) the increased use of fuel efficient vehicles has driven down fuel tax revenues per mile driven; (2) the tax, long stuck at 18.4 cents per gallon, is not indexed for inflation and has not been raised for over a decade; and (3) there is no political will to take the obvious step of setting the fuel tax at a level sufficient to maintain and build our country's infrastructure. Instead, the federal government has met the revenue shortfall by taking money from other funds. Thus, "what drivers may not see or understand is that even though higher fuel prices mean that they are paying a higher price for driving *that does not mean that they contribute more towards the cost of roads*." (Dannin 2011:97)

The failure since 1994 to keep the federal fuel tax at the same effective level, let alone increase it to levels that would pay for much-needed repair, maintenance, and new construction, continues a legacy of opposition to using taxes to fund highways (U.S. Department of Transportation, Federal Highway Administration, n.d.). Instead, states and cities have turned to privatization of infrastructure to fund new construction, provide for upgrades and repairs, and generate revenue to fund other public needs. However, infrastructure privatization is also highly unpopular (Dannin 2011:97).

Budget Shortfalls

Throughout the Great Recession, governments at all levels struggled with revenue shortfalls. "In fiscal year 2012 some 42 states and the District of Columbia have closed, or are working to close, $103 billion in budget gaps. These gaps come on top of the large shortfalls the states faced in fiscal years 2009 through 2011" (McNichol, Oliff, and Johnson 2011). While much of the gap can be attributed to the loss of tax revenues and costs associated with high levels of unemployment persisting for years, revenues and spending in some cases have been affected by state Taxpayer Bill of Rights (TABOR) amendments (Lav 2010).

States such as California and Arizona turned to sale and leaseback of government buildings as a way to provide revenue for current operations. According to the California Legislative Analyst's Office, this approach would impose large long-term costs on the state:

> After taking into account the one-time revenue that the state would receive in the first year and converting the future costs into today's dollars, we estimate the transaction would cost the

state between $600 million and $1.5 billion. The Legislature will need to weigh how these costs compare to other alternatives for addressing the state's budget shortfall. In our view, taking on long-term obligations—like the lease payments on these buildings—in exchange for one-time revenue to pay for current services is bad budgeting practice as it simply shifts costs to future years. Therefore, we encourage the Legislature to strongly consider other budget alternatives. And, more specifically, we recommend the Legislature reject the sale–leaseback if the sales revenue is at the lower end of the range presented in this report—near the Governor's revenue estimate, for example—as the costs would be equivalent of long-term borrowing at double digit interest rates. (Taylor 2010:3–4)

Vilification of Public Employee Pay and Benefits

A March 2011 CNN poll found that people's estimate of government spending underestimates spending on the military and grossly overestimates spending on Medicare, Medicaid, Education, Foreign Aid, Government Pensions, Food Assistance, Housing Assistance, and Public Broadcasting. In the case of Public Broadcasting, people overestimate government support by 500%. The study showed that those estimates affect support for cutting or increasing government support for the programs (CNN 2011).

Some of the impetus for privatization also seems to have come from anger about public employee pensions, pay, and benefits. Public employees were widely regarded as being overpaid at a time when unemployment and underemployment were high and as being entitled to generous pensions and other retirement benefits.

In addition, while public sector workers were more likely to retain defined benefit pensions, an increasing number of private sector workers with pensions had only defined contribution retirement funds, such as 401(k)s, many with no employer contribution. In other words, as the first of the baby boomers were retiring amidst the Great Recession, the public that had just seen their 401(k)s vanish were neither sympathetic nor interested in making good on promises to public sector employees. Their anger was fueled by persistently high and long-term unemployment that had left many people with no income or benefits and had led to cuts or elimination of benefits for those who had jobs.

By the 2010 elections, fears about the economy and state budgets led to election victories by anti-tax candidates who pledged to cut budgets at all levels of government. Those victories were often coupled with cuts affecting public employees. For example,

In New Jersey, outrage over state deficits helped Republican Chris Christie defeat incumbent Democrat Jon Corzine last November. A few weeks after Mr. Christie's victory, a Quinnipiac University poll found that three-fourths of state voters supported a wage freeze for state workers, and 61% favored layoffs. Last month, Gov. Christie signed a set of bills that would, among other things, cut pension benefits for future employees. (Dougherty 2010)

So great was the anger directed against public employees, who were seen as greedy and overpaid, that it was impossible to find sympathy for them—people who had deferred income in exchange for a promise that the money was being placed in their retirement plans. Worse, many public sector employers had failed to pay into public sector pensions, which essentially left their employees with IOUs. New Jersey, for example, owed $53.9 billion to public employee pension funds.

Various studies compared pay and benefits for public sector employees, taking into account levels of education and training and hours worked, and found that most public sector employees—especially the most highly educated—were actually paid less than comparable private sector employees and that a larger percentage of their compensation came in the form of higher benefits, especially pensions and health care (Keefe 2010a, 2010b, 2011; Allegretto and Keefe 2010).

Anger directed against public sector employees over retirement benefits also demonized them as incompetent, inefficient, and overpaid or, more charitably, as not sharing the economic pain visited on those who had lost their retirement savings. Governor Christie and others successfully cast public employees as greedy and spoiled, which directed outrage toward those workers. Ironically, many public sector workers faced being left with no retirement income or health care because many public employees, unlike most private sector workers, are entitled to no or only a partial Social Security benefit. In other words, calling for public employees to share the general pain by accepting cuts in pay and benefits could mean inflicting far deeper pain on many public employees.

Some state and local governments took more direct action against public employees and their benefits. For example, in June 2011 the city of Half Moon Bay, California, contracted out half of its jobs. Along with cuts in the past five years, these actions eliminated 75% of city jobs. A key motivation was reducing obligations to the California Public Employees Retirement System. "The practical argument is that contracting for services can cut government costs, often because of less generous retirement benefits in the private sector" (Mendel 2011).

Attacks on Public Employee Unions and Collective Bargaining

A number of states, many of which had strong histories of supporting public sector collective bargaining, enacted or proposed new laws or took other actions to eliminate or limit public sector collective bargaining rights. Among the states were Alaska, Arizona, Colorado, Florida, Idaho, Indiana, Iowa, Kansas, Massachusetts, Michigan, Nebraska, New Hampshire, New Mexico, Nevada, Ohio, Oklahoma, Tennessee, Washington, and Wisconsin (Wisniewski 2011; Epstein 2011; Winston & Strawn 2011). Attacks on public sector employees and bargaining in some states, such as the agenda led by Governor Walker in Wisconsin, galvanized national opposition. In addition, some union members who had supported Walker's election, in particular firefighters and police, turned out in force to oppose taking away public sector collective bargaining rights.

In July 2011, Michigan enacted new legislation on public sector collective bargaining and teacher tenure. The legislation required arbitrators to give the greatest weight to ability to pay (as defined in the legislation) and internal comparability. It also forbade collective bargaining on decisions about teacher placement and its effects on individuals or a bargaining unit; content, standards, or procedures concerning reductions in force or its effects; employee evaluations and their development or effects on individuals or bargaining units; classroom observations; and compensation. Furthermore, decisions to discharge or demote a tenured teacher could be challenged only on the grounds that the decision was arbitrary or capricious; tenure and seniority could not be used in making personnel decisions except to break a tie; and, if a teacher was wrongfully discharged, the only remedy was reinstatement with no right to lost wages, lost benefits, or any other economic damages (Feldscher 2011; State of Michigan 2011 House Bill Nos. 4625, 4626, 4627).

Cutbacks on public sector bargaining played out differently in other states. In Nevada, the state senate and assembly unanimously passed legislation that excluded all state employees in professional or managerial jobs, such as physicians, civil lawyers, and employees with authority to hire, fire, discipline, and negotiate labor contracts, from collective bargaining. The new legislation also allowed the state of Nevada to reopen collective bargaining agreements during fiscal emergencies (Carlile 2011).

In Indiana, where Republicans had a 60–40 house majority and a 37–13 senate supermajority, the Senate Labor Committee chair combined limits on teacher collective bargaining with teacher merit pay and state-funded vouchers for students to attend private schools. In addition, teacher collective bargaining was limited to salaries, benefits, and total number of work days (Davies 2011).

A major driver of these and other laws, including some to be discussed in this chapter, has been legislation drafted and promoted by the American Legislative Exchange Council (ALEC) (NPR Fresh Air 2011a, 2011b). Writing in *The Nation*, Rogers and Dresser stated that "privatization is so central to ALEC's agenda that it has built a fake board game, Publicopoly, on its website, where the curious can find model legislation and other resources on privatizing basically everything" (2011). According to Sullivan, ALEC is "a membership organization of state legislators and powerful corporations and associations, such as the tobacco company Reynolds American Inc., ExxonMobil and the National Rifle Association. Another member is the billion-dollar Corrections Corporation of America—the largest private prison company in the country" (2010). ALEC provides a forum for writing model bills for legislators, with businesses and legislators at the same table. The membership fee for state legislators is $50 a year and tens of thousands of dollars a year for private corporations (Sullivan 2010; Hodai 2010). More than 200 of ALEC's model bills were enacted in 2009 (Sullivan 2010).

One of ALEC's partners in promoting privatization is the Reason Foundation's Leonard Gilroy. Gilroy has also been an active participant in crafting state privatization reports. He co-authored ALEC's State Budget Reform Toolkit (2011), which provides states with templates for privatizing, either by enacting legislation or issuing executive orders. The Toolkit's recommendations include embracing the expanded use of privatization and competitive contracting and establishing state privatization and efficiency councils. The Toolkit also provides model legislation to achieve these goals, including the Competitive Contracting of Public Services Act, the Council on Efficient Government Act, and the Taxpayer Privatization Dividend Act.

AFSCME Local 3111 President Sheri Van Horsen compared ALEC's recommendations to a number of legislative and other actions taken by the state of Arizona and found that nearly 20 recommendations in its State Budget Reform Toolkit had been put into effect or become law in Arizona. Among them were several provisions promoting privatization:

- ALEC recommended establishing state privatization and efficiency councils, and Governor Brewer signed an executive order to form the Commission on Privatization and Efficiency on May 25, 2010 (State of Arizona 2010a).

- ALEC recommended expanding the use of privatization, and the legislature in 2010 and 2011 attempted to privatize state and city services.

- ALEC recommended selling real property assets, and in 2009 the state sold taxpayer-owned buildings and the Capitol.

- ALEC recommended enacting a Taxpayer Bill of Rights, and in 2010 and 2011 the legislature attempted to implement such a bill (Democratic Diva 2011).

Privatization of Public Services During the Great Recession

Privatization can be used to replace public employees with private sector employees, a goal that is strongly supported by those committed to an unrestrained free market or to companies that want to expand into work performed by public employees. Privatization could also be used as a tool to affect the outcome of elections. Public sector employees and union members have tended to be politically active and to vote Democratic (Bice and Poston 2011). As a result, targeting public sector jobs and unions in 2012 could affect the balance of political power by weakening support for Democratic candidates.

Privatization Legislation and Initiatives

Several varieties of legislation promoting privatization have been introduced during the Great Recession. One example, drafted by ALEC, is its Taxpayer Privatization Dividend Act, which states that its main purpose is to set up a commission on privatization to award "ownership and control of a public service to the private sector while retaining public responsibility, or eliminating regulations."

One of the earliest states to adopt such a provision was Arizona. Governor Jan Brewer's Executive Order 2010-10 includes a number of provisions promoted in ALEC's draft legislation (Arizona COPE 2011). Laws establishing state councils on efficient government have been introduced in Virginia, Maryland, Arizona, Kansas, Oregon, Illinois, and South Carolina. In each case, the concepts in the bill mirror the ALEC proposal. In some cases—South Carolina, Arizona, and Illinois—the state bills read as copies of ALEC's model legislation. Virginia's, Oregon's, Maryland's and Kansas' bills, to varying degrees, contain language directly from ALEC's model (Rogers and Dresser 2011).

In July 2011, Pennsylvania Governor Tom Corbett announced that he would create a privatization commission, but the details had not been made public as of this writing (Bumsted 2011).

A second type of legislation, inspired by ALEC's model legislation, would exempt employees of private contractors who perform work on public projects from prevailing wage and collective bargaining laws (Rogers and Dresser 2011).[1] This sort of legislation was proposed in states such as

Ohio, Illinois, and Indiana (Davies 2011). For example, the Ohio House proposed that the "Director of Budget & Management and the authorized representative of a responsible state agency may take any action and execute any contract (defined to include contracts for services and leases) for the provision of a public service to more efficiently and effectively provide public services." Such a contract could not exceed 75 years (§ 126.602(C)(5)), and exempted employers "working at or on a project to provide a public service" from paying prevailing wages and from collective bargaining.[1]

Left unclear was how such a law would square with the National Labor Relations Act (NLRA), which has jurisdiction over the collective bargaining rights of private sector employees. Under the NLRA's successorship doctrine, the employees' union in the public sector could have enforceable rights to continue to represent those employees if they continued to perform the same work in the private sector. In addition, if the employees were not represented by a union at the time their work was privatized, they would have NLRA rights to choose union representation. Indeed, in early 2011 a federal district court struck down a new Illinois law that limited overtime and collectively bargained pay rates for work that was privatized, finding the law was preempted by the NLRA (*Local 727* 2011).

The Ohio House proposed § 126.604: "The gross receipts and income of a successful proposer derived from providing public services under a contract through a project owned by the state shall be exempt from taxation levied by the state and its subdivisions. . . ." (Cincinnati Federation of Teachers, n.d.:23). The provisions exempting private contractors from state taxes may have been intended to place private contractors on the same footing as public agencies, which do not pay taxes. Pro-privatization groups, such as the Business Coalition for Fair Competition, argue that public agencies and nonprofit organizations "unfairly compete with private, for-profit businesses by engaging in commercial activities, but not paying taxes" (Business Coalition for Fair Competition, n.d.).

Around the same time, Arizona, South Carolina, South Dakota, and Utah amended their constitutions to require a secret ballot vote whenever a state or federal law permitted a union election. In May 2011, the National Labor Relations Board (NLRB) announced that it would sue Arizona and South Dakota because the amendments were preempted by the NLRA, which allows decisions about union representation to be made by secret ballot or designations, such as signing union authorization cards (NLRB 2011a, 2011b). The NLRB deferred instituting a lawsuit against South Carolina and Utah to conserve taxpayer resources.

The Promises of Privatization—Better Quality at Lower Prices
Privatization has long been promoted as a free market solution to providing superior services and products. The confluence of the Great Recession and the election of conservative governors and legislators in many states generated support for privatizing public services and infrastructure. During the Great Recession, a number of states considered or actually turned to some form of privatization to continue to provide services to their citizens despite limited budgets (Beckett 2011). Privatization initiatives took a number of forms, including vouchers that could be used toward the cost of private school education, hiring private contractors to administer government agencies or assets (either with the public employees remaining in place or by replacing public employees with private employees), outright sales, sales and leaseback, and long-term leases of public infrastructure.

A driving force behind many of these initiatives has been the Reason Foundation, a libertarian organization (Reason Foundation, n.d.). According to SourceWatch's "Alec Exposed" website, the Reason Foundation's projects include Privatization.org (SourceWatch, n.d.). The Reason Foundation is a member of the Atlas Economic Research Foundation Network, which connects a global network of more than 400 free-market organizations in over 80 countries to the ideas and resources needed to advance the cause of liberty" (AERFN, n.d.). According to Media Matters, Reason Foundation funders who have donated more than a quarter million dollars are the Sarah Scaife Foundation ($2,016,000), David H. Koch Charitable Foundation ($1,522,212), Lynde and Harry Bradley Foundation ($962,500), Claude R. Lambe Charitable Foundation ($857,000), Carthage Foundation ($366,000), and John M. Olin Foundation ($276,500) (Media Matters, n.d.).

The Reason Foundation's influence on events during the Great Recession can be captured in the roles of its director of government reform, Leonard Gilroy. As previously mentioned, he is co-author of ALEC's 2011 State Budget Reform Toolkit. He is also co-author of a May 2011 Commonwealth Foundation/Reason Foundation "Yellow Pages" report advocating privatization in Pennsylvania, an advisor to Arizona's Commission on Privatization and Efficiency, and an advisor to the New Jersey Privatization Task Force. Each of these initiatives is discussed in more detail in this chapter.

State Councils on Privatization: New Jersey. New Jersey made national news when, on March 11, 2010, newly elected Governor Chris Christie issued an executive order creating a privatization task force to address the state's financial crisis. Since then, other states have established privatization councils or announced plans to do so. New Jersey is further along in that process and may presage the course of actions likely to be seen elsewhere.

The executive order's statement of reasons for creating the task force is ultimately related to complaints connected to collective bargaining and public sector unions. The problems listed in the executive order include decisions made by the prior administration that limited actions the state could take to rein in costs, including

- being "hindered by legal impediments, many of which were needlessly self-imposed by the prior administration";

- agreeing to "an unreasonable 'memorandum of agreement' ('MOA') that purports to prevent the State from taking common sense management approaches to achieve personnel efficiencies in the near term";

- "delaying previously negotiated wage increases until after the end of the prior administration, [which] has resulted in the State having reduced flexibility to manage its workforce and effectively increased the costs that will be associated with achieving near-term savings by ensuring rounds of litigation in order to preserve basic managerial prerogatives with respect to the size and composition of the State workforce"; and

- "needlessly" limiting the flexibility needed "to manage its wage and salary payments and the size of its workforce . . . while simultaneously preventing meaningful managerial control of the State workforce."

The executive order then charged the privatization task force to focus "on a number of critical issues, including (a) which government functions are or may be appropriate for privatization; (b) current legal and practical impediments to privatization; (c) ensuring that the scope and quality of services is not inappropriately diminished; and (d) such other matters as may be referred to the Task Force by the Governor" (New Jersey Executive Order 2010; "Governor Christie Creates Task Force" 2010). In other words, the thrust of the charge was that no options other than privatization were to be considered.

The members appointed to the task force were Richard A. Zimmer (chair), a former congressional representative; Todd Caliguire, a Republican politician and president of ANW/Crestwood, a global stationery distributor; Kathleen Davis, executive vice president and chief operating officer of the Chamber of Commerce of Southern New Jersey; John Galandak, president of the New Jersey Commerce and Industry Association; and P. Kelly Hatfield, a former Summit, New Jersey, Council and Board of Education member and microbiologist with an interest in environmental issues and developmental disabilities.

The six advisors to the New Jersey task force were Leonard C. Gilroy, the Reason Foundation; Arthur Maurice, New Jersey Business and Industry Association; Peter J. McDonough, Jr., director of communications to former New Jersey Governor Christine Todd Whitman, consultant to ProtectingAmerica.org, and adjunct professor at the Eagleton Institute of Politics at Rutgers University–New Brunswick; E.S. Savas, professor, Baruch College, City University of New York, and longtime advocate of privatization; Beth Leigh Mitchell, New Jersey assistant attorney general; and Todd Wigder, New Jersey deputy attorney general ("Governor Christie Creates Task Force" 2010).

Two months later, the task force issued its report guided, it said, by its understanding of the mandate "to undertake a comprehensive review of opportunities for privatization within state government and to identify impediments to privatization." The report shows the efforts made by the task force to fulfill its mandate, as well as the difficulty of determining cost savings for a wide range of state services in such a brief period. The report attributes the state's past privatization failures to "poorly conceived concepts, unclear goals, superficial due diligence, inexperienced or undercapitalized contractors, lax or nonexistent government oversight, government officials with clear conflicts of interest, and government mis-conduct" and says that "lessons learned from these failures have informed the recommendations in this report" (New Jersey Privatization Task Force 2010).

There are reasons to be skeptical about those claims. The report does not show that those lessons resulted in a thorough vetting of how public services should be provided. For example, the report states that more than $210 million would be saved by privatizing work that had traditionally been performed by government workers, yet a large percentage of oppor-tunities for savings are identified only as TBD (to be decided/determined). Even worse, the report does not explain how each of the amounts identi-fied as savings was calculated. It is obvious that the task force did not even try to identify costs; it was interested only in savings. It did make the excuse that it could make accurate cost and savings calculations only after privatization had taken place, but, even though true, there must be some mechanism for making plausible calculations as to the effects of privati-zation before it is decided. Otherwise, privatization might actually cost more and result in a lower quality of service.

This problem is not unique to the task force. Although some people hold strong views as to whether the private sector is superior to public provision, most people have a general belief that, before public services are privatized, there should be competition or cost–benefit analyses to determine who can provide better-quality services for less money. However, as in this case, often there is no comparison of cost and quality. Even when there is a comparison, significant costs are often not included or are even excluded and quality is generally not assessed. Two studies provide examples of the problem.

In the first study, on privatization operations in the Department of Labor (DOL) from 2004–2007, the Government Accountability Office (GAO) found that the DOL had no process to assess how privatization had operated and had "excluded a number of substantial costs in its reports to Congress—such as the costs for pre-competition planning, certain transition costs and staff time, and post-competition review activities (GAO 2008). The GAO also found that the DOL's reports of savings were unreliable, contained inaccuracies, and used projections instead of actual numbers that were available to it.

Among the costs that the DOL failed to include were those that would be incurred by the people of New Jersey or any other government when privatizing public services. The GAO found that costs of voluntary separation payments to employees who lost their jobs and monitoring contractor performance were not taken into consideration. The DOL had also not included—and probably could not assess—nonquantifiable, but real, costs of losses in morale, productivity, and trust between current employees and management. Overall, the GAO concluded that the costs that could be quantified were twice as high as reported; therefore, the DOL had greatly overstated savings from privatization. The GAO pointed out that these problems were not limited to the DOL. The DOL's reports had followed Office of Management and Budget regulations, which actually directed that these and other costs be excluded from cost–benefit analyses (GAO 2008). The GAO's findings reveal the same sorts of problems identified in an earlier study of the privatization of the Internal Revenue Service's mailrooms (Dannin 2008).

The authors of the New Jersey Privatization Task Force report (the Zimmer Commission) acknowledged the importance of including costs in their report but then limited the sorts of costs they would consider:

> However, in order to accomplish a true "apples-to-apples" comparison between public sector providers and a private contractor, it is essential that all costs associated with the current governmental structure, including pension and other overhead costs, be ascertained and included in the analysis. (New Jersey Privatization Task Force 2010)

Despite that caveat, there is no evidence that the task force followed through on its own instruction. Rather, the report's focus is on impediments to privatization, many of which are actually traditional good government reforms such as civil service protections (which the task force saw as superseded by collective bargaining) and collectively negoti-ated protections for laid-off workers, including severance pay and benefits through the Displaced Workers Pool. For example, the protections to be accorded employees were limited to their inclusion in a "nonadversarial" process of competing for their own jobs. In doing so, the task force failed to consider the importance of first involving employees and union repre-sentatives in a process of improving the efficiency of their operations. That failure means any decision would be based on a comparison of costs of an inefficient operation and would mean that costs were higher than they needed to be. The task force also included no process for bringing back privatized work that proved to be more expensive or of poorer quality. It also failed to include the cost of oversight or even to recognize the impor-tance of oversight.

It is not difficult to see that, adversarial or nonadversarial, the process would generate costs to morale and productivity and a long-lasting loss of trust between current employees and management. In other words, the task force's focus and approach guaranteed that it would overlook the sorts of real costs to the people of New Jersey that the GAO found in its study. Indeed, the task force included the administration of workers' compensation claims as an impediment to privatization, although no re-lationship to privatization was articulated. It also identified obligations under collective bargaining to negotiate the effects of privatization on employees as a cost, which can be accurate, but ignored the benefits that could come from a good-faith effort to work with state employees to im-prove state operations as a first step. And even though the task force said that it was committed to avoiding past mistakes, its report failed to show how its processes would prevent future failures.

The bulk of the report is devoted to what it calls "privatization opportunities" accompanied by anticipated cost savings, even though the report cautioned that it was impossible to estimate savings until "New Jersey policymakers embrace PPPs [public–private partnerships] and pass broad-based enabling legislation to facilitate them" (New Jersey Privatization Task Force 2010). The task force report includes those figures despite ac-knowledging that it did no analysis "due not only to the fact that the actual cost of a privatized alternative will often not be known until the end of a full-fledged competitive bidding process, but also because New Jersey state government agencies have difficulty calculating with precision the full cost of functions currently performed at the state level" (New Jersey Privatization Task Force 2010:14). Indeed, a large percentage of the services identified for privatization have costs labeled TBD. At no point did the task force present the factors on which it based its estimated savings.[2] As a result, it is difficult to understand how the task force concluded that it had identified savings of $210 million.

Similar initiatives have appeared around the country. For example, on January 21, 2010, Arizona Governor Jan Brewer issued corrected Executive Order 2010-04 (State of Arizona 2010a) establishing a Commission on Privatization and Efficiency (COPE), superseded by Executive Order 2010-10, issued May 25, 2010 (State of Arizona 2010b). On July 21, 2011, COPE issued its privatization recommendations (Arizona COPE 2011). Arizona's commission follows ALEC's model for state privatization commissions. As in New Jersey, Arizona's commission was also composed of people who strongly supported privatization (cell-out-arizona 2008; Democratic Diva 2011) and included the Reason Foundation's Leonard Gilroy as a participant.

The Commonwealth Foundation/Reason Foundation "Yellow Pages" Report. On July 19, 2011, Pennsylvania Governor Tom Corbett also announced the creation of a panel to examine privatizing public services and selling state assets (Bumsted 2011). However, he included no details about its membership or charge. The groundwork for that announcement may have been laid two months earlier in May 2011, when the Commonwealth Foundation and Reason Foundation issued a "Yellow Pages" report that recommended privatization as the remedy for Pennsylvania's financial woes (Gilroy, Kenny, Currie, and Stelle 2011).

The "Yellow Pages" authors claimed, "In well-structured privatization initiatives the government and taxpayers gain accountability they rarely have with public agencies" (Gilroy, Kenny, Currie, and Stelle 2011:4). This statement may puzzle those who are aware that state agencies are held accountable through mechanisms such as freedom of information acts, open meetings acts, citizen oversight panels, state and federal due process and equal protection obligations, civil service regulations, and other laws (Dannin 2006). The report embodies the view that the private sector is the best and most efficient way to provide accountability, apparently even when there is no competition.

The "Yellow Pages" report's vision of what is required of a well-structured privatization initiative rests on its view that a service found in a phonebook's Yellow Pages is most likely "not an inherently governmental function and government should consider buying [the service] rather than using taxpayer dollars to hire and manage public employees." The report also contends that public agencies and services are a drain on the country's finances and that "[e]nding taxpayer-subsidized competition with private businesses also frees up resources for agencies to complete their mission, and saves taxpayers money" (Gilroy, Kenny, Currie, and Stelle 2011:4).

There is no question that the Reason Foundation and its allies have been successful at promoting privatization and free market ideas. The Pennsylvania "Yellow Pages" report may also prove to be highly influential. It is therefore worth examining how they make their case for privatization. The report makes strong claims about privatization; however, it is short on evidence to support those claims. For example, the report claims that private historical sites are more popular than public sites (Gilroy, Kenny, Currie, and Stelle 2011:7–8) and cites the Commonwealth Foundation article, "Private Historical Sites Are More Popular" (Currie 2010), to support that claim.

Currie's article contains a list of sites under the headings of private and private–public partnerships (Table 1) next to a photo of the cover of a *History Channel* magazine issue on "10 Must Visit U.S. Historic Sites" (History Channel 2010). Currie seems not to have noticed that her "top ten list" includes 27 places. She also seems untroubled about a list of historical sites that includes "the Philly Cheesesteak Sandwich." Currie's essay, quoted in full, says of this "top ten list":

> Unfortunately, the ability of [sic] non profit groups, private philanthropy and individual entrepreneurship have to preserve our historic sites and natural resources is largely overlooked.

> The perception that privately run historic sites or parks are of lesser quality is entirely unfounded and exposes what little people really know about sites of public interest.

> The Shriver House Museum and General Lee's Headquarters Museum in Gettysburg are entirely privately owned and operated and are the only museums in Pennsylvania to make the History Channel's "10 Must Visit U.S. Historical Sites." In fact, over half of the attractions listed are either private–public partnerships or privately owned and operated.

> Countless examples exist of the private sector stepping in to create and save historical places, including Muir Woods National Monument. This redwood forest exists today because of businessman and philanthropist, William Kent, who upon being threatened with eminent domain donated his land to the Federal Government—asking it be declared a national monument dedicated to his favorite naturalist, John Muir.

> Sadly, many of our government managed natural and historical treasures, like Muir Woods National Monument, are in danger

of closing. This can be prevented by allowing private individuals and companies to lease or buy these places.

The moral of the story is those sites that taxpayers are forced to support are often inferior to those run by the private sector. Citizens should be able to choose which museums and historical sites to patronize. (Currie 2010)

Currie makes strong claims about privatization and the future of historical sites but without examining the causes of financial problems or the effects of placing public land under private control. The most important cause of underfunded government and government infrastructure is policy choices to lower marginal tax rates and create generous tax breaks for the wealthiest. The historical effects of private ownership or control of natural monopolies are not encouraging.

Overall, Currie's article on historical sites provides no comfort that these issues are being researched or analyzed. Rather, the assertions seem to be based on ideology alone. Her claims are certainly puzzling when compared to the sites listed. First, the list includes far more than ten sites

TABLE 1

Private	Private–Public Partnership
Old State House	Faneuil Hall Marketplace
Bravard [sic] Museum of History	USS Constitution Museum
and Natural Science	Lexington Battle Green Historic Houses
Shriver House Museum	Yellowstone National Park
Gen. Robert Lee's Headquarters Museum	Grand Central Terminal
Custer Battlefield Museum	Betsy Ross House
Crazy Horse Memorial	Muir Woods National Monument
The National Civil Rights Museum	
Sun Studio	
Graceland	
Beale Street	
Rockefeller Center	
Empire State Building	
Philly Cheesesteak Sandwich	
Texas History Wax Museum	
River Walk	
Enchanted Springs Ranch	
Society of the Cincinnati	
Yosemite Adventures	
Yosemite Mountaineering School	
Gold Prospecting Adventures	

included on a national top ten list of historical sites. No doubt some people would advocate their favorite cheesesteak shop on a top ten list, but it seems unlikely the History Channel would. Currie seems not to have been motivated to research these discrepancies, including asking whether she had the correct list, even though it appears someone at the Commonwealth Foundation had a copy of the magazine.

The real History Channel top ten list (History Channel 2010; Gerber 2010) includes Boston, Cape Canaveral, Gettysburg, Little Bighorn, Memphis, New York City, Philadelphia, San Antonio, Washington, D.C., and Yosemite. The History Channel created an interactive companion website, *Hit The Road: Historic Destinations* (History Channel 2010), which links to features such as area attractions. It is those area attractions that appear on the Commonwealth Foundation's expanded list rather than the History Channel's actual top ten list.

A second example is the "Yellow Pages" claim: "One recent example of the lack of good management in state facilities is the 'misplacement' of over 1800 artifacts by the Pennsylvania Historical and Museum Commission" (Gilroy, Kenny, Currie, and Stelle 2011:8). The claim references a news article in the *Pittsburgh Tribune-Review*, whose headline suggests that a serious problem exists in managing historical artifacts. The text of the article, however, does not actually support that proposition (Bumsted and Zlatos 2010). In fact, the article questions whether the missing artifacts were actually missing and says that many public museums are actually run by volunteers or private organizations. In other words, the article could be taken as support for the conclusion that allowing public museums and historical sites to be run by volunteers and private ventures is not good stewardship.

None of these issues was hidden in the news story. In fact, the first paragraph makes it clear that there was uncertainty as to whether or how many objects might be missing. For example, it says that the inventory list used was 12 years old and that the commission staff was able to locate 300 of the missing objects in one afternoon, suggesting that there was a problem using an ancient inventory list. The news story also suggests that part of the problem was that the commission's budget had been cut from $58 million to $26 million for the past four years, causing cuts in staff from 443 full-time positions to 228.

In other words, if the goal was making accurate claims in support of findings and recommendations, the authors of the "Yellow Pages" report would have searched for the facts, but they apparently did not. For example, there was an audit report, but the "Yellow Pages" did not cite the audit report or the press release on the audit report, even though both were available online (Wagner 2011). Auditor General Jack Wagner said that the deep budget cuts the commission has experienced in recent years were a contributing factor to the lax oversight and dated inventory system. The commission's annual appropriation declined by 54% in three years, from $58.4 million in fiscal year 2006–2007 to $27 million in 2009–2010. As a result, the museum's staffing has declined from 443 full-time positions to 228 during the corresponding period ("Auditor General Jack Wagner Says" 2010).

The top ten list and missing artifacts claims are just two examples of bold statements made in the "Yellow Pages" report, even though there is no support for their accuracy. In most cases, though, the claims made in the "Yellow Pages" report cite nothing to support its claims. Though deeply flawed, the report is likely to be highly influential with Governor Corbett's privatization commission when it is appointed because its point of view is congenial to Corbett's.

Accountability. Accountability is an important way to understand whether work should be done by the private or public sector. Theoretically, in the private sector, choice and competition are supposed to create a form of accountability by disciplining those who do not provide quality goods and services. Put another way, the possibility of failure, based on customer decisions, is supposed to drive improvement at lower cost.

However, competition does not exist in all instances because, in some circumstances, there is a natural monopoly. In these cases, when there is no competition, there is no market accountability. The response to this problem has been to create accountability through oversight mechanisms such as open meetings and freedom of information acts, civil service regulations, and oversight of various sorts. In other words, public sector accountability is part of our system of democratic governance.

If government services are privatized when no competition exists or can exist, there is no accountability through competition, and no public sector accountability mechanisms apply. As a result, privatization can leave the public welfare and purse unguarded. Oversight and accountability are still needed, but no mechanisms have been put in place to protect the public. That is precisely the situation that has developed in some states through the policies of governors elected during the Great Recession.

Newly elected Ohio Governor John Kasich set up a private Web portal, FixOhioNow.com, to solicit résumés for government positions. Kasich's office claims that, because the website is privately funded, résumés are not subject to the state's public records law (Beckett 2011; Reporters Committee, n.d.)—a claim of dubious legal or constitutional merit:

In the Ohio House, the budget was a grab bag for would-be private providers of public services. David Brennan, owner of Ohio's largest operator of charter schools and multimillion-dollar contributor to GOP coffers, dispatched his lobbyist, Tom Needles, to secure an audacious deal. Needles walked away with authority to create a new breed of for-profit charter schools funded by taxpayers with no requirement to report how the public dollars are spent. (Hallett 2011)

David Brennan's White Hat Management may be the sort of educational entrepreneurship advocated by ALEC, but the reality has not been encouraging:

During the last few years, White Hat has been embroiled in litigation brought by its franchisees and the Ohio Department of Education concerning the management of the schools, its financial practices, and its public obligations as a state actor. According to a ProPublica report, "Government data suggest that schools with for-profit managers have somewhat worse academic results than charters without management companies, and a number of boards have clashed with managers over a lack of transparency in how they are using public funds. Only 2 percent of White Hat's students have made the progress expected under federal education law." (Dannin 2012)

Conclusion

The way in which public services are and will be provided has undergone major changes in recent years. Since the 2010 elections, privatization has increasingly become a major issue throughout the United States. Privatization has made national news where there have been major demonstrations and protests, as in Wisconsin, or where governors have aggressively promoted privatization and unions and the public have resisted, as in New Jersey. More recently, revelations about the role of ALEC in promoting privatization and eliminating or limiting public sector collective bargaining rights have shed light on the impetus toward privatization.

These recent events mean that privatization is now on the national radar screen. Of longer-term importance will be changes affecting the people who provide those services. If public sector employees—or private sector employees who perform work formerly done by public sector workers—no longer have decent benefits and civil service, union, and other protections, how will this affect states and the country as a whole?

Will this work remain a calling that attracts those who want to work for the public benefit? Will the quality of the work be degraded, or will it even continue to exist? And if the work is performed by private sector employees with inferior pay and working conditions and few protections, what will be the political and economic effects?

Endnotes

[1] Ohio Revised Code, Chapter 4115: Wages and Hours on Public Works (http://codes.ohio.gov/orc/4115). This legislation includes provisions on maximum hours and prevailing wage, including health and life insurance benefits and workers compensation. Chapter 4117 includes provisions on public employee collective bargaining (http://codes.ohio.gov/orc/4117). According to the Ohio Legislative Service Commission analysis, "The bill specifies that prevailing wage laws do not apply to any projects and public employee collective bargaining laws do not apply to any employees working at or on a project to provide a public service" (Ohio Legislative Service Commission 2010).

[2] For a more comprehensive critique of the task force report, see Keefe and Fine (2011).

References

Allegretto, Sylvia A., and Jeffrey Keefe. 2010 (Oct.). "The Truth about Public Employees in California." Center on Wage and Employment Dynamics. <http://www.employmentpolicy.org/sites/www.employmentpolicy.org/files/truth_public_employees.pdf>. [November 14, 2011].

American Legislative Exchange Council (ALEC). 2011. "State Budget Reform Toolkit." <http://www.alec.org/wp-content/uploads/Budget_toolkit.pdf>. [November 14, 2011].

Anti-Defamation League. No date. "Tax Protest Movement." <http://www.adl.org/learn/ext_us/TPM. asp?xpicked=4&item=21>. [November 14, 2011].

Arizona Commission on Privatization and Efficiency (COPE). 2011. "Report to Governor Janice K. Brewer: Recommendations." <http://www.azcope.gov/FinalreportJuly2011.pdf>. [November 14, 2011].

Atlas Economic Research Foundation Network (AERFN). No date. "North American Institute Directory." <http://atlasnetwork.org/wp-content/uploads/2011/02/Atlas_Directory_02162011.xlsx>. [November 14, 2011].

"Auditor General Jack Wagner Says Historical and Museum Commission Not Properly Protecting State Historic Artifacts." 2010 (Oct. 28). <http://www.auditorgen.state.pa.us/Department/Press/WagnerSaysMuseumCommNotProtectingHistory.html>. [November 14, 2011].

Beckett, Christine. 2011. "Government Privatization and Government Transparency: What Happens When Private Companies Do the Governing?" *The News Media & The Law*, Vol. 35, no. 1 (Winter), p. 21 <http://www.rcfp.org/news/mag/35-1/government_privatization_and _government_transparency_21.html>. [November 14, 2011].

Bel, Germà, Xavier Fageda, and Mildred E. Warner. 2010. "Is Private Production of Public Services Cheaper than Public Production? A Meta-Regression Analysis of Solid Waste and Water Services." *Journal of Policy Analysis and Management*, Vol. 29, no. 3, pp. 553–77.

Bel, Germà, Robert Hebdon, and M.E. Warner. 2007. "Local Government Reform: Privatization and Its Alternatives." *Local Government Studies*, Vol. 33, no. 4, pp. 507–15.

Bender, Keith, and John Heywood. 2010 (Apr.). "Out of Balance? Comparing Public and Private Sector Compensation over 20 Years." Center for State and Local Government Excellence & National Institute on Retirement Security. <http://www.nirsonline.org/storage/nirs/documents/final_out_of_balance_report_april_2010.pdf>. [March 28, 2012].

Bice, Daniel, and Ben Poston. 2011 (Feb. 28). "Missing Senators Rely Heavily on Union Campaign Dollars." *Journal Sentinel.* <http://www.jsonline.com/news/state politics/117078618.html>. [November 14, 2011].

Bumsted, Brad. 2011. "Corbett Panel to Look at Selling State Assets, Privatizing Services." *Pittsburgh Tribune-Review.* July 19. <http://www.pittsburghlive.com/x/pittsburghtrib/news/state/s_747456.html>. [November 14, 2011].

Bumsted, Brad, and Bill Zlatos. 2010 (Oct. 29). "Audit: Pennsylvania Museums' Artifacts 'Likely Lost Forever.'" *Tribune-Review.* <http://www.pittsburghlive.com/x/pittsburghtrib/news/regional/s_706638.html>. [November 14, 2011].

Business Coalition for Fair Competition. No date. "How Does Government Unfairly Compete?" <http://www.governmentcompetition.org/howgovtcompetes.html>. [November 14, 2011].

Carlile, William H. 2011 (Jun. 28). "Collective Bargaining: Nevada Governor Signs Measure Curbing Public Sector Supervisors' Bargaining Rights." *BNA Government Employment Relations Reporter*, Vol. 49, p. 834.

cell-out-arizona. 2010 (Dec. 8). "Governor's Commission on Privatization Recommends … Privatization." *Tucson Citizen.* <http://tucsoncitizen.com/cell-out-arizona/2010/12/08/governor%e2%80%99s-commission-on-privatization-recommends%e2%80%a6 privatization>. [November 14, 2011].

Cincinnati Federation of Teachers. No date. "Proposed Budget Provisions Affecting Collective Bargaining Rights Public Sector Employment: Comparison Between SUB. H.B. No. 153 and AM. SUB. S.B. No. 5." <http://www.cft-aft.org/ohbudget/camparsinaffectcb.pdf>. [November 14, 2011].

CNN Politics. 2011 (Mar. 31). "Reality Check: What We Really Know about the Budget." <http://www.cnn.com/2011/POLITICS/03/31/gallery.reality.budget/index.html>. [November 14, 2011].

Currie, Katrina. 2010 (Mar. 18). "Private Historical Sites Are More Popular." Commonwealth Foundation. <http://www.commonwealthfoundation.org/policyblog/info/private-historical-sites-are-more-popular>. [November 14, 2011].

Dannin, Ellen. 2006. "Red Tape or Accountability: Privatization, Public-ization, and Public Values." *Cornell Journal of Law and Public Policy*, Vol. 15, no. 1 (Fall), pp. 111–63.

Dannin, Ellen. 2008. "Counting What Matters: Privatization, People with Disabilities, and the Cost of Low-Waged Work." *Minnesota Law Review*, Vol. 92, pp. 1348–89.

Dannin, Ellen. 2011. "Crumbling Infrastructure, Crumbling Democracy: Infrastructure Privatization Contracts and Their Effects on State and Local Governance." *Northwestern*

Journal of Law and Social Policy, Vol. 6, no. 1 (Winter), pp. 47–105. <http://www.law. northwestern.edu/journals/njlsp/v6/n1/2/2Dannin.pdf>. [November 14, 2011].

Dannin, Ellen. 2012. "Privatizing Government Services in the Era of Alec and the Great Recession." *University of Toledo Law Review*. Forthcoming.

Davies, Tom. 2011 (Mar. 13). "GOP Taking Wide Swipe at Hoosier Unions." *Pittsburgh Post-Tribune*. <http://posttrib.suntimes.com/news/4296115-418/gop-taking-wide-swipe-at-hoosier-unions.html>. [November 14, 2011].

Democratic Diva. 2011 (Jul. 25). "A Concise and Useful Analysis of ALEC's Influence in Arizona." Democratic Diva.com. <http://www.democraticdiva.com/2011/07/25/a-concise-and-useful-analysis-of-alecs-influence-in-arizona/>. [November 14, 2011].

Dougherty, Conor. 2010 (Apr. 1). "Cash-Poor Cities Take on Unions." *Wall Street Journal*. <http://online.wsj.com/article/SB10001424052748704059004575127991641216702.html>. [November 14, 2011].

Epstein, Jennifer. 2011 (Mar. 8). "Idaho OKs Bill Limiting Bargaining." Politico. <http://www. politico.com/news/stories/0311/50892.html>. [November 14, 2011].

Feldscher, Kyle. 2011 (Jul. 19). "Gov. Rick Snyder Signs Major Changes to Teacher Tenure into Law." AnnArbor.com. <http://annarbor.com/news/gov-rick-snyder-signs-major-changes-to-teacher-tenure-into-law>. [November 14, 2011].

Gerber, Greg. 2010 (Mar. 11). "Go RVing Top 10 Destinations Guide Distributed to History Viewers." <http://rvdailyreport.com/news/id/4812/go-rving-top-10-destinations-guide-distributed-to-history-viewers>. [November 14, 2011].

Gilroy, Leonard, Harris Kenny, Katrina Currie, and Elizabeth Stelle. 2011 (May 26). "'Yellow Pages' Privatizing Government in Pennsylvania: Private Sector Solutions for the Keystone State." Commonwealth Foundation/Reason Foundation. <http://reason.org/files/pennsylvania_yellow_pages_privatization.pdf>. [November 14, 2011].

Government Accountability Office (GAO). 2008. "Department of Labor: Better Cost Assessments and Departmentwide Performance Tracking Are Needed to Effectively Manage Competitive Sourcing Program." GAO-09-14. <http://www.gao.gov/htext/d0914.html>. [April 6, 2012].

"Governor Christie Creates Task Force to Develop a Comprehensive Approach to Workforce Privatization." 2010 (Mar. 11). Press release. <http://www.state.nj.us/governor/news/news/552010/approved/20100311b.html>. [November 14, 2011].

Hallett, Joe. 2011 (Jun. 5). "Commentary: Lawmakers Ought to Slow Down the Push to Privatize." *The Columbus Dispatch*. <http://www.dispatch.com/live/content/editorials/stories/2011/06/05/lawmakers-ought-to-slow-down-the-push-to-privatizehtml?sid=101>. [November 14, 2011].

Hefetz, Amir, and M. Warner. 2004. "Privatization and Its Reverse: Explaining the Dynamics of the Government Contracting Process." *Journal of Public Administration, Research and Theory*, Vol. 14, no. 2, pp. 171–90.

History Channel. 2010. "Top 10 Destinations." <http://www.history.com/interactives/historic-destinations>. [November 14, 2011].

Hodai, Beau. 2010 (Jun. 21). "Ties That Bind: Arizona Politicians and the Private Prison Industry: A Revolving Cast of Lobbyists and Legislators Blur the Line Between Public

Service and Corporate Profits." *In These Times.* <http://www.inthesetimes.com/article/6085/ties_ that_bind_arizona_politicians_and_the_private_prison_industry>. [November 14, 2011].

Keefe, Jeffrey. 2010a (Jul. 30). "Are N.J. Public Employees Overpaid?" Employment Policy Research Network. <http://www.employmentpolicy.org/sites/www.employment policy.org/files/NJ%20Public%20Employee%20Comp.pdf>. [November 14, 2011].

Keefe, Jeffrey. 2010b (Sep. 15)."Debunking the Myth of the Overcompensated Public Employee: The Evidence." Employment Policy Research Network. <http://www.employmentpolicy.org/sites/www.employmentpolicy.org/files/Debunking%20 the%20Myth.pdf>. [November 14, 2011].

Keefe, Jeffrey. 2011 (Feb.). "Are Wisconsin Public Employees Over-Compensated?" Employment Policy Research Network. <http://www.employmentpolicy.org/sites/www.employment policy.org/files/wisconsin.pdf>. [November 14, 2011].

Keefe, Jeffrey, and Janice Fine. 2011. "In the Public Interest? Safeguarding New Jersey's Public Investments: A Response to the New Jersey Privatization Task Force Report." New Jersey AFL-CIO. <http://www.njaflcio.org/files/njaflcio/Legislative/ Safeguarding%20 New%20Jersey%27s%20Public%20Investments%20Keefe%20 and%20Fine.pdf>. [November 14, 2011].

Lav, Iris J. 2010 (Mar. 15). "A Formula for Decline: Lessons from Colorado for States Considering TABOR." Center for Budget and Policy Priorities. <http:// growthandjustice.typepad.com/files/10-19-05sfp.pdf>. [November 14, 2011].

Local 727, International Brotherhood of Teamsters v. *Metropolitan Pier & Exposition Authority,* Case No. 10 C 3484 (N.D. Ill. Mar. 31, 2011).

McNichol, Elizabeth, Phil Oliff, and Nicholas Johnson. 2011 (Jun. 17). "States Continue to Feel Recession's Impact." Center on Budget and Policy Priorities. <http:// www.cbpp.org/cms/index.cfm?fa=view&id=711>. [November 14, 2011].

Media Matters Action Network. No date. "Conservative Transparency: Reason Foundation." Media Matters Action Network. <http://mediamattersaction.org/transparency/ organization/Reason_Foundation/funders>. [November 14, 2011].

Mendel, Ed. 2011 (Jun. 13). "Outsource Jobs: New Way to Cut Pension Costs?" CalPensions. <http://calpensions.com/2011/06/13/outsource-jobs-new-way-to-cut-pension-costs>. [November 14, 2011].

National Labor Relations Board (NLRB). 2011a (May 6). "NLRB Initiates Litiga- tion Against the State of Arizona on Amendment Limiting Method for Choosing Union Representation." Press release. <http://www. nlrb.gov/news/nlrb-initiates- litigation-against-state-arizona-amendment-limiting-method-choosing-union-repres>. [November 14, 2011].

National Labor Relations Board (NLRB). 2011b (Jan. 14). "State Constitutional Amendments Fact Sheet." Press release. <http://www.nlrb.gov/news-media/ backgrounders/state-amendments-and-preemption-0>. [November 14, 2011].

National Public Radio Fresh Air. 2011a (Jul. 21). "National Chairman of ALEC Responds to Report." <http://www.npr.org/2011/07/21/138575665/national-chairman-of- alec-responds-to-report>. [November 14, 2011].

National Public Radio Fresh Air. 2011b (Jul. 21). "Who's Really Writing States' Legislation?" Interview with John Nichols. <http://www.npr.org/2011/07/21/138537515/how- alec-shapes-state-politics-behind-the-scenes>. [November 14, 2011].

New Jersey Executive Order No. 17 (March 11, 2010). <http://www.state.nj.us/infobank/circular/eocc17.pdf>. [November 14, 2011].

New Jersey Privatization Task Force. (May 31, 2010). "Report to Governor Chris Christie, Executive Summary. <http://www.nj.gov/governor/news/reports/pdf/2010709_NJ_Privatization_Task_Force_Final_Report_%28May_2010%29.pdf>. [November 14, 2011].

Ohio Legislative Service Commission. 2010. "Bill Analysis, Sub. H.B. 153, 129th General Assembly as Pending in H. Finance and Appropriations (LSC 129 1066-2)." <http://www.legislature.state.oh.us/analysis.cfm?ID=129_HB_153&hf=analyses129/h0153-i-129.htm# Toc289844403>. [November 14, 2011].

Ohio Revised Code, Chapter 4115: Wages and Hours on Public Works. <http://codes.ohio.gov/orc/4115>. [November 14, 2011].

Ohio Revised Code, Chapter 4117: Wages and Hours on Public Works. <http://codes.ohio.gov/orc/4117>. [November 14, 2011].

Rogers, Joel, and Laura Dresser. 2011. "ALEC Exposed: Business Domination Inc." *The Nation*, August 1–8. <http://www.thenation.com/article/161977/alec-exposed-business-domination-inc>. [November 14, 2011].

Reason Foundation. No date. "Frequently Asked Questions." <http://reason.org/about/faq/#q6>. [November 14, 2011].

Reporters Committee for Freedom of the Press. No date. "Open Government Guide." <http://www.rcfp. org/ogg/index.php?op=compare&outline=R1B4&all=true>. [November 14, 2011].

SourceWatch. "Privatization.org." <http://www.sourcewatch.org/index.php?title =Reason_Foundation>. [November 14, 2011].

State of Arizona Executive Order 2010-04 (January 21, 2010). 2010a. <http://azmemory.lib.az.us/cdm4/item_viewer.php?CISOROOT=/execorders&CISOPTR=694&CISOBOX=1&REC=9>. [November 14, 2011].

State of Arizona Executive Order 2010-10 (May 25, 2010). 2010b. <http://www.azcope.gov/press_releases/ExecutiveOrder.pdf>. [November 14, 2011].

State of Michigan 96th Legislature Regular Session of 2011. Enrolled House Bill No. 4625. <http://www. legislature.mi.gov/documents/2011-2012/billenrolled/House/pdf/2011-HNB-4625.pdf>. [November 14, 2011].

State of Michigan 96th Legislature Regular Session of 2011. Enrolled House Bill No. 4626 <http://www. legislature.mi.gov/documents/2011-2012/billenrolled/House/pdf/2011-HNB-4626.pdf>. [November 14, 2011].

State of Michigan 96th Legislature Regular Session of 2011. Enrolled House Bill No. 4627 <http://www. legislature.mi.gov/documents/2011-2012/billenrolled/House/pdf/2011-HNB-4627.pdf>. [November 14, 2011].

Sullivan, Laura. 2010 (Oct. 28). "Prison Economics Help Drive Ariz. Immigration Law." NPR Morning Edition. <http://www.npr.org/templates/story/story.php?storyId=130833741>. [November 14, 2011].

Taylor, Mac. 2010 (Apr. 27). *Evaluating the Sale-Leaseback Proposal: Should the State Sell Its Office Buildings?* Report by the Legislative Analyst's Office, pp. 3–4. <http://www.lao.ca. gov/reports/2010/edu/sale_leaseback/sale_leaseback_042710.pdf>. [November 14, 2011].

U.S. Department of Transportation, Federal Highway Administration. No date. "Highway History: When Did the Federal Government Begin Collecting the Gas Tax?" <http:// www. fhwa.dot.gov/infrastructure/gastax.cfm>. [November 14, 2011].

Wagner, Jack. 2011 (Oct.). "A Special Performance Audit of the Pennsylvania Historical and Museum Commission: Accountability of Historic Artifacts." <http://www .auditorgen.state.pa.us/reports/performance/special/speHistoricalMuseumComm 102810.pdf>. [November 14, 2011].

Winston & Strawn, LLP. 2011. "Labor & Employment Practice, Labor News, Select Events and News from the World of Organized Labor." <http://www.winston.com/siteFiles/ Publications/April2011_Labor_Newsv2.html#State>. [November 14, 2011].

Wisniewski, Mary. 2011 (Mar. 10). "Factbox: Several States Beyond Wisconsin Mull Union Limits." <http://www.reuters.com/article/2011/03/11/us-usa-unions-states-idUST RE7295QI20110311?feedType=RSS&virtualBrandChannel=11563>. [November 14, 2011].

Chapter 5

The Great Recession's Impact on African American Public Sector Employment

William M. Rodgers III

Rutgers University

and

The National Poverty Center

The Great Recession generated the largest contraction in total nonfarm employment since World War II. From December 2007 to June 2009, defined as a recession by the National Bureau of Economic Research (NBER), more than 7.4 million (5.4%) jobs were lost, causing the national unemployment rate to jump from 5.0% to 9.5%. Men were hardest hit due to the widespread losses in construction and manufacturing. Their unemployment rate climbed from 4.5% to 9.8%, compared to an increase of 4.3% to 7.5% for women. Women's losses were muted by private sector growth in the education and health services sectors.

The deterioration in the labor market status of African Americans, especially men, was even worse.[1] African American men started the recession with a jobless rate of 10.0%. During the 18-month downturn, their unemployment rate almost doubled, peaking at 17.5%.[2]

Numerous labor supply, labor demand, and institutional reasons exist as to why African Americans bore the brunt of the recession. They range from labor supply explanations that focus on educational attainment, skills, and experience to labor demand problems such as being concentrated in industries and geographic areas that were hardest hit by the downturn. Labor market discrimination also contributed to the disparate impacts.[3] Another explanation for the disparate impacts, which has received little attention, is the contraction in public sector employment.

Pressures on State and Local Governments

During the recession, the budgets of state and local governments came under tremendous pressure. Record declines in tax revenue and large structural budget deficits led to large and widespread budget cuts. Unlike the federal government, state and local governments must balance their budgets each fiscal year. To do so, they must cut spending, raise taxes, or both.

Early in the Great Recession, states tended to rely on making across-the-board and targeted cuts and tapping rainy day funds. As the recession deepened, states expanded their use of across-the-board and targeted cuts. They also began to implement fee increases, local aid reductions, layoffs, and furloughs. Due to the nature of state budget construction, as the economy began its slow recovery in fiscal year (FY) 2010, even more states chose to use layoffs and furloughs to either reduce or eliminate their budget shortfalls. In FY 2011, the use of layoffs and furloughs began to moderate.

Local governments used similar strategies. From FY 2009 to FY 2011, personnel cuts were the most widely used tools, followed by the delay and cancellation of capital projects. The most common city personnel–related cuts were (1) hiring freezes, (2) salary/wage reductions or freezes, (3) layoffs, (4) early retirements, (5) furloughs, (6) decreased health care benefits, (7) revisions to union contracts, and (8) reduced pension benefits.

The impact of the type and timing of cuts shows up in the Bureau of Labor Statistics' (BLS) published payroll data. In FY 2008, more than 2.2 million private sector jobs were lost, but public sector employment experienced a modest increase. In FY 2009, both sectors contracted, according to Current Employment Survey data (available online at http:// www.bls.gov). It is important to note that the mandate to carry out the decennial census led, albeit modestly, to continued federal employment growth.

During FY 2010, a twist occurred between the private and public sectors. Private sector employment began to expand, while public sector employment began to contract. This pattern continued in FY 2011. The public sector contractions would have been larger had the variety of state and federal stimulus and emergency packages such as the American Recovery and Reinvestment Act (ARRA) not been implemented.[4]

Potential Impact on African Americans

Have African Americans experienced a disparate impact as a result of state and local budget cuts? It is a distinct possibility because African Americans comprise a disproportionate share of public sector workers. Employment in the public sector has historically helped provide minorities with opportunities in the workforce.

The National Urban League's Equality Index (Hardy 2011) illustrates these points. The index consists of five components: economics, health, education, social justice, and civic engagement. In 2011, the civic engagement index was the only component that was at parity. In fact, it has been at parity since the league first published the index in 2005. A major reason for parity in the civic engagement index is that African Americans have greater representation than whites in federal executive branch (nonpostal) employment and state and local government employment. If the federal, state, and local cuts have had a disparate impact on African Americans, the civic engagement index could fall from parity, leading to an overall decline in the league's equality index.

What should be expected? *A priori*, the answer is not clear. It lies in the type of public sector jobs that were cut, the relative education and experience of public sector African Americans, and the rules that govern displacement. Further, there is less occupational segregation in the public sector than in the private sector. More African Americans are in occupations that are involved with hiring and firing decisions in the public sector. This higher stature and the existence of internal labor markets could help to mute or minimize the budget cuts' disparate racial effects.

Methodology and Major Findings

To explore whether African Americans have been hurt more than other workers by public sector cuts, I analyzed a variety of sources: published BLS data, published EEOC-4 data on state and local employment (full time, part time, and new hires), and microdata from the 2006, 2008, and 2010 Displaced Worker Surveys (DWS) of the Current Population Survey. The major findings are as follows.

Aggregate BLS Employment Data

- In 2007, African Americans comprised 14.6% of government employment. By 2009, their share had dropped to 14.2% of public sector jobs. It remained at 14.2% in 2010.

- African Americans in the private sector also experienced a small decline in their share, falling from 10.9% to 10.5%. Some of the lost ground was recovered in 2010. Their share ticked up slightly to 10.7%.

Aggregate EEOC-4 Data

- The aggregate EEOC-4 data on state and local governments with at least 100 employees indicate that during the recession African Americans expanded their full-time, part-time, and new-hire shares in the public sector. However, this is largely because they experienced smaller losses than whites.

The DWS evidence contains a very different narrative than what the aggregate data show:

- Even after controlling for personal characteristics, including industry and occupation at the time of displacement and local economic conditions, the probability of displacement of public sector African Americans relative to public sector whites increased from no gap prior to the recession to a gap of 2.8 percentage points during the recession.

- This gap that emerged equals the adjusted private sector black–white displacement gap, which prior to the recession equaled 1.7 and 1.9 percentage points and widened to 2.8 percentage points during the recession.

- Public sector African Americans have a 22.0% lower probability of re-employment relative to white public sector respondents. It exceeds the 16 percentage point gap in the private sector.

- This 22-point disadvantage is due solely to unemployment and not to movement out of the labor force.

In the first section that follows, I describe the macroeconomic context. Next, I describe the tools that states used to balance their budgets during the recession and weak recovery. I then present evidence from the EEOC-4 files. Finally, I offer an analysis of microlevel data from the 2006, 2008, and 2010 Displaced Worker Surveys of the Current Population Survey and then summarize my analysis and conclusions.

Macroeconomic Context

The NBER has defined the Great Recession as spanning from December 2007 to June 2009. Real gross domestic product (GDP) contracted by 5.0% from the fourth quarter of 2007 to the second quarter of 2009.[5] Nonfarm payroll employment fell by more than 7.4 million (5.4%). These losses were more than double the average during the last six recessions. The divergence emerged in the seventh to ninth months of the recession, which coincides with the freezing of U.S. financial markets.

As a result, the official U.S. unemployment rate almost doubled, increasing from 5.0% to 9.5%. A new feature of this recession was the doubling of the number of Americans who were working part time but wanted full-time work, along with those who dropped out of the labor force but if offered a job would take it. When these individuals are added, the resulting more-comprehensive unemployment rate started at 8.8% and ended the recession at 16.6%.[6]

Disparate Impact

The recession rewrote the rules through its disparate impact on Americans. Men bore the brunt of the recession. Some analysts call the Great Recession a "Mancession." For example, white men and women had similar pre-recession unemployment rates of 4.5% and 4.3%, respectively. Men's unemployment rate jumped to 9.8%, however, while the unemployment rate of women rose to only 7.5%. Americans with the most education were not immune to joblessness. The college graduate unemployment rate doubled.

Sectoral Variation

Much of this new joblessness can be attributed to the sectors that were hit and the fact that Americans were extremely vulnerable to an economic downturn. The largest job losses occurred in construction (19.8%) and manufacturing (14.6%). The only broad industrial sector that added jobs was the education and health services sector, which expanded by 3.3%.

There were also other aspects of the economy that deepened the recession's impact. Americans entered the recession with household debt at an all-time high. The share of Americans who were employed just prior to the recession (December 2007) was similar to the level at the beginning of the November 2001 recovery. Real earnings and income had also been stagnant over this pre-recession period. Basically, Americans had little cushion to withstand the recession.

Impact on African Americans

One basic recession rule that remained in place was the outcome that African Americans bore a disproportionate burden of the downturn. The unemployment rate of African Americans was already close to 10.0% at the recession's start. By the recession's eighth month, when the crisis moved beyond the finance and construction sectors and became a personal consumption or aggregate demand recession, the African American unemployment rate crossed the 10.0% threshold.

Macro Trends

Where have the macroeconomy and labor market headed since then? The NBER designated June 2009 as the start of the recovery. The recovery can be divided into two segments: jobless and "pothole" recovery periods. A jobless recovery occurs when economic growth is positive but not large enough to create positive job growth. A pothole recovery occurs when economic growth is slightly higher but only large enough to generate monthly job growth that is no greater than 130,000 to 150,000, the range needed to account for natural population growth. As a result, only workers with the greatest skill, education, and strongest networks obtain jobs, while others either face prolonged job searches or they leave the labor force. The problem facing the economy over these two periods has been the slow pace of economic growth. Real GDP growth has not been consistent with robust job creation (e.g., at least 200,000 per month). All of real GDP growth's major components have been slow to recover, but growth in personal consumption, which comprises 70.0% of real GDP, seems to be the primary culprit that is inhibiting job creation.

Implications for Unemployment

More specifically, from June 2009 to February 2010, real GDP grew at a tepid rate of 2.3%. During this jobless segment of the recovery, private sector employment continued to fall (1.1% decline). With real GDP growth having crossed the 3.0% threshold since February 2010—a modest result—private sector job creation began to grow in the pothole recovery at an anemic 2.6% clip.

What do these macro trends mean for U.S. unemployment? For the unemployment rate to begin to fall, average monthly job creation must exceed 130,000 to 150,000. This threshold corresponds to the growth in jobs needed to accommodate natural increases in the population and immigration. During the jobless recovery, the unemployment rate instead continued to rise because private sector employment was still contracting at an average monthly loss of 145,000. The unemployment rate peaked at 10.1% in October 2009. Since February 2010, the unemployment rate has neither risen nor fallen because average monthly jobs growth equals 138,000, which is right in the middle of the break-even range. At this writing, the unemployment rate has remained above 9.0%.[7] State and local tax revenues have been slow to recover.

State and Local Budget Cutting Methods and Public Sector Employment

Table 1 summarizes the strategies that states used from FY 2006 to FY 2011 to reduce or eliminate their budget gaps. Although the NBER-defined recession did not start until December 2007, two months into FY 2008, states such as Rhode Island and Maine were already taking steps to address their budget gaps.[8] The most common approaches were to use targeted cuts and rainy day funds. During the recession's first year, states expanded their use of targeted cuts, rainy day funds, and other remedies (see the notes in Table 1). Layoffs, user fees, and agency reorganization became more common.

In FY 2009 (October 2008 to September 2009), states really began to feel the effects of the recession's impact on their finances. During that fiscal year, 71.0% of states used targeted cuts, 45.0% tapped their rainy day funds, 43.0% pursued across-the-board cuts, 35.0% reduced local aid, one third used furloughs and layoffs, and 12.0% implemented early retirement and agency reorganization. Only 6.0% of states chose privatization as a strategy. With respect to local governments, the National League of Cities (Hoene and Pagano 2011) reports that two thirds of city governments surveyed made personnel cuts to address budget shortfalls.

Even though the economy began to recover in the second half of FY 2010, revenue shortfalls still required state and local governments to use

TABLE 1
Methods for Reducing or Eliminating State Budget Gaps (Percentage of States)

FY	Fees	Layoffs	Furloughs	Early retirement	Across-the-board cuts	Targeted cuts
2006	0%	2%	2%	2%	2%	6%
2007	4%	2%	2%	0%	2%	2%
2008	4%	6%	2%	2%	12%	18%
2009	24%	31%	33%	12%	43%	71%
2010	47%	53%	43%	12%	53%	67%
2011	28%	40%	38%	12%	40%	68%

FY	Reduce local aid	Reorganize agencies	Privatization	Rainy day funds	Other
2006	2%	2%	2%	6%	6%
2007	0%	0%	0%	2%	8%
2008	2%	4%	2%	16%	18%
2009	35%	12%	6%	45%	45%
2010	43%	27%	6%	37%	57%
2011	32%	24%	10%	18%	60%

Source: Assorted years of The Fiscal Survey of States, a report by the National Governors Association and the National Association of State Budget Officers, Washington, DC (http://www.nasbo.org).

Notes: Based on data from National Governors Association's fiscal survey of states. The NGA obtains the information from the National Association of State Budget Officers. "Other" methods include higher education–related fees (7), court-related fees (9), transportation/motor vehicle–related fees (8), business-related fees (6), salary reductions (9), cuts to state employee benefits (13), lottery expansion (4), gambling/gambling expansion (4), and other (15). Specific methods covered by the "other" category are reported in "Notes to the Tables" in each report. For example, in FY 2011, other actions in Illinois included tax amnesty payments of $266 million and in New Jersey changes in available tax credits. The numbers in parentheses refer to the number of states that used these methods in FY 2011.

a variety of fiscal tools to reduce or eliminate their budget gaps. Most notable were the increased use of layoffs, furloughs, fees, reduced local aid, and agency reorganization. City governments' use of layoffs and hiring freezes also increased.

Based on these patterns of behavior, if African Americans experienced a disparate employment impact, it would have lagged the private sector contraction and occurred in FY 2009, FY 2010, and FY 2011. These dates correspond to October 2008 through September 2009 (the last part of the recession), October 2009 through September 2010 (the start of the weak or jobless recovery), and October 2010 through September 2011 (the pothole recovery).

Public Sector Drag on Employment Growth

This delayed use of employment-cutting strategies is a partial reason total nonfarm employment has lagged or failed to exceed the key monthly increase of 130,000 to 150,000.[9] Just as private sector employment growth began to re-emerge, public sector employment began to contract. Table 2 reports private and public sector employment by fiscal year. The table shows that in FY 2008 and FY 2009, more than 8 million private sector jobs were lost. During these fiscal years, state and local employment expanded, but starting in FY 2009, state and local government employment contracted by 30,000 and 67,000, respectively.

At the state level, the losses were concentrated in general public sector employment. Education continued to expand. At the local level, the losses were also more general: 10,000 in education and 67,000 in general local governments. State and local employment continued to contract in FY 2010 and FY 2011. In those two fiscal years, state and local employment fell by 78,000 and 423,000, respectively. For the latter year, the losses were still concentrated in general government but did accelerate in local education (226,000).

Public Versus Private Sector Losses

It is important to note that in percentage terms the losses are smaller than the FY 2008 private sector losses, the first year of the recession. The public sector losses of 1.3% to 1.5% are approximately one quarter of the peak private sector contraction of 5.5%. At this writing, it is unclear whether the losses will accelerate in FY 2012, remain in the 1.3% to 1.5% range, or become smaller. The outcome will depend on the ability of state and local governments to raise revenue and address the costs of employee-related health care coverage and pensions.

Public Sector Impact on African Americans

Aggregate BLS data suggest that public sector budget cuts had a small disparate impact on African Americans. In 2007, African Americans comprised 14.6% of government employment. By 2009, the share had dropped to 14.2% of public sector jobs. The percentage remained at 14.2 in 2010. Numerically, that rate corresponds to a drop in African American public sector employment from 3.1 million in 2009 to 3.0 million in 2010.

White public sector employment actually increased from 2007 to 2009 (16.6 million to 16.8 million). However, white public sector employment did fall in 2010 to 16.7 million. African Americans in the private sector also experienced a small decline in their share of private sector employment, falling from 10.9% to 10.5%. Some of the lost ground was recovered in 2010 when the share ticked up slightly to 10.7%.

Evidence from the Aggregate EEOC-4 Files

This section utilizes 2007 and 2009 full-time, part-time, and new-hire data reported to the EEOC by state and local governments to disaggregate the previous patterns by gender, occupation, and full-time status. The report, "Job Patterns for Minorities and Women in State and Local Government (EEOC-4)," contains labor force data from state and local governments with 100 or more employees within the 50 U.S. states and

TABLE 2

Public Employment by Level and Type

(in Thousands, Except for Change Percentage)

	Total nonfarm	Private	Govt.	Federal	State		Local	
					All state	Education	All local	Education
Panel A: Month and year								
Oct 06	136,506	114,438	22,068	2,731	5,097	2,308	14,240	7,950
Oct 07	137,772	115,470	22,302	2,734	5,132	2,325	14,436	8,028
Oct 08	135,804	113,245	22,559	2,773	5,186	2,363	14,600	8,096
Oct 09	129,505	106,971	22,534	2,845	5,156	2,378	14,533	8,087
Oct 10	130,015	107,713	22,302	2,847	5,146	2,394	14,309	7,980
Oct 11	131,588	109,579	22,009	2,821	5,078	2,404	14,110	7,861
Nov 11	131,708	109,719	21,989	2,817	5,073	2,406	14,099	7,855
Panel B: FY change, number								
FY07	1,266	1,032	234	3	35	17	196	78
FY08	−1,968	−2,225	257	39	54	38	164	69
FY09	−6,299	−6,274	−25	72	−30	15	−67	−10
FY10	510	742	−232	2	−10	16	−224	−107
FY11	1,573	1,866	−293	−26	−68	11	−199	−119
Panel C: FY change, percentage								
FY07	0.90%	0.90%	1.10%	0.10%	0.70%	0.74%	1.40%	0.98%
FY08	−1.40%	−1.90%	1.20%	1.40%	1.10%	1.63%	1.10%	0.85%
FY09	−4.60%	−5.50%	−0.10%	2.60%	−0.60%	0.63%	−0.50%	−0.12%
FY10	0.40%	0.70%	−1.00%	0.10%	−0.20%	0.66%	−1.50%	−1.32%
FY11	1.20%	1.70%	−1.30%	−0.90%	−1.30%	0.45%	−1.40%	−1.49%

Note: Author's tabulations from the BLS Current Employment Statistics Survey (http://www.bls.gov).

the District of Columbia. Agencies are required to provide information on their employment totals and employee job categories and salaries, disaggregated by sex and race/ethnic group as of June 30 in the survey year. The public sector data have been collected biennially since 1993 in every odd-numbered year. Thus, a drawback to using the EEOC information is that 2011 data were not available at this writing. As a result, I was not able to show the lagged impact of the recession and weak recovery on public sector employment. Timing is another limitation. The EEOC June 30 reporting period differs from the fiscal year reporting period used in documenting methods used to reduce or eliminate state budget gaps.

Gender and Occupation Effects on African Americans

Table 3 reports the African American percentage of state and local government employment by gender, occupation, and year. Table 4 reports the actual calculated changes. The conclusion to be drawn is that the budget cuts did not seriously erode the relative presence of African Americans in state and local government in this time period. In fact, their presence in most full- and part-time occupations and their presence in the new-hire pool increased. In 2007 and 2009, African American men comprised 15.0% and 15.6%, respectively, of full-time employment. The share increased because white and African American employment fell 4.7% and 0.7%, respectively.

The percentage of African American males increased in each of the following occupations: professional, administrative support, paraprofessionals, and skilled craft and service maintenance occupations. The major contributors to the share increases were the losses of white men in professional (32,000), administrative support (7,370), skilled craft (15,172), and service/maintenance (16,846) occupations. African American men experienced sizable absolute losses in protective service, but they were not large enough to erode their occupation share.

Relative to all women, African American women's share of full-time state and local employment increased from 22.3% to 23.4%. The driver behind this shift is that white women's employment fell 3.7%, while African American women's employment increased 1.8%. African American women gained ground in seven of the eight occupations, with the largest increases in professional, technician, para-professional, administrative support, and service occupations. The share gains in professional and technician occupations were due to actual gains combined with white women losing jobs in these occupations. In the other occupations, such as administrative support, the shares of African American women increased because those workers did not experience the large absolute percentage contractions that white women faced.

TABLE 3
African American Share of State and Local Employment
by Occupation and Gender, 2007 and 2009

	Men		Women	
	2007	2009	2007	2009
Panel A: Total full time				
Officials/Admin	9.0%	9.2%	15.3%	15.4%
Professionals	11.0%	11.7%	18.5%	19.8%
Technicians	11.5%	11.9%	20.9%	21.6%
Protective Service	13.7%	13.8%	33.1%	33.5%
Para-professionals	24.1%	26.9%	28.7%	30.7%
Admin Support	17.7%	18.8%	19.6%	20.6%
Skilled Craft	14.8%	15.3%	27.1%	26.1%
Service/Maintenance	26.9%	28.1%	39.2%	40.5%
Total Full Time	15.0%	15.6%	22.3%	23.4%
Panel B: Total part time				
Officials/Admin	7.1%	7.0%	10.3%	9.6%
Professionals	10.1%	10.7%	11.1%	11.4%
Technicians	9.6%	9.6%	13.8%	13.9%
Protective Service	10.4%	9.8%	30.7%	20.1%
Para-professionals	16.8%	18.0%	17.5%	18.2%
Admin Support	15.6%	16.4%	14.7%	15.9%
Skilled Craft	18.2%	12.5%	16.2%	10.8%
Service/Maintenance	15.1%	15.9%	16.7%	18.4%
Total Part Time	13.8%	14.1%	15.9%	15.8%
Panel C: New hires				
Officials/Admin	9.1%	11.1%	14.0%	16.1%
Professionals	11.6%	14.4%	19.2%	20.5%
Technicians	12.7%	15.1%	21.2%	25.0%
Protective Service	15.9%	17.5%	35.9%	36.0%
Para-professionals	24.9%	28.6%	31.6%	32.4%
Admin Support	16.0%	17.9%	18.7%	19.2%
Skilled Craft	16.2%	16.3%	21.4%	25.8%
Service/Maintenance	30.2%	30.5%	43.6%	42.6%
Total New Hires	17.8%	19.3%	24.7%	25.7%

Note: Author's calculations from the EEOC 4 state and local reports for 2007 and 2009 EEOC-4. The entries for African American men are the percentages of all men. The entries for African American women are relative to all women. This includes Asians, Latinos, and Indians.

TABLE 4
Change from 2007 to 2009 in State and Local Public
Employment by Occupation, Race, and Gender

	White		Black	
	Number	%	Number	%
Panel A: Men				
Total full time/ Occupation	**-113,637**	**-4.70%**	**-3,592**	**-0.70%**
Officials/Admin	-11,800	-5.90%	-817	-3.70%
Professionals	-32,199	-6.00%	332	0.40%
Technicians	-15,056	-7.10%	-1,196	-3.60%
Protective Service	-13,342	-1.80%	-2,361	-1.70%
Para-professionals	-1,852	-2.90%	2,774	10.70%
Admin Support	-7,370	-9.00%	-264	-1.10%
Skilled Craft	-15,172	-5.00%	-1,165	-1.80%
Service/Maintenance	-16,846	-6.60%	-895	-0.70%
Total part time/ Occupation	**-15,389**	**-3.70%**	**-1,945**	**-2.50%**
Officials/Admin	387	2.30%	10	0.70%
Professionals	2,579	6.50%	704	13.30%
Technicians	-1,664	-6.90%	-189	-6.30%
Protective Service	-3,840	-6.00%	-1,084	-12.90%
Para-professionals	-2,405	-4.00%	672	4.60%
Admin Support	682	1.40%	617	5.50%
Skilled Craft	-4,050	-18.90%	-2,774	-49.60%
Service/Maintenance	-7,078	-5.30%	99	0.40%
Total new hires/ Occupation	**-63,740**	**-26.80%**	**-12,112**	**-18.90%**
Officials/Admin	-2,025	-17.50%	27	2.10%
Professionals	-13,767	-29.10%	-459	-6.10%
Technicians	-4,927	-27.30%	-354	-10.80%
Protective Service	-18,932	-24.10%	-2,746	-15.20%
Para-professionals	-1,986	-18.80%	-260	-5.70%
Admin Support	-4,565	-32.50%	-831	-23.10%
Skilled Craft	-6,796	-28.70%	-1,535	-27.70%
Service/Maintenance	-10,742	-31.30%	-5,954	-29.50%

(continued, next page)

TABLE 4 (continued)
Change from 2007 to 2009 in State and Local Public
Employment by Occupation, Race, and Gender

	White		Black	
	Number	%	Number	%
Panel A: Women				
Total full time/ Occupation	**−65,933**	**−3.70%**	**11,066**	**1.80%**
Officials/Admin	−1,214	−1.10%	−28	−0.10%
Professionals	−6,774	−1.10%	12,257	7.20%
Technicians	−1,274	−1.00%	1,154	2.70%
Protective Service	−5,722	−4.30%	−2,555	−3.10%
Para-professionals	−7,109	−4.40%	3,232	3.90%
Admin Support	−40,788	−7.70%	−3,033	−1.90%
Skilled Craft	207	1.40%	−175	−2.80%
Service/Maintenance	−3,259	−5.00%	214	0.40%
Total part time/ Occupation	**−14,135**	**−2.90%**	**−5,127**	**−4.60%**
Officials/Admin	747	6.60%	−58	−4.00%
Professionals	3,388	3.60%	969	7.00%
Technicians	−137	−0.50%	−44	−0.80%
Protective Service	−3,261	−12.50%	−7,205	−52.00%
Para-professionals	−4,121	−4.00%	328	1.30%
Admin Support	−6,187	−4.80%	371	1.40%
Skilled Craft	154	1.50%	−804	−36.90%
Service/Maintenance	−4,718	−5.20%	1,316	6.20%
Total new hires/ Occupation	**−60,750**	**−28.90%**	**−20,029**	**−22.40%**
Officials/Admin	−1,738	−22.60%	−85	−5.80%
Professionals	−14,645	−22.40%	−1,591	−8.30%
Technicians	−3,387	−21.20%	−137	−2.50%
Protective Service	−6,915	−33.50%	−4,639	−30.50%
Para-professionals	−4,781	−21.20%	−2,570	−18.50%
Admin Support	−25,455	−40.10%	−7,034	−36.60%
Skilled Craft	−654	−30.70%	−72	−10.40%
Service/Maintenance	−3,175	−25.40%	−3,901	−27.30%

Note: Author's calculations from the EEOC-4 state and local reports for 2007 and 2009.

Part-Time Shares

Shifting to part-time employment, African American men maintained their share during the recession. Skilled craft is the exception. The percentage of African Americans in this occupation fell from 18.2% to 12.5%. Almost half of African American men in that occupation lost their jobs. Positive growth in professional, para-professional, service/maintenance, and administrative support and larger white male losses in these occupations helped prevent African American men from losing share. African American women's lost presence in part-time protective service (30.7% to 20.1%) and skilled craft was countered by increases in service/maintenance, administration support, and para-professional occupations.

Finally, and potentially most telling about the future presence of African Americans in the public sector, Panel C of Table 3 indicates that African American men and women both increased their new-hire shares significantly. The percentage of African American males hired in five of the eight occupations grew. African American women increased their presence in the pool of new hires in seven of eight occupations. The gains are solely due to smaller absolute percentage declines than the declines for white men and women. For example, African American men's share in protective service increased because new white male hires contracted by 24.1% and new African American male hires contracted by only 15.2%.

Evidence from the 2006, 2008, and 2010 CPS Displaced Worker Surveys

The EEOC-4 data have several drawbacks. They provide an aggregate portrait for each year. Thus, we cannot observe the displacement process. The EEOC-4 analysis does not control for worker characteristics and local labor market conditions that influence the chances of displacement. In an attempt to address these drawbacks, this section presents an analysis of the determinants of displacement and re-employment status by class of worker and race. One limitation of this analysis is that the samples in each survey are too small to estimate displacement and re-employment rates by race, gender, and class of worker simultaneously.

I used the 2006, 2008, and 2010 Displaced Worker Surveys (DWS) of the Current Population Survey (CPS). Each survey attempts to capture employee terminations that are the result of employer business decisions. A dislocation that is unrelated to the performance or choices of the given employee can have three reasons: plant closing, layoff, or abolition of a job. The 2010 survey window coincides with the Great Recession. In January 2010, interviewees were asked:

> During the last three calendar years, that is, January 2007 through December 2009, did (name/you) lose a job or leave

one because: (your/his/her) plant or company closed or moved, (your/his/her) position or shift was abolished, insufficient work or another similar reason?

For the 2006 and 2008 surveys, the calendar years for the question correspond to January 2003 through December 2005 and January 2005 through December 2007, respectively. Job losers are categorized as respondents who reported a job loss in the three calendar years prior to the survey. Based on this information, I constructed an estimate of the three-year job loss rate as the number of reported job losers divided by the number of workers who were either employed at the survey date or reported a job loss but were not employed at the survey date.

The Farber Study

Using the 2010 DWS, Farber (2011) provided the most comprehensive estimates of the recession's impact on job displacement.[10] His analysis of the surveys from 1984 to 2010 indicated that displacement rates for the 2007 through 2009 period were at record levels. Approximately one in six workers (16%) reported a job loss from January 2007 through December 2009. The rate jumped to this level from 8.5% in the periods from January 2003 through December 2005 and January 2005 through December 2007.

Farber estimated displacement rates by educational attainment and age cohort. Workers with college degrees had a lower likelihood of displacement, but even their chances of displacement increased from 2007 to 2009. Older workers (45 to 64 years of age) had displacement rates of approximately 8.0% from 2003 to 2007 compared to 9.3% to 10.2% for 20- to 24-year-olds. During the recession, from 2007 to 2009, the displacement rates jumped to 17.6% for 20- to 24-year-olds and 14.4% to 15.4% for 45- to 64-year-olds.

Farber also documents the recession's impact on post-displacement labor force attachment. Post-displacement attachment shifted from employment to unemployment. In the two three-year periods (2003–2005 and 2005–2007) prior to the recession, the post-displacement employment fraction of the population of displaced workers was 66.0%. In the period covering the recession (2007–2009), the percentage of workers who found employment after displacement fell to 47.4%. The percentage who were unemployed doubled from 20% to 40%, while the percentage who exited the labor force remained constant. Farber showed a similar dynamic across categories of educational attainment and age.

Extending the Farber Results

Building on Farber's findings, this section estimates displacement rates and post-displacement labor force outcomes by class of worker and race.

I was most interested in comparing public sector African Americans to private sector African Americans, and public sector African Americans to public sector whites. Tables 5a and 5b report summary statistics for private sector and for federal, state, and local government respondents. During the recession, African American public sector respondents had higher displacement rates than white public sector workers.

Relative to African American private sector respondents, the odds of displacement were much lower for federal workers, the same for state workers, and higher for local workers. These relations held in the surveys prior to the recession. The lower levels of educational attainment and experience (age serves as a proxy) of local government respondents contributed to their higher displacement rate.

The summary statistics also report post-displacement labor force status at the time of the survey. Was a displaced respondent employed, unemployed, or not in the labor force? Prior to the recession, African American public sector respondents tended to have lower re-employment rates than white public sector respondents, but sizable gaps emerged during the recession. For example, African American state and local re-employment rates dropped from more than two thirds in the periods prior to the recession to between 43.2% and 50.6%. Compared to private sector African Americans, state and local public sector African Americans have higher re-employment rates.

These comparisons are not fully informative because I did not control for the characteristics (e.g., age and educational attainment) of the respondents. For example, African American employees in local government are younger and have less education than other groups. Their average age is 38 years compared to averages that range from 40 to 45 for other public sector and private sector respondents. Only one fifth have a bachelor's degree. One third to one half of African Americans and whites in federal and state government and the private sector possess bachelor's degrees. Even one third of whites in local government have such degrees. This fact explains why they have higher displacement rates and low re-employment rates. If sizable differences remain once controls are added, then we might begin to conclude that the rules and human resource policies that govern public sector layoffs changed during the recession such that African American public sector workers became systematically disadvantaged.

Probit Analysis

To adjust the displacement rate gaps for personal characteristics and local labor market conditions, I estimated probit models for which the dependent variable is a dummy variable that equals 1 if the individual experienced displacement, or zero. Dummy variables for race and ethnicity, class of worker, gender, educational attainment, and marital status were also included. Age and the metropolitan area unemployment rate were included in their linear form. A second model added detailed information about the industry and occupation at the time of displacement. To assess whether African American public sector workers had higher odds of displacement than white public sector workers, I limited the samples to public sector respondents and re-estimated the probit models.

Table 6 reports black–white gaps (differences) in the probability of displacement. Each row corresponds to a different outcome: displacement, post-displacement employment, and unemployment. The standard errors are in parentheses. For example, row 1 of Panel A reports the unadjusted black–white displacement rate gap. The estimate in the column labeled "All 2006" indicates that African Americans have a 2 percentage point higher likelihood of displacement than a white respondent. The difference expanded to 2.2 percentage points in the 2008 survey and increased further to 2.4 percentage points in the 2010 survey.

For public sector respondents, the unadjusted black–white gap was basically zero in 2006 and 2008, but a 3.6% gap emerged in 2010. After controlling for personal characteristics, the odds that public sector African Americans faced displacement relative to public sector whites during the recession fell from 3.6% to 2.8%. Panel C shows that even after adding occupation and industry information, a gap of 2.7% remained.

Impact of Layoff Rules

The most troubling feature of this 2.7 percentage-point gap is that it was not significantly different from the overall black–white displacement gap of 3.1%, which started as a pre-recession adjusted gap of 1.8 and 1.9 percentage points. These findings suggest that the more formal rules of layoff in the public sector ceased to generate race-neutral displacement outcomes between blacks and whites in the public sector.

Are the 2.7 to 3.1 percentage point gaps economically meaningful? One way of answering this question is to compare the gap to the average displacement rates of public sector African Americans. Table 5 shows the average public sector displacement rates of African Americans during the recession as 6.8% for federal workers, 9.8% for state workers, and 17.5% for local workers. Thus, the recession's black–white displacement gap of 2.7% is 39.7%, 27.6%, and 15.4% of the average displacement rates of federal, state, and local public sector African Americans, respectively.

Another way to answer this question is to use the estimated relationships from the probit models and the changes in the predictor variables' means from 2006/2008 to 2010 to generate predicted increases in the

TABLE 5a
Survey Summary Statistics from the Displaced Worker Survey Panel A: Private and Federal

	Private sector				Federal government			
	White		African American		White		African American	
Variable	2008	2010	2008	2010	2008	2010	2008	2010
Layoff = 1	0.031	0.070	0.052	0.101	0.047	0.060	0.038	0.068
Post-displacement (Employed = 1)	0.734	0.713	0.532	0.393	0.853	0.781	0.821	0.604
Post-displacement (Unemployed = 1)	0.262	0.284	0.468	0.603	0.137	0.192	0.179	0.396
Post-displacement (NILF* = 1)	0.004	0.003	0.000	0.004	0.010	0.027	0.000	0.000
Search duration	20.387	33.509	24.457	33.611	15.610	18.835	23.441	44.036
Unemployment duration	18.732	29.677	20.201	33.611	14.376	16.506	21.765	38.331
Male = 1	0.615	0.598	0.487	0.480	0.435	0.424	0.373	0.350
Age	45.851	45.179	43.723	43.202	43.387	43.643	41.564	42.154
College graduate = 1	0.475	0.482	0.302	0.334	0.572	0.593	0.403	0.392
Some college = 1	0.285	0.302	0.374	0.323	0.255	0.237	0.316	0.293
Widowed = 1	0.013	0.013	0.018	0.019	0.017	0.012	0.005	0.010
Divorced = 1	0.139	0.106	0.119	0.214	0.120	0.112	0.157	0.101
Separated = 1	0.015	0.019	0.055	0.054	0.010	0.017	0.045	0.060
Never married = 1	0.166	0.175	0.322	0.319	0.218	0.212	0.334	0.380
Metro area unemployment rate	5.255	8.981	5.278	8.874	5.465	9.129	5.541	8.981

*NILF: Not in labor force.

Note: Author's tabulations from the 2006, 2008, and 2010 Displaced Worker Surveys of the Current Population Survey. The sample includes all respondents between 20 and 64 years of age at the time of the survey. The summary statistics for 2006 are available on request. They are not shown because they are similar to the 2008 summary statistics.

TABLE 5b

Survey Summary Statistics from the Displaced Worker SurveyPanel B: State and Local Government

	White				African American			
	State		Local		State		Local	
Variable	2008	2010	2008	2010	2008	2010	2008	2010
Layoff = 1	0.037	0.058	0.092	0.144	0.042	0.098	0.122	0.175
Post-displacement (Employed = 1)	0.894	0.771	0.789	0.590	0.792	0.506	0.678	0.432
Post-displacement (Unemployed = 1)	0.064	0.205	0.195	0.392	0.208	0.494	0.314	0.552
Post-displacement (NILF* = 1)	0.042	0.025	0.016	0.018	0.000	0.000	0.008	0.017
Search duration	15.953	23.819	19.127	32.237	21.384	29.973	20.933	35.631
Unemployment duration	13.528	21.622	16.077	28.569	16.653	16.506	21.765	33.931
Male = 1	0.387	0.394	0.532	0.527	0.339	0.370	0.484	0.475
Age	43.758	43.887	40.536	40.970	43.745	43.368	38.400	38.568
College graduate = 1	0.553	0.561	0.320	0.327	0.454	0.365	0.170	0.204
Some college = 1	0.244	0.233	0.322	0.322	0.302	0.267	0.337	0.347
Widowed = 1	0.015	0.015	0.013	0.014	0.013	0.028	0.111	0.106
Divorced = 1	0.114	0.102	0.119	0.117	0.135	0.159	0.157	0.101
Separated = 1	0.013	0.016	0.018	0.020	0.043	0.046	0.050	0.046
Never married = 1	0.158	0.155	0.261	0.268	0.308	0.318	0.433	0.455
Metro area unemployment rate	5.771	9.580	5.664	9.469	5.704	9.650	5.642	9.438

*NILF: Not in labor force.

Note: Author's tabulations from the 2006, 2008, and 2010 Displaced Worker Surveys of the Current Population Survey. The sample includes all respondents between 20 and 64 years of age at the time of the survey. The summary statistics for 2006 are available on request. They are not shown because they are similar to the 2008 summary statistics.

TABLE 6

Black–White Difference in the Probability of Displacement and Post-Displacement Employment Status

Dependent variable	All			Public sector only		
	2006	2008	2010	2006	2008	2010
Panel A: Unadjusted						
Layoff	0.0200 (0.0038)	0.0218 (0.0038)	0.0239 (0.0045)	0.0102 (0.0072)	0.0021 (0.0070)	0.0363 (0.0098)
Post-Displacement Employment	−0.1419 (0.0219)	−0.1261 (0.0216)	−0.1503 (0.0171)	−0.2661 (0.0704)	−0.0916 (0.0710)	−0.2563 (0.0543)
Post-Displacement Unemployment	0.0914 (0.0188)	0.1096 (0.0194)	0.1406 (0.0173)	0.2201 (0.0676)	0.1168 (0.0718)	0.2653 (0.0542)
Panel B, Adjusted #1: Gender, age, education, marital status, area unemployment rate						
Layoff	0.0166 (0.0049)	0.0194 (0.0049)	0.0275 (0.0059)	0.0098 (0.0075)	−0.0058 (0.0068)	0.0284 (0.0105)
Post-Displacement Employment	−0.0911 (0.0245)	−0.1112 (0.0245)	−0.1476 (0.0210)	−0.2414 (0.0876)	−0.0713 (0.0846)	−0.2083 (0.0634)
Post-Displacement Unemployment	0.0978 (0.0242)	0.1188 (0.0242)	0.1472 (0.0210)	0.2035 (0.0827)	0.0996 (0.0843)	0.2180 (0.0631)
Panel C, Adjusted #2: Occupation and industry dummy variables added						
Layoff	0.0175 (0.0049)	0.0187 (0.0049)	0.0312 (0.0060)	0.0083 (0.0066)	−0.0062 (0.0063)	0.0266 (0.0096)
Post-Displacement Employment	−0.0904 (0.0253)	−0.1167 (0.0254)	−0.1592 (0.0220)	−0.2843 (0.1360)	−0.2052 (0.1258)	−0.2188 (0.0719)
Post-Displacement Unemployment	0.0972 (0.0250)	0.1257 (0.0252)	0.1595 (0.0220)	0.2883 (0.1317)	0.2774 (0.1408)	0.2338 (0.0719)

Note: Author's calculations of the 2006, 2008, and 2010 microdata files of the Current Population Survey's Dislocated Worker Survey. Entries are the discrete change (difference) in the probability of an outcome between non-Latino African Americans and non-Latino whites. The estimates come from probit models that include dummy variables for Latino and other races. Non-Latino whites are the excluded group. The Adjusted #1 models control for gender, age, educational attainment, marital status, and the metropolitan area unemployment. The Adjusted #2 models add dummy variables for occupation and industry. Standard errors are in parentheses.

displacement rate and compare them to the actual change in the displacement rate. An examination of the summary statistics in Table 5 indicates that the metropolitan unemployment rate was the only predictor variable that significantly changed. The average metropolitan area unemployment rate for African American local government respondents increased from 5.6% in 2008 to 9.4% in 2010, a 3.8 percentage point increase.

Unemployment Not an Explanation of Differential Displacement

How much did this 3.8 percentage-point increase contribute to the actual increase in the local public sector displacement rate of 5.3 percentage points (12.2% to 17.5%)? The answer is not at all because the metropolitan-area unemployment rate had no impact on the displacement chances of local government respondents. In the 2010 survey, the estimated change in the probability of displacement for a local public sector worker associated with a 1 percentage-point increase in the metropolitan area unemployment rate equaled 0.0013, with a standard error of 0.0011. The estimated change was basically zero.[11]

Alternative Explanations of Differential Displacement

Other explanations for the emergence of an unexplained black–white displacement gap need to be explored. For example, the attempts to weaken the collective bargaining power of public sector unions in key states such as Wisconsin, New Jersey, and Ohio are well documented. This erosion in power could raise displacement rates for all public sector workers and have a disparate impact on African Americans if unions can no longer reduce the effects of discrimination. I might also have excluded a characteristic that has become correlated with race and predicts displacement.[12]

What else changed during the recession that might explain the higher public sector African American displacement rate? Table 7 shows that prior to the recession, more than 50% of public sector displacement was due to the position being abolished. During the recession, the reason for public sector displacement shifted from plant closure to insufficient work. The shift was larger for African Americans. Future research could identify whether displacement rules differ when insufficient work drives employee cutbacks and how this mechanism would have a disparate impact on African Americans.

Post-Displacement Outcomes

What happens after displacement? Do African Americans have more difficulty obtaining employment? Table 6 reports African American differences in re-employment status. Public sector African Americans face a sizable re-employment disadvantage relative to white public sector respondents. Unlike the emergence of a displacement rate gap, re-employ-

TABLE 7
Reason for Displacement by Class of Worker

	Public			Private		
	Plant or company closed or moved	Insufficient work	Position or shift abolished	Plant or company closed or moved	Insufficient work	Position or shift abolished
Panel A: All						
2006	0.179	0.229	0.592	0.432	0.349	0.219
2008	0.096	0.364	0.541	0.361	0.397	0.242
2010	0.065	0.405	0.529	0.261	0.535	0.204
Panel B: African American						
2006	0.249	0.226	0.524	0.369	0.382	0.248
2008	0.092	0.417	0.491	0.349	0.443	0.208
2010	0.066	0.488	0.446	0.274	0.543	0.184

Note: Author's calculations of the 2006, 2008, and 2010 microdata files of the Current Population Survey's Dislocated Worker Survey.

ment for African Americans in the public sector was a major challenge even before the recession.

The existence of a large gap in the 2006 survey, followed by a narrowing in the 2008 survey and an expansion of the gap in the 2010 survey, may be due to the jobless recovery that developed after the eight-month recession from March 2001 to November 2001. However, this explanation seems unlikely because the private sector re-employment rates in the 2006 survey are considerably lower than in the 2010 survey. An interesting point to note is the symmetry between the employment and unemployment gaps, indicating very little movement out of the labor force. Displaced African Americans and white respondents continue to look for work.

Another important comparison to make is that the black–white re-employment gap among public sector respondents is larger than the black–white re-employment gap among private sector respondents. This needs further investigation, particularly in light of this chapter's EEOC-4 analysis (Table 3), which suggests that African Americans comprise an increasing share of new hires in state and local governments.

Summary and Conclusions

Numerous studies have documented the costs that the Great Recession has had on Americans, especially the most vulnerable. However, to date there has been little focus on how state and local budget cuts affected African American public sector employment opportunities. Why is this important? African Americans comprise a disproportionate share of public sector workers and the public sector has historically helped to provide African Americans opportunities in the workforce. The National Urban League's Equality Index illustrates these points. The index consists of five components: economics, health, education, social justice, and civic engagement.

The civic engagement sub-index is the only component at parity. In fact, it has been at parity since the league first published the index in 2005. A major reason for parity in the civic engagement sub-index is that African Americans have greater representation in federal executive branch (nonpostal) employment and state and local government employment than whites.

A priori, it is not clear as to the effect of the federal, state, and local public sector cut's impact on African American public sector employment. The answer lies in the type of public sector jobs that were cut, the relative education and experience of public sector African Americans, and the rules that govern displacement. The role of public sector unions is important for understanding each of these stories.

African Americans may still face greater risk of displacement than their white peers, but the latter's greater experience and education may help to insulate them from the budget cuts. Further, there is less occupational segregation in the public sector than in the private sector. More African Americans are in occupations that are involved with hiring and layoff decisions. This higher stature and the existence of internal labor markets could help to mute or minimize the budget cuts' effects.

To explore whether African Americans have been hurt more than whites by public sector cuts, I analyzed published BLS data, published EEOC-4 data on state and local employment (full time, part time, and new hires), and microlevel data from the 2006, 2008, and 2010 Displaced Worker Surveys (DWS) of the Current Population Survey (CPS). The major findings are as follows.

According to the aggregate BLS employment data, in 2007, African Americans comprised 14.6% of government employment. By 2009, the share had dropped to 14.2% of public sector jobs. The percentage remained at 14.2% in 2010. African Americans in the private sector also experienced a small decline in their share of private sector employment, falling from 10.9% to 10.5%. Some of the lost ground was recovered in 2010. The share then ticked up slightly to 10.7%.

The aggregate EEOC-4 data on state and local governments with at least 100 employees indicate that African Americans expanded their public sector presence during the recession. However, this expansion is largely because they experienced smaller losses than whites. Most notable are the losses in protective services that African Americans and whites both experienced. The DWS evidence contains a very different narrative than the aggregate data. Even after controlling for personal characteristics, including industry and occupation at the time of displacement and local economic conditions, the probability of displacement of public sector African Americans relative to public sector whites increased from no gap prior to the recession to 2.8 percentage points during the recession. This gap that emerged equals the private sector black–white displacement gap, which prior to the recession equaled 1.7 and 1.9 percentage points and widened to 2.8 percentage points during the recession.

These findings suggest that the more formal rules of public sector displacement ceased to generate race-neutral displacement outcomes between public sector African Americans and whites. Future research needs to examine actual layoff practices to improve understanding of the emergence of the unexplained black–white public sector displacement gap. For example, the attempts to weaken the collective bargaining power of public sector unions in key states such as Wisconsin, New Jersey, and Ohio are well documented. This erosion in power could raise displacement rates for all public sector workers and have a disparate impact on African Americans if unions can no longer reduce the effects of discrimination. Additionally, this analysis may have excluded a characteristic that has become correlated with race and predicts displacement.

The source of the higher African American public sector displacement rates during the recession might be due to changes in the reason for displacement. During the recession, the reason for public sector displacement shifted from plant closure to insufficient work, with the shift being larger for African Americans. Future research needs to identify whether displacement rates differ under the insufficient work reason and how that translates into disparate impacts on African Americans.

The chapter concluded with an examination of whether the recession has made it more difficult for African Americans to obtain employment after displacement. Public sector African Americans face a sizable re-employment disadvantage relative to white public sector respondents. Unlike the emergence of a displacement rate gap, re-employment for African Americans in the public sector was a major challenge even before the recession.

An interesting finding is the symmetry between the employment and unemployment gaps, indicating that there is very little movement out of the labor force. Displaced African Americans and white respondents continue to look for work. Another important comparison to make is that the black–white re-employment gap among public sector respondents is larger than the black–white re-employment gap among private sector respondents. This finding needs further investigation, particularly in light of this chapter's EEOC-4 analysis, which suggests that African Americans comprise an increasing share of new hires in state and local governments.

As in any study, the answers to the posed questions raise a new series of questions. What types of jobs are re-employed public sector respondents accepting? If they do find work, is it in the public or private sector? Are they working full time or part time? Are re-employment earnings lower? If so, how much lower?

Farber (2011) reported that in the 2010 survey, job losers who found new jobs earned on average 17.5% less in their new jobs. The comparable estimate for losers of full-time jobs was 21.8%. Are the re-employment earnings of public sector workers the same, or is the gap larger?

The answer depends on whether the new job is in the public or private sector. If the new job is in the public sector, then the stricter pay structure there (owing to the role of unions) may minimize some of the losses that re-employed individuals are experiencing in the private sector. If the new job is in the private sector, representing a sector switch, then the individual may suffer a sector-specific loss in earnings and a loss due to having no union representation.

Another important issue is whether the new jobs have benefits. This question is a key concern because one of the historical attractions to public sector careers is that the benefits tend to be better than in the private sector. The more supportive benefits serve as an incentive given the public sector's lower average earnings, especially in local government jobs.

The challenge with trying to utilize the 2010 DWS alone to answer these new questions is sample size. The number of displaced public sector respondents who found employment is too small to generate any reliable estimated impacts, especially if the focus is on African Americans. Researchers must either wait for the next few DWS rounds or create their own microlevel data from surveys of public sector workers.

Endnotes

[1] The unemployment rate of African American women increased from 8.1% to 12.7%.

[2] Over the same period, the unemployment rate of African American women increased from 8.1% to 12.7%.

[3] EEOC data on the number of receipts and reasonable charges trended upward during the recession. Some of this could also be due to increased enforcement by the Obama administration. However, the data contain an increase in these measures during 2001, the previous recession. The number of receipts was 30,510 (FY 2007), 33,937 (FY

2008), 33,579 (FY 2009), and 35,890 (FY 2010). The number of reasonable charges was 1,016 (FY 2006), 993 (FY 2007), 1,061 (FY 2008), 1,201 (FY 2009), and 1,330 (FY 2010). The number of successful conciliations increased, too. The data are compiled by the Office of Research, Implementation, and Planning. The data come from the EEOC's Integrated Mission System.

[4]Independent estimates conclude that ARRA created or saved 2 to 3 million jobs. See, for example, *The Economic Impact of the American Recovery and Reinvestment Act of 2009* (Council of Economic Advisors 2011).

[5]Over the same period, the Federal Reserve's industrial production series fell by 17% (http://www.federalreserve.gov/releases/g17/table1_2.htm).

[6] This measure corresponds to the BLS's U-6 definition of unemployment. See, for example, The Employment Situation, Table A-15. Alternative Measures of Labor Under-utilization (http://www.bls.gov).

[7] In November 2011, the unemployment rate fell to 8.6%, but the drop was largely due to the continued departure of individuals from the labor force (http://www.bls.gov).

[8] See Hatch 2004 for an analysis of the public sector employment trends during the 1991–1992 and 2001 recessions and their aftermaths. She shows the lagged impact that tax revenue has on the public sector.

[9] Growth above this level accommodates the natural increase in the labor force from immigration and entrance of newly minted high school and college graduates.

[10] For previous work that uses the DWS see, for example, Farber 1993, 1997, 1998, 2005; Podgursky and Swaim 1987; Kletzer 1989; Topel 1990; Gardner 1995; Neal 1995; Aaronson and Sullivan 1998; and Hipple 1999. Fallick 1996 and Farber 2004 provide literature reviews of previous research.

[11] The detailed results are available from the author on request.

[12] For the probit models in Table 6, I estimated additional models that included strategies states used in FY 2008 and FY 2009. The previous conclusions are robust to these additions to the model. In the 2010 model, the layoff strategy is the only strategy measured with precision. The estimated partial derivative of 0.011 indicates that states that used layoff strategies in FY 2008 and FY 2009 to address their budget gaps have displacement rates 1.1 percentage points higher than states that did not use layoffs. The displacement rate for the sample of respondents is 13.49%. All other estimated partial derivatives are small and not measured with precision. The signs make sense. For example, early retirement, privatization, and reorganization each have negative signs. Under early retirement strategies, older and more expensive workers are replaced with younger and cheaper workers. For privatization, the negative sign suggests that the potentially displaced workers are rehired as contractors. Agency reorganization probably just re-allocates work-ers in the same agency or another agency. The partial derivatives for fees, across-the-board cuts, targeted cuts, lower state aid, rainy day funds, and other tools do not exceed 0.0045. Again, each partial is not measured with precision. The fact that these estimated partials are zero is consistent with an explanation that these strategies either raise funds or find ways unrelated to employment to balance the budget.

References

Aaronson, Daniel, and Daniel G. Sullivan. 1998. "The Decline of Job Security in the 1990s: Displacement, Anxiety, and Their Effect on Wage Growth." *Federal Reserve Bank of Chicago Economic Perspectives*, Vol. 22 (1st Quarter), pp. 17–43.

Council of Economic Advisors. 2011 (Dec. 9). *The Economic Impact of the American Recovery and Reinvestment Act of 2009 Eighth Quarterly Report.*

Fallick, Bruce. 1996. "A Review of the Recent Empirical Literature on Displaced Workers." *Industrial and Labor Relations*, Vol. 50 (October), pp. 5–16.

Farber, Henry S. 1993. "The Incidence and Costs of Job Loss: 1982–91." *Brookings Papers on Economic Activity: Microeconomics*, pp. 73–119.

Farber, Henry S. 1997. "The Changing Face of Job Loss in the United States, 1981–1995." *Brookings Papers on Economic Activity: Microeconomics*, pp. 55–128.

Farber, Henry S. 1998. "Has the Rate of Job Loss Increased in the Nineties?" *Proceedings of the Fiftieth Annual Winter Meeting of the Industrial Relations Research Association*, Vol. 1, pp. 88–97.

Farber, Henry S. 2004. "Job Loss in the United States, 1981–2001." *Research in Labor Economics*, Vol. 23, pp. 69–117.

Farber, Henry S. 2005. "What Do We Know About Job Loss in the United States? Evidence from the Displaced Workers Survey, 1981–2004." *Economic Perspectives*, Federal Reserve Bank of Chicago (2nd Quarter), pp. 13–28.

Farber, Henry S. 2011. *Job Loss in the Great Recession: Historical Perspective from the Displaced Workers Survey, 1984–2010.* Working Paper #564, Princeton University Industrial Relations Selection.

Gardner, Jennifer M. 1995. "Worker Displacement: A Decade of Change." *Monthly Labor Review*, Vol. 118 (April), pp. 45–57.

Hatch, Julie. 2004. "Employment in the Public Sector: Two Recessions' Impact on Jobs." *Monthly Labor Review*, Vol. 127 (October), pp. 38–47.

Hardy, Chanelle P., ed. 2011. *The State of Black America 2011.* New York: National Urban League, pp. 24–35.

Hipple, Steve. 1999. "Worker Displacement in the mid-1990s." *Monthly Labor Review*, Vol. 122 (July), pp. 15–32.

Hoene, Christopher W., and Michael A. Pagano. 2011. *Research Brief on America's Cities.* Washington, DC: National League of Cities.

Kletzer, Lori. 1989. "Returns to Seniority after Permanent Job Loss." *American Economic Review*, Vol. 79 (June), pp. 536–43.

National Governors Association and the National Association of State Budget Officers. 2006, 2007, 2008, 2009, 2010, 2011. *The Fiscal Survey of States.* NGA and NASBO: Washington, DC.

Neal, Derek. 1995. "Industry-Specific Capital: Evidence from Displaced Workers." *Journal of Labor Economics*, Vol. 13 (October), pp. 653–77.

Podgursky, Michael, and Paul Swaim. 1987. "Job Displacement Earnings Loss: Evidence from the Displaced Worker Survey." *Industrial and Labor Relations Review*, Vol. 41 (October), pp. 17–29.

Topel, Robert. 1990. "Specific Capital and Unemployment: Measuring the Costs and Consequences of Job Loss." *Carnegie Rochester Conference Series on Public Policy*, Vol. 33, pp. 181–214.

CHAPTER 6

Trends in the Relative Compensation of State and Local Government Employees

KEITH A. BENDER

AND

JOHN S. HEYWOOD

University of Wisconsin–Milwaukee

Introduction

Levels of compensation help determine both the competence and efficiency of governmental services. Excessive levels waste resources, depriving governments of the opportunity to address other costly objectives or to reduce burdens to taxpayers. Insufficient levels make it difficult or impossible to attract workers of the quality needed to provide the services demanded by citizens. The process that determines the compensation of state and local government workers is unavoidably influenced by administrative and political processes. The fundamental issue remains how well these processes work.

Comparability with the private sector stands as the most generally accepted standard by which economists and compensation specialists make such judgments. This standard recognizes that both equity and efficiency argue that public sector compensation should be comparable to that of similar workers performing similar tasks in the private sector. Equity requires that workers not be paid differently for identical work simply because their employer is the government. Efficiency requires that the compensation be just adequate to attract the appropriate supply and quality of workers.

In this chapter, we examine the extent to which state and local government compensation in the United States meets the comparability standard and highlight trends over the past three decades. We next briefly discuss the criterion of comparability and compare it to alternative standards. We also review the academic literature that compares state and local compensation to identify measurement issues and the quality of available information.

After that, we present a straightforward application holding basic wage determinants constant to examine the comparability differential in pay between the government (state and local) and private sectors. We first compare average worker characteristics across the private, state, and local sectors. Next, we estimate the comparability differentials in pay annually for the past several decades and show a relative deterioration in state and local earnings over the 1990s.

We follow that with a description of fringe benefit levels and composition in the public and private sectors. We adjust the earnings comparability estimates since 2000 to gain a general flavor for overall compensation comparability, and then we highlight the challenges of making such an adjustment and suggest alternative approaches. Our general conclusion is that state and local government workers have not generally been overcompensated and that the comparability standard has probably been roughly met on average.

We go on to suggest that perhaps the most pressing issues in public compensation policy are not about average compensation but about the very different distributions in the public and private sectors. The public sector earnings distribution shows far more compression than that in the private sector. As a consequence, it is easy to find groups of workers earning above comparable wages as well as many earning below comparable wages. Thus, if the public sector hopes to pay large portions of its workers comparably, instead of being approximately right on average, more effort may be warranted on readjusting pay within the public sector.

We conclude that the standard of comparability and patterns of compensation might support such a readjustment within the public sector. However, the standard of comparability typically fails to support uniform reductions in public sector compensation such as those that have been taking place.

The Standard of Comparability

The principle of comparability contends that public sector workers should earn compensation matching that earned by similar workers doing similar work in the private sector. In the promulgated standards of the U.S. government, the standard of comparability in the setting of public sector compensation has at least a 150-year history (Smith 1987:177). The natural variation in state and local governments means that compensation of their workers depends on state-specific legislation and cannot easily be summarized. Nonetheless, many states incorporate comparability standards either into dispute resolution processes (Hill and DeLacenserie 1991) or as a central principle in the legislation of compensation. Indeed, a variety of states have established surveys designed to support legislated or implied comparability standards (Belman, Franklin, and Heywood 1994). While these surveys of private employers are often limited to earnings, some include fringe benefit costs (Belman and Heywood 1996).

Despite the persistent policy importance of the standard of comparability, much of the history of concern over public compensation has been fear that it was too low, not that it was too high. Kearney and Carnevale summarize the evidence prior to the mid-1960s by saying, "Until the rise of unions in the public sector, public employees were consistently underpaid relative to similar workers in the private sector" (2001:156). Only after this period did public sector earnings begin to increase relative to their private sector counterparts. Thus, by the late 1970s, economists became very interested in whether comparability had been achieved. The earliest econometric study by Smith (1976) found that state and local sector workers enjoyed a negligible earnings advantage of one to two percentage points. This small overall advantage reflected generally negative differentials for men and positive differentials for women.

The People Approach

The approach that Smith pioneered represents one of the two major methodologies for examining comparability. Her approach became known as the people approach. The object was to standardize for known earnings determinants associated with a particular worker: the education, training, experience, job location, broad occupation, and other worker characteristics. After standardizing for these earnings determinants, remaining differences in mean earnings between state and local public sector and private sector workers represent the public earnings differential. An earnings differential at or near zero would be evidence of comparability on average.

The pattern of results from such studies has not dramatically changed since Smith's early work but does depend on the particular sample, time period, and characteristics used to standardize across workers (Bender 1998). Belman and Heywood (1995) used data from the Current Population Survey, finding variation across seven major states. They found that in six states the adjusted differential for local government workers was actually negative (public sector workers earned less than comparable private sector wages) and that for state workers the differential was positive in four states and negative in three.

Lee (2004) used the National Longitudinal Survey with its panel data structure and particularly detailed worker characteristics. The simplest regression estimates suggest that female state workers earn 3% less than comparable private workers and that male state workers earn 8% less than comparable private workers. Female local government workers also earn about 3% less, while male local government workers earn essentially the same as private sector workers. Adjusting for detailed measures of ability (such as intelligence tests) generally causes these differentials to move toward zero. Examining individual workers as they change sectors (fixed-effect estimates) suggests some positive public sector differentials for females but largely no difference for men.

More recently, Lewis and Galloway (2011) used the large sample sizes of detailed census data to examine differentials in each state after adjusting for worker characteristics. They combined state and local government workers within a state and so generated only a single public differential for each state. Lewis and Galloway concluded, "Most state and local governments pay less than private firms in the same state for similar workers" (2011:2). While they presented differentials that range from –15.2% in Kansas to +13% in Nevada, fully 44 of the 50 states emerged with negative differentials (an earnings advantage for private sector workers) and most differences within a handful of percentage points of zero (comparability).

Borjas (2003) tracked public sector earnings differentials from the 1960s to 2000. His data suggest a fairly steady pattern over time for men but a declining relative position for women in the public sector. By the end of that time period, the differentials were similar for both genders at about –9% in the local sector and –12% in the state sector.

While our summary is by no means an exhaustive review, it makes clear that the detailed results are somewhat mixed. The results depend on time period, data source, and methodology. Yet the estimated earnings differential for state and local government workers is typically ten percentage points or less and seemingly negative more often than positive.

The critical point to take from the people approach to estimating earnings differences is that the characteristics of state and local government employees differ dramatically from those of the private sector. State and local governments consist disproportionately of occupations that demand more skills and earn higher wages. As a consequence, the typical state or local government employee has substantially more education, training, and experience compared to the typical private sector worker. Adjusting for these differences is required to compare apples to apples. Indeed, adjusting for these differences typically explains most of the observed earnings advantage of the typical state and local worker.

The Position Approach

The people line of research can be contrasted with the second broad methodology of detailed position comparisons. In the position approach, efforts are made to compare duties of each job and to find positions with comparable duties in both the public and private sectors. Junior accountants are compared to junior accountants and computer operators to computer operators. The earnings differences across sectors within these narrow positions are then aggregated to construct measures of central tendency.

The idea of comparing similar positions and duties is appealing but requires judgment in matching positions that appear comparable but may not be identical. Even if the judgment is accurate, some positions and duties simply will not have reasonable equivalents across sectors. Firefighters or police may not have a private sector equivalent. Indeed, Belman and Heywood (2004a) showed that of the 509 detailed three-digit census occupation definitions, approximately 150 are unique to either the public or the private sector. These occupations account for as much as 31% of the public workforce.

Examining the Wisconsin State Wage Survey, Belman, Franklin, and Heywood (1994) found 124 occupational definitions that appear in the private sector and either the state or local sector. These common occupations account for only 20% of all private sector occupations and only 43% of all state government workers. Many of the tasks being done by the private and public sectors appear to be done uniquely in only one of those sectors.

Despite these problems of comparison, a number of position-based studies of comparability have been undertaken. Among the more complete was that undertaken by Bureau of Labor Statistics (BLS) researcher Michael Miller (1996). The BLS designed the Occupational Compensation Survey Program to allow one-to-one comparison of workers performing essentially the same job through wide portions of the economy, including state and local governments. This involved matching detailed job descriptions to 44 occupations broken into seven categories.

The BLS results are instructive:

> Contrary to comparisons based on overall averages or broad occupational groups, private industry paid better for virtually all professional and administrative occupational job levels and for the majority of technical and clerical job levels. For blue-collar workers the situation was mixed. (Miller 1996:22)

The patterns made clear that at the bottom of skill and responsibility hierarchies, state and local government employees had an advantage but in the middle and upper portion, private workers had an advantage. Indeed, among the 80 comparisons possible among the white collar jobs, private industry paid better than state and local governments in four out of every five positions.

Individual studies within states illustrate some of the potential pitfalls of aggregating data. Ballard and Funari (2009) showed data from the American Community Survey as reported by the Michigan House Fiscal Agency. They reported that the average earnings of state of Michigan employees exceed those of private sector workers. Yet, when comparing earnings within educational category (less than high school, high school degree, some college, etc.), State of Michigan employees earned less within every one of the eight educational categories. This reflects the composition fallacy known as Simpson's Paradox. The average state worker appears to earn more only because the state hires more of those in the highly educated categories, who tend to earn more—not because workers with the same education earn more in the public sector.

Other Views on Comparability

It seems fair to conclude that the central tendencies revealed by both approaches to comparability, people and positions, suggest that the earnings of state and local workers are not excessive. There exist, of course, alternate standards for setting governmental compensation but, in the end, these may be of only modest assistance. One view is that public sector compensation should be judged by ability to pay. This involves the difficult task of measuring that ability and distinguishing inability from reluctance. Certainly communities can face financial stringency, but arguments for public sector wage relief may reflect an unwillingness to tax adequately or discretionary decisions to spend on other objectives. Thus, if a government has a budget deficit but a low tax rate, what is the ability to pay?

Yet none of these difficulties means that public sector workers are, or should be, immune to conditions around them. In the recent recession and its continuing fallout, many state governments instituted unpaid furloughs, reducing the level of compensation. In local governments, not only have there been furloughs, but some jurisdictions have explicitly tied compensation to measures of revenue, such as the sum of taxes, fees, and state aid (see Kertscher 2009 for an example). While we will discuss additional recent responses of policy makers, it is important to note that Freeman (1987) showed that public sector pay differs over time as much as private sector pay does. In the end, over any reasonable time period, even jurisdictions with agreed-upon low ability to pay may not be able to reject comparability completely. If a local jurisdiction decides it does not have the ability to pay and permanently reduces wages below the level of the private sector and of other nearby jurisdictions, it will simply be unlikely to attract needed workers, which may compel re-adopting comparability.

A second frequently mentioned standard other than comparability contends that the government should be a model employer. Governments have seen this model as one of advocating and demonstrating employment policies such as due process, merit systems, pensions, health insurance, and anti-discrimination measures. Thus, wage regression estimates frequently suggest that the extent of earnings discrimination is smaller in public sectors (Hoffnar and Greene 1996; Heywood 1989). Estimates frequently indicate that women workers, for example, earn more than their private sector counterparts even when men do not (Asher and Popkin 1984). According to the model employer view, women workers who receive higher wages compared to the private sector may nonetheless receive the appropriate wage if this public sector premium is offsetting discrimination they would otherwise face in the private sector. The implication that model employer wages should be higher can easily be reversed when making other comparisons with the private sector. A government might lower earnings for workers whose private sector counterparts have elevated wages reflecting less than competitive markets. Beyond trying to remedy imperfections in the private markets, this view also argues that in a system that relies on employer-based health insurance and retirement, public employers should be at the forefront in making sure that both are provided.

In the end, the model that a public employer should set remains in the eye of the beholder. As Belman and Heywood (1996) detail, in a variety of overseas settings, politicians have attempted to set public pay lower in the hope that it would become a standard for bargainers in the private sector and serve as an informal income policy and a tool for macroeconomic policy. In the face of the complexity and ambiguity of both ability to pay and the model employer, the standard of comparability provides both more certainty and more applicability across a range of settings.

Perceptions and Recent Policy

Unfortunately, the nuances of comparability and the measurement of comparability rarely make it to the popular press. *USA Today* routinely reports on aggregate pay and benefit differences between the public and private sectors. Thus, Cauchon (2009) writes that the average compensation of public sector workers (sum of earnings plus fringe benefits) was $11.90 per hour more than that of private sector workers.

Individual newspapers in local areas report similar differences in average compensation within their area. The *Sun Journal* (2009) in Lewiston, Maine, highlighted that state workers in Maine had average compensation (including benefits) that was around 9% higher than the average in Maine's private sector. While recognizing that this did not prove waste, the editorial board called the difference unsustainable and something that should change.

Despite the tone of these and similar articles, the averages they report provide no evidence on the issue of whether public sector workers are overcompensated. The tone also appears hard to reconcile with the concerns expressed by public administrators that low pay has hurt the morale and quality of the public sector workforce. Administrators are also concerned that it will be difficult to replace the baby boomers about to retire and that the general appeal of government jobs has declined markedly since the late 1980s (Lewis and Frank 2002).

The tone set by the popular press matches that of many state and local elected officials. Elected officials responded to the budget shortfalls associated with the Great Recession by reducing the pay and benefits of public sector employees. Initial responses in the vast majority of states included layoffs and furloughs that cut labor costs and reduced compensation (see the National Conference of State Legislatures 2009) and a prediction for more such responses in the next round of budgets. As it turned out, many states went beyond those measures, substantially increasing government employees' contributions to fringe benefits, cutting those benefits, and even removing provisions that allow union bargaining over benefits.

For example, in the first six months of 2011, 25 states enacted significant revisions to their state retirement plans, with others still pending. The two most common changes increased employee contributions for health insurance and pensions in 15 states and increased age and service requirements for retirement benefits in 14 states (Snell 2011). Indeed, at the height of budget sessions in the spring of 2011, *Business Week* published an article titled "For Governors, Public Unions are the Enemy," isolating six governors' efforts to implement "pay cuts, benefits cuts, salary cuts and loss of collective bargaining rights" (Jones 2011). Indeed, several states recently have substantially reduced the ability of public sector unions to collectively bargain (for example, in Indiana, Ohio, New Jersey, and Wisconsin) with the anticipation that the extent of union coverage may decline within the public sectors of those states.

The critical object of any comparability exercise is an effort to compare similar workers doing similar duties—and has been for decades. It is well recognized that the average public sector and private sector workers are not similar workers doing similar duties. This is well known to compensation specialists, who repeatedly show that the typical state or local sector worker has more education and tenure and greater responsibilities. As but a single example, more than half of the jobs in the state of Michigan workforce actually *require* at least a bachelor's degree to apply (Ballard and Funari 2009). Thus, the fact that public sector workers receive greater average compensation than private sector workers should be no more surprising than the fact that those with more skills and education earn more. The analysis of comparability should examine the difference between sectors *after* controlling for the differences in the workers and their jobs.

In summary, both the politically charged newspaper reports and the handwringing public administrators could be correct. Public sector workers could earn more on average than private sector workers (because of the former's greater skill and education) but still less than they would earn if they took their skills to the private sector. The critical economic and policy issue is not the first issue (which is largely irrelevant) but rather the second issue. We now turn to investigate that second issue.

A New Examination of the Data

Basics on the Data, Construction of Variables, and Methodology

We present a new examination of data using the standard people-based approach that has been commonly used at least since Smith (1976). Our examination uses data from the annual outgoing rotation groups (ORG) of the Current Population Survey (CPS). The CPS is a monthly survey of 50,000 to 60,000 households conducted by the Bureau of the Census for the Bureau of Labor Statistics. The annual ORG data come from all households that are in the last month of their final four-month period as participants in the survey.[1] ORG data are standardized for question continuity by the National Bureau of Economic Research and are publicly available (http://www.nber.org/cps/).

We used the full set of years available at this time, 1979 to 2010. An exception arose when controlling for union coverage, data that are available only since 1983. This approach allows both a recent snapshot of the current degree of comparability and a picture of the historical pattern over the past three decades.

CPS data provide earnings but not fringe benefit information. We used alternative data to adjust the measures of earnings comparability we derived from the CPS but defer that discussion until the next section of this chapter. The earnings data identify usual weekly earnings, which we divided by usual weekly hours to convert to hourly wages. We limited the sample to those working full time by excluding people working less than 35 hours per week.[2] We also excluded resulting average wage calculations that are less than $1 per hour and more than $500 per hour.

An important data note is that some CPS observations have allocated data for earnings and hours. The survey imputes (rather than measures) earnings when data on hours and earnings are not reported. We excluded all such allocated data to avoid the issue of match bias in the resulting estimates (Hirsch and Schumacher 2004).

CPS data also clearly identify workers who are employed by either a state or local government. We kept the two levels of government separate in all of our estimations to present an estimate of comparability for each level for each year. The earnings of workers at these two levels were compared to private sector workers who are employed (not self-employed) in the for-profit sector.

Our basic methodology estimated the log of hourly earnings with a set of relevant earnings determinants provided by the CPS. Among the determinants were the two critical sectors, state and local government. The use of log earnings as the dependent variable follows both from the basic theory of the human capital model and from repeated experience, finding that it generally provides a superior fit to the data. Such log earnings models provide consistent estimates of the proportional impact of wage determinants under the assumption that the distribution of the error term is independent of the regressors. While we followed the dominant strategy, we recognize that when this assumption is violated, alternative estimations may be superior (Blackburn 2007). We emphasize that the general tenor of our results does not vary greatly with alternative treatments of how to estimate the impact of state and local employment on earnings.

Descriptive Statistics and a First Look

Table 1 isolates the available earnings determinants and presents their means for three time periods. When we examine the data across all years in the last column, we note that workers in the state and local sector are disproportionately female, married, black, and unionized compared to the private sector. Critically, they are also older and have much more education. In the private sector, only 23% of workers have completed college; in the state sector, 48.8% are college graduates and in the local sector, 48.2% have finished college. The most common occupations in the state and local sectors include teachers, social workers, nurses, and university professors (Belman and Heywood 2004a).

Means of these variables are also presented for the first and last year in our time series to show how they have changed over time. Although educational credentials have increased in all sectors, the gap between the state and local sectors and the private sector has remained enormous. The comparison shows an aging of the workforce that is most pronounced in the state sector, a sharp decline in private sector union coverage, and an increasing concentration of women in the state and local sectors.

Knowing that workers in the state and local sectors are more highly educated, it should not be surprising to find they are paid more on average. We computed the mean wage in each of the government sectors and compared it to that in the private sector. In Figure 1, we present for each year the percentage difference in mean wages. There appears to be a mild hump-shaped relationship over the past quarter century (28 annual waves of the CPS). It started as a ten percentage point wage advantage for state and local workers in 1983 that rose to around 20% by the early 1990s and then declined to a steadier 15 percentage point wage advantage toward the end of the time series.

TABLE 1
Means of Variables from the Current Population Survey (ORG)

Variable	1983			2010			All years		
	Private	State	Local	Private	State	Local	Private	State	Local
Male	60.7%	51.5%	50.1%	59.7%	43.2%	43.7%	60.0%	47.4%	45.8%
Married	65.6%	67.5%	71.6%	58.3%	63.6%	65.3%	60.4%	64.5%	38.2%
White	79.8%	77.9%	78.4%	66.2%	72.6%	72.3%	73.1%	74.8%	74.9%
Black	8.9%	13.2%	13.4%	9.1%	12.3%	11.7%	9.6%	14.0%	13.4%
Other race	2.7%	3.2%	1.7%	6.9%	5.3%	4.4%	4.3%	4.5%	3.1%
Hispanic	8.6%	5.8%	6.5%	17.8%	9.9%	11.7%	13.0%	5.7%	8.6%
No high school degree	18.1%	8.3%	10.5%	10.3%	2.1%	2.7%	13.6%	3.9%	5.3%
High school degree	40.5%	29.7%	26.1%	30.4%	16.7%	18.9%	36.2%	22.3%	23.0%
Some college	23.1%	21.2%	18.7%	29.2%	24.0%	25.4%	27.2%	25.0%	23.5%
College degree	11.3%	14.8%	16.2%	21.7%	29.4%	27.5%	16.3%	23.4%	23.5%
Post-college degree	7.1%	26.1%	28.5%	8.4%	27.8%	25.5%	6.7%	25.4%	24.7%
Age	35.8	38.6	39.8	40.3	44.3	43.9	37.5	41.8	41.8
Covered by union contract	20.7%	40.6%	55.5%	8.5%	38.8%	51.9%	12.8%	38.5%	52.3%

FIGURE 1
Comparing Unadjusted Wages (Not a Comparability Exercise)

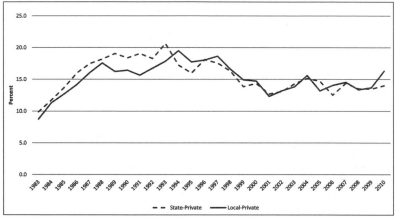

Note: These are the annual percentage difference between the average wage earned among all U.S. state and among all U.S. local government workers when compared to the average wage earned among private sector workers.

We now explore how much of the raw wage difference remains after adjusting for basic earnings determinants. In our initial specification, we regressed the log wage against the education variables, personal characteristics, and indicator variables for each state of residence. Including this set of state indicators controls for differences in cost of living and earnings patterns and allows more similar circumstances to be compared between public and private sector workers.[3] We estimated this specification for each year first in a sample that included all private sector workers and the state government workers and in a second sample that included all private sector workers and the local government workers. Each model includes an indicator for government workers.

To give a flavor of these estimates, we show the results for 2010 in the first two columns of Table 2. The first column shows the comparison of the private sector workers to the workers in state government. In the table, we converted the coefficients that would otherwise be expressed in log wage dollars into the percentage increases or decreases in actual wages associated with the variables.[4] Thus, the regression suggests that men earn 20% more than women, that high school graduates earn 23% more than dropouts, and that college graduates earn 98% more than dropouts (essentially double), holding all other variables constant.

The estimate for 2010 shows that state workers were paid 6.6% less than their otherwise equal private sector counterparts. Column 2 shows the analogous estimate for the comparison of local government and private sector workers. In 2010, local government workers were paid 3.7%

TABLE 2
OLS Regression Results for 2010 ORG Data

Variable	State vs. private	Local vs. private	State vs. private	Local vs. private	State vs. private	Local vs. private
Public sector worker	−0.066* (−9.68)	−0.037* (−6.68)	−0.113* (−16.58)	−0.097* (−16.90)	−0.070* (−10.10)	−0.020* (−3.13)
Male	0.201* (51.00)	0.208* (53.94)	0.193* (49.20)	0.201* (52.46)	0.165* (40.45)	0.163* (40.71)
Married	0.109* (27.03)	0.104* (26.61)	0.108* (26.97)	0.103* (26.49)	0.087* (23.49)	0.082* (22.85)
Black	−0.136* (−22.94)	−0.131* (−22.83)	−0.141* (−24.07)	−0.137* (−23.92)	−0.104* (−18.59)	−0.105* (−19.27)
Other race	−0.123* (−17.81)	−0.122* (−17.99)	−0.121* (−17.67)	−0.120* (−17.71)	−0.110* (−17.06)	−0.113* (−17.78)
Hispanic	−0.201* (−40.66)	−0.196* (−40.45)	−0.200* (−40.72)	−0.195* (−40.51)	−0.162* (−34.21)	−0.157* (−34.05)
High school degree	0.230* (30.65)	0.235* (31.65)	0.222* (29.80)	0.228* (30.97)	0.162* (23.50)	0.163* (24.07)
Some college	0.461* (54.99)	0.466* (56.32)	0.454* (54.53)	0.460* (55.98)	0.297* (38.94)	0.302* (40.17)
College degree	0.981* (94.26)	0.979* (95.70)	0.987* (95.19)	0.981* (96.36)	0.617* (65.34)	0.628* (67.31)
Post-college degree	1.536* (109.40)	1.529* (111.98)	1.550* (110.61)	1.522* (112.24)	0.986* (78.32)	1.003* (81.31)
Age	0.052* (53.67)	0.052* (54.78)	0.051* (52.75)	0.051 (53.88)	0.043* (47.69)	0.043* (48.90)
Age squared	−5.1E−4* (−46.21)	−5.1E−4* (−47.23)	−5.0E−04* (−45.52)	−5.0E−04* (−46.52)	−4.1E−4* (−46.37)	−4.2E−4* (−41.60)
Covered by union contract	—	—	0.177* (27.14)	0.162* (26.90)	0.219* (34.83)	0.224* (37.76)
Occupational controls incl.	No	No	No	No	Yes	Yes

Notes: Other variables controlled for, but not reported, are a constant term and state of residence. The excluded racial category is white. The excluded educational category is no high school degree. * indicates statistical significance at the 1% level. When occupations are included, the following categories are controlled for: managerial; business/financial operations; computer and math; engineering; science; social services; arts, sports, etc.; legal; education, library sciences; healthcare practitioner; protective service; food preparation and serving; cleaning and maintenance; personal care and service; sales; office and administrative support; farming, fishing, forestry; construction and extraction; installation, maintenance and repair; production; and transportation.

less than their private sector counterparts. Thus, despite average wages around 13% or 14% higher (see Figure 1 again), the adjusted wage gap is statistically significant in the opposite direction. The adjusted wage gap provides an estimate of comparability; the estimate suggests that state and local workers are on average underpaid, controlling for other determinants of wages.

As always, the exact estimate is sensitive to the inclusion or exclusion of particular variables. For example, the estimated state and local government percentage wage gaps are larger if one uses broad regional dummies (not reported) instead of specific states as we do. Yet, neither this nor other changes alter the basic pattern of the adjusted wage gap typically being lower for state and local government workers. The major driver in this basic pattern is the fact that government workers have jobs that demand more education, a fact not accounted for by the raw averages.[5] Thus, the overall averages frequently used, for instance in the press, are misleading because even if those with college degrees earn less in the public sector, they earn more than those without college degrees.

We present two variants on the initial earnings equations in Table 2 that include occupational controls and a control for unionization. The proper use of occupational controls and unionization is much disputed in the academic literature on public wage differentials. As a theoretical matter, even relatively broad occupational groups can be highly specific to either the public or private sector (Belman and Heywood 1988).

There are very few blue-collar production workers in the public sector and virtually no fire and police workers in the private sector. The statistical consequence of controlling for nearly exclusive occupations is essentially to throw out large segments of the workforce from the comparability exercise (see Belman and Heywood 2004a for a proof). This approach may be appropriate but is done at the cost of not offering any judgment on those workers who are in occupations unique to the sector.

Linneman and Wachter (1990) argued that the odds that public sector workers are unionized and work for large employers are so much higher that it makes no sense to bring these characteristics over when asking what they would earn in the private sector. They recommended excluding unionization and size as controls. Belman and Heywood (1993) showed that, compared to workers in the private sector, public sector workers would be more likely to work for large employers and be unionized if they were in the private sector (given the characteristics of public sector workers). Thus, completely excluding unionization as a control is likely inappropriate.

More fundamentally, there exists a general debate over the inclusion of job attributes such as occupations, unionization, firm size, or other characteristics. For example, occupational controls may account for working conditions and the associated compensating differentials. While workers moving from specific occupations in the public sector may not move to the same occupation in the private sector, they may be moving to ones with a different set of working conditions. Thought of this way, controlling for occupation is part of standardizing for similar jobs, even if not for similar workers.

Duncan and Stafford (1980) have argued that a large share of the union premium in the private sector also represents compensating wage differentials for working conditions. Although it is not available in our data, firm size provides a similar point. Evidence indicates that workers get less job satisfaction working for very large employers and that they receive higher wages from those employers (Idson 1990; Schmidt and Zimmermann 1991). Thus, while a typical public sector worker who changed sectors would likely find himself or herself working for a private sector employer smaller than the typical public sector employer, controlling for employer size is part of standardizing for positions (Belman and Heywood 1990). In total, if one takes what Belman and Heywood (1996) identify as a hybrid approach, trying to standardize for both people and positions as best one can, these and perhaps other job characteristics belong in the underlying earnings estimates. As one more example, job security is frequently discussed with the presumption that it is greater in the public sector. Again, a measure of job security might be profitably included but is absent from typical data sources.[6]

We present first a variant adding a union control and then a second variant that also adds occupational controls as alternative attempts to more closely compare employees doing similar work. Using occupational controls is somewhat problematic for our time series because the system of occupational classifications changed in 2000 in a way that makes maintaining a consistent set of classifications difficult. We did the best we could by adopting the latter set of classifications and cross-walking back to the earlier years to maintain the same approximate classification. But we recognize the imprecision we have introduced and the problem associated with occupations that are nearly exclusive to either the public or private sector.

We show the results for 2010, including unionization, in Table 2, columns 3 and 4. They show a double-digit negative differential for each sector. Estimates that also include occupational controls, in columns 5 and 6, show smaller but still significant negative differentials, which suggests public sector workers earn less than comparable wages. Interestingly, the estimate for state workers is slightly more negative and that for local workers is slightly less negative in this final estimate compared to the original estimate without either unionization or occupational controls.

The Pattern of Earnings Comparability over Time

Figure 2 presents the hourly earnings differentials for the state and local sectors for each year using the original specification, which does not include the occupational or union controls. An estimate of approximately zero is taken as an indicator of close comparability. The earnings differentials for both the state and local sectors over time show a hump-shaped pattern. Over much of the early period, state workers appear to be less underpaid than the local workers, but this difference vanishes by the later years. The state government differential starts at –7% to –8% early in the period, creeps up toward zero in the early 1990s, but then shows a sharp decline and levels off in the past decade at about the original –7%. The local government differential becomes several percentage points positive in the late 1980s and early 1990s, but drops even more dramatically as the decade continues.

Recall that Borjas (2003), using a broadly similar approach, found differentials of around –10% in 2000, the last year of his data. Our second specification, which includes unionization (Figure 3), shows consistently negative differentials, the same hump over time with a sharp decline over the 1990s, and differentials that remain in negative double digits. The final specification, which includes both unionization and occupational controls (Figure 4), continues to chronicle the hump shape and decline

FIGURE 2
Adjusted Wage Differential

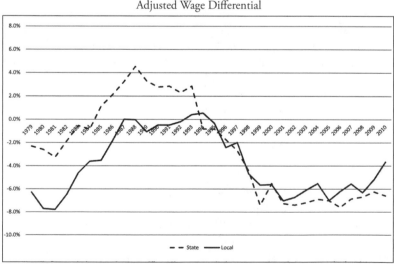

Note: The figure graphs the estimated percentage differential between state or local government workers and private sector workers from OLS regressions controlling for the independent variables in Table 2 but with no controls for union coverage or occupation.

FIGURE 3
Alternative Adjusted Wage Differential (Including Unionization)

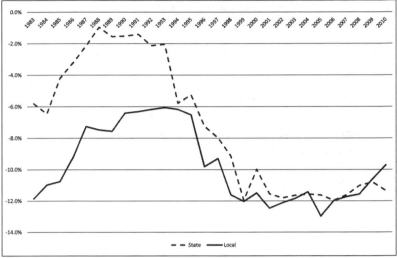

Note: The figure graphs the estimated percentage differential between state or local government workers and private sector workers from OLS regressions controlling for the independent variables in Table 2, including a control for union coverage but no control for occupation.

FIGURE 4
Alternative Adjusted Wage Differential (Including Unionization and Occupations)

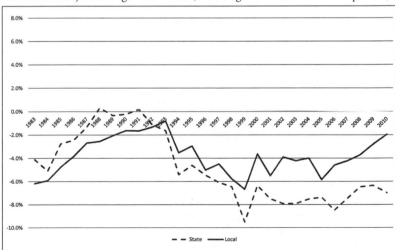

Note: The figure graphs the estimated percentage differential between state or local government workers and private sector workers from OLS regressions controlling for the independent variables in Table 2, including a control for union coverage and a common set of occupations across all years.

and broadly mimics the first estimation. Thus, the broad pattern we identify of a deteriorating position of state and local workers was presented before by Borjas, and we isolated that things have not changed dramatically in the decade since the last year examined by Borjas.[7]

Obtaining a Working Estimate with Which to Proceed

While it seems that earnings are below comparability in the state and local sectors, one objective is to make a comparison that includes other forms of compensation, including pensions and insurance. To do this, we need a reasonable working estimate of the extent to which state and local earnings are comparable with the private sector. In the spirit of providing both a manageable degree of variation and still give some nuance, we averaged the estimated earnings differential for 2000 to 2010 using both our basic methodology of not including union and occupational controls and both of our variants including those controls.

The original methodology showed average differentials of –6.8% for state workers and –5.9% for local workers. The first variant presented larger averages over the past decade, with –11.4% for state workers and –11.6% for local workers. The final variant presented averages of –7% for state workers and –4% for local workers. These estimates are shown in Table 3 and are the ones we will build on when adding in the role of fringe benefits.

The Role of Fringe Benefits

Next, we adjusted the estimates of wage comparability to account for differences in fringe benefits between state and local governments and the private sector. Ideally, data such as the CPS would include a measure of the value of such benefits for each worker or the cost spent on each worker. However, worker survey data on such values might be very unreliable because few workers accurately know the monetary value of their fringe benefits. Perhaps as a consequence, the CPS does not contain measures of the value of fringe benefits. It shares this characteristic with all the major individual worker survey data that labor economists commonly use. Additional aggregate data must be used, but the insights gained from the wage comparability exercise can be applied.

We started with the basic realization that if fringe benefits comprise the same share of state and local compensation as they do of private compensation, then the wage differential provides a suitable measure of total compensation comparability. To see this point, imagine every worker across all sectors receives fringe benefits as a fixed proportion of their total compensation and so of earnings. Using the wage determinants to examine the fringe benefits would result in the same percentage differential as

TABLE 3
Average Wage Differentials from 2000 to 2010 Across Three Estimations

	State–private	Local–private
Without union or occupation controls	–6.8%	–5.9%
With union control	–11.4%	–11.6%
With union and occupation controls	–7.3%	–4.0%

were estimated using wages. We exploit this fact to adjust the wage differential with actual data, which show that fringe benefits as a share of total compensation in state and local government differ from that in the private sector.[8]

To make the adjustment, we take data from the National Compensation Survey (NCS). The NCS is not a survey of workers but of employers. Collected by the Bureau of Labor Statistics, it details the cost of employee compensation and is used to construct the frequently used Employment Cost Index. NCS estimates the current cost of fringe benefits, not the generosity of those benefits. If the public sector is more efficient at providing benefits, its costs may be lower.[9] This is similar to the point that larger firms may be more efficient at providing benefits and helps support the notion that a proper comparability exercise should standardize for the size of the employer. The survey provides data for all firms in the private sector, for private sector firms larger than 100 employees, and for the sum of state and local government combined. Thus, we cannot contrast the pattern between the two levels of government; however, the data are easily available (ftp://ftp.bls.gov/pub/special.requests/ocwc/ect/ececqrtn.pdf).

As shown in Figure 5, we graphed earnings as a share of total compensation (earnings plus fringe benefits) for the period of our time series. The first point is that the shares of the public and private sector are within a few percentage points over the entire period. Indeed, until 2005, there was essentially no difference between the earnings shares of the public sector and that of private sector firms with over 100 employees. The gap emerges in the past few years of our time series and ends up around two percentage points. The public sector routinely has a lower share of compensation spent on earnings (a higher share spent on fringe benefits) than the entire private sector (all employer sizes).

The information most relevant to our adjustment is the share of total compensation provided by earnings. As we emphasized earlier, if earnings were the same share of total compensation in both state and local government and the private sector, the best estimate of the percentage difference in total compensation, holding constant worker and job characteristics,

FIGURE 5
Relative Importance of Wages and Salary as a Percentage of Total Compensation

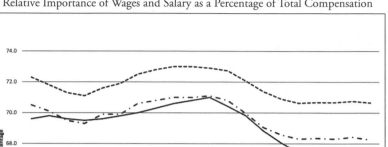

would be exactly that estimated in the last section. Table 4 averages the earnings and fringe benefit shares for two private sector samples and for the combination of state and local government over the past decade to match our earnings differential, which was similarly averaged in Table 3. The total private firm sample has earnings that are approximately 71.5% of total compensation, while the large firm private sector sample has an earnings share of 69.3% and the state and local sample has an earnings share of about 68.2%. Again, these shares make clear that fringe benefits are a larger share of compensation in state and local government, although not dramatically different.

In the previous section, we held worker and job characteristics constant and estimated a resulting percentage difference in wages in Table 3. For state and local workers, these estimates varied (depending on specification) from −4% to −11.6%. As an illustration, take the most negative estimate, which is that the ratio of local to private wages is .884. If workers in each sector had earnings as the same share of total compensation, that ratio would be our best estimate of the ratio of total compensation. Yet, because the share of benefits for workers in state and local governments is larger, the appropriate ratio of total compensation will be larger (less negative or even positive) than that for earnings alone. The implied adjustment multiplies the ratio of local to private wages, .884, by the ratio of private earnings share to local earnings share.[10] Using the all private

TABLE 4
Earnings and Fringe Benefits as Shares of Total Compensation
(Averaged over 2000–2010)

Sector	Fringes as a share of compensation	Earnings as a share of compensation
Total private sector	.2851	.7149
Large firms in private sector (100+ workers)	.3072	.6928
State and local government	.3180	.6820

sector earnings share, the second ratio is 1.048 (.7149/.6820) and, when multiplied by the earnings ratio, yields a total compensation ratio of .926. This implies a total compensation differential of –7.3%. Thus, assuming the determinants of fringe benefits match the estimated determinants of hourly earnings and adjusting for the fact that state and local compensation is more heavily oriented toward benefits, the local government workers receive less than comparable total compensation in this specification.

Table 5 presents the state and local total compensation differentials, with this methodology applied to both state and local governments and using all three of the earnings differentials and both the full private sample and large firm private sample earnings to compensation ratios from Table 4. Each of these adjustments results in a total compensation differential that adds to the relative position of state and local workers. The resulting estimates for the total compensation differential range from essentially 0% to –10%, with all but one of the estimates across state and local workers being negative. In short, incorporating fringe benefits makes state and public workers appear somewhat less poorly compensated, but our range of estimates suggest they remain modestly undercompensated relative to private sector workers.

Our assumption that the determinants of fringe benefit values follow the determinants of wages could be debated, but it recognizes a crucial point. Fringe benefits should be expected to be higher if public sector workers are more highly educated and doing jobs that command higher earnings. In the private sector, fringe benefits are greater for the more educated and, because the public sector consists disproportionately of the educated, if it mimics the private sector we would expect the average level of fringe benefits to be higher in the public sector. As with earnings, the average comparison of fringe benefit levels between the public and private sector reveals nothing about comparability in compensation between the two levels. Our adjustment process recognizes this point and serves to emphasize, at minimum, that simple fringe benefit levels across sectors should not be compared because it is not a comparability exercise.

TABLE 5
Estimated Total Compensation Differentials

	State	Local
Earnings estimates without occupation or union (all private sector fringes sample)	–2.3%	–1.4%%
Earnings estimate without occupation or union (larger firm private sector fringes sample)	–5.3%	–4.4%
Earnings estimate with union (all private sector fringes sample)	–7.1%	–7.3%
Earnings estimate with union (larger firm private sector fringes sample)	–10.0%	–10.2%
Earnings estimate with occupation and union (all private sector fringes sample)	–2.8%	0.6%
Earnings estimate with occupation and union (larger firm private sector fringe sample)	–5.8%	–2.5%

Driving this point home is the realization that much of the difference in the average cost of fringe benefits between sectors reflects simple differences in provision of the benefits. Table 6 uses the March 2010 CPS and shows that approximately three fourths of public sector workers receive an employer- or union-provided pension and health insurance. The comparable figures in the private sector have dropped to only 44% receiving a pension and only 55% receiving health insurance. Thus, should comparability require simply that a state or municipal employer provide these benefits to only half of its workers?

Clearly, it would be illegal if a private sector employer engaged in randomly providing only half of its employees a pension and health insurance. This observation strikes us as an important point in thinking about the meaning of comparability. It cannot logically be a simple mindless mimicry of private sector averages. If it is thought that most public sector employees should provide health insurance to their full-time workers, the private sector comparables might then become workers at firms that also provide health insurance. Further research on this seems clearly needed.

Table 6 also presents May 2010 CPS responses to a question asking workers whether their employer or union pays all, part, or none of their provided health insurance. While this measure is very crude, it suggests that those in the public sector are equally likely to have their employer pay part, less likely to have their employer pay none, and more likely to

TABLE 6
Percentage of Workers Participating in Pension and Health
Insurance Benefits from the March 2010 CPS, by Sector

| | Private | | | State and local government | | |
	All	Small (<100)	Big (>100)	All	Small (<100)	Big (>100)
% pension	43.7%	26.6%	55.9%	73.0%	58.3%	74.9%
% health insurance	55.2%	40.0%	66.0%	74.3%	60.2%	76.1%
Proportion of health insurance costs paid by employer/union						
All	18.7%	28.0%	14.7%	22.4%	30.8%	21.6%
Part	76.2%	65.5%	80.9%	75.0%	66.9%	75.8%
None	5.0%	6.6%	4.4%	2.6%	2.3%	2.6%

have their employer pay all. Nonetheless, the differences are modest. Thus, 18.7% of private sector employees say their employer pays all compared to 22.4% of public sector employees. We emphasize this can only be descriptive because no attempt to equalize worker or employer characteristics has been undertaken. Moreover, there are no comparable questions regarding contributions to pensions. Yet we note that public sector employees are far more likely to contribute to their defined benefit plan than are private sector employees, but also that such plans are themselves far more common in the public sector.[11] At a minimum, when taken with the provision numbers, this hints that differences in employee contributions play a far smaller role in benefit differences between sectors than do differences in the provision of benefits in the first place.

Comparability and Distributional Considerations

It is well known that public sector earnings show far less dispersion than those of the private sector. The high wages are not as high and the low wages are not as low (Poterba and Rueben 1994; Bender 2003; Belman and Heywood 2004b). This raises fundamental issues about the extent of comparability between public and private compensation. Indeed, it is possible to have a mean compensation differential of zero but no public sector workers being paid their private sector equivalent. The total cost of some public employees would be comparable, but it would merely consist of some public workers being paid too little and others being paid too much. In this section, we explore this important issue regarding comparability.

As a first exploration, we repeated our annual estimates of the state and local differentials for three groups: those without a college degree, those with a college degree, and those with more than a college degree (advanced or professional degree). The results, using our initial specification without occupational or union controls, are shown in Figures 6 and 7. The state–private earnings differential is shown in Figure 6; for those without college, it shows a hump shape reaching its largest positive value in the late 1980s and early 1990s at about 7%. It then drops to around zero by 1998 and stays near zero until the last four years of the time series, when it begins to rise.

This result is in very sharp contrast to the results for the college-educated group and those with more than college education. Each of these differentials tends to be negative throughout the time series but only modestly until the early 1990s. They then drop precipitously, leveling off at approximately –12% for the college educated and –16% for those with more than college. Thus, it seems clear that the position of those in the public sector with college degrees or more is far worse than those without college relative to the private sector and that this is a phenomenon of the past 15 years.

As an illustration, the less than college group's differential in 1994 is about 3%, while that for those with more than college is about –5%. In 2010, the differential for the less than college group is again around 3%, while that for the group with more than college is –18%. Perhaps most important, if one looks to the very beginning of the time series, all three education-based differentials are remarkably similar and the overall pattern over time is one of growing dispersion by level of education.

The local–private pattern is shown in Figure 7. Again all three educational levels have similar single-digit negative differentials at the beginning of the time series. The differential for the least educated grew to become positive in the late 1980s and early 1990s and then returned to about zero. Those of the more educated groups dropped to increasingly larger negative differentials. Thus, in both cases, the governmental differentials show greater dispersion over time by education. While the reason for this is unclear, one conjecture is that public sector compensation has simply not reflected the growing educational wage differential in the private sector. Perhaps skill-biased technical change has increased the wages of the educated more than those of the less educated in the private sector. But this development may simply not have been matched by the public sector. As a consequence, the public sector over these years seems to have become a great place to be a janitor and a poor place to be a certified public accountant or lawyer.

FIGURE 6

State–Private Percentage Differential by Educational Degree

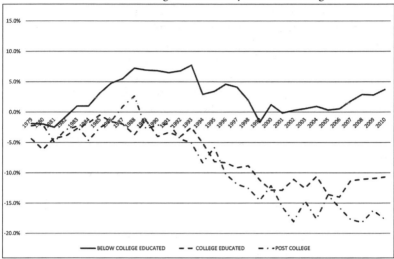

Note: The figure graphs the estimated percentage differential between state government workers and private sector workers by educational degree from OLS regressions controlling for the independent variables in Table 2 but with no controls for union coverage or occupation.

FIGURE 7

Local–Private Percentage Differential by Educational Degree

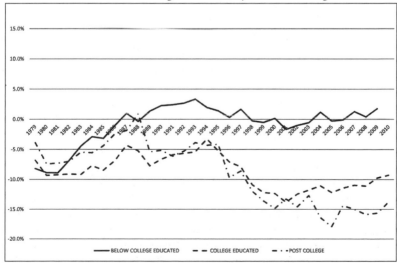

Note: The figure graphs the estimated percentage differential between local government workers and private sector workers by educational degree from OLS regressions controlling for the independent variables in Table 2 but with no controls for union coverage or occupation.

We attempted two other types of comparisons to gain a sense of the difference in dispersion between the public and private sectors. First, we simply calculated over time the ratio of the earnings of workers at the 90th percentile of the earnings distribution to those at the median, the 50th percentile of the earnings distribution. We did this for each year in our entire time series and did it separately for workers in the private sector, state government, and local government. The results are in Figure 8 and show that at the beginning of the time series, the 90:50 ratio is similar across all three sectors. Those at the 90th percentile in the private sector earned about 1.9 times as much as those at the median, while those at the 90th percentile of the two public sectors earned about 1.8 times more than those at the median.

Over the course of nearly three decades, the ratio increased for all three sectors but only modestly for the two public sectors, increasing by about .1 and thus averaging about 1.9 toward the end of the time series. However, the private sector ratio increased by .4 and tops 2.3 by 2010. Thus, this standardization within sectors shows that earnings at the top of the private sector distribution have increased dramatically compared to the earnings at the top of the public sector distribution. This finding seems consistent with our evidence that the public differential has become large and negative for those with college degrees because the public sector has not matched the increasing return to education evident in the private sector. Yet holding to a strict standard of comparability that mimics the earnings of the private sector might generate within the public sector both the growth of the working poor and the growing concentration of earnings at the top of the distribution, as has emerged within the private sector.[12] Obviously, normative evaluations may differ, and our point is not to argue for this outcome but merely to make clear the implications of the comparability standard.

In the second investigation, we estimated quantile regressions at the 10th, 50th, and 90th percentiles of the overall wage distribution. We used the original earnings specification, which controlled for neither unions nor occupations. This pattern of earnings differentials is shown in Figures 9 and 10. The point of these estimates is that they standardize for the relevant controls, but instead of estimating their influence through the point of means, they do so at specific places in the wage differential.

The pattern of results is clear. All three differentials show the pattern of a hump and a decline from the early 1990s, and the position of the relative differentials remains consistent. Examining the state differential, those at the bottom of the distribution, the 10th percentile, have an earnings advantage relative to their private sector counterparts. Larger in the 1980s, the advantage has shrunk to around 3% over the past decade, but it remains an advantage.

FIGURE 8

Dispersion at the Top End of the Distribution by Sector

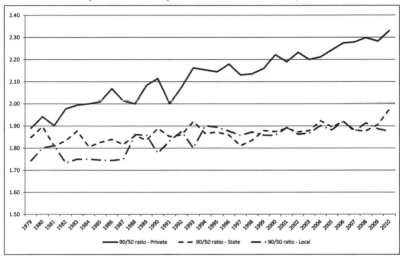

Note: The figure plots the 90/50 ratio of average hourly wages for private, state, and local workers who report working full time and have hourly wages between $1 and $500.

FIGURE 9

Quantile Regression Estimates of the State–Private Differential

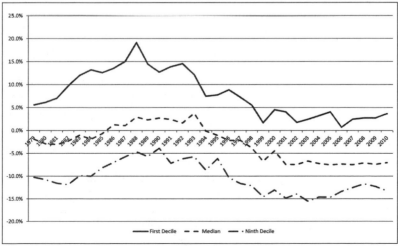

Note: The figure graphs the estimated percentage differential between state government workers and private sector workers from quantile regressions controlling for the independent variables in Table 2 but with no controls for union coverage or occupation.

FIGURE 10

Quantile Regression Estimates of the Local–Private Differential

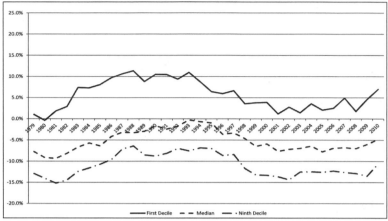

Note: The figure graphs the estimated percentage differential between local government workers and private sector workers from quantile regressions controlling for the independent variables in Table 2 but with no controls for union coverage or occupation.

Median estimates do not look much different from our original mean regressions, with the differential turning negative and remaining about –7% over the past decade. The differential at the 90th percentile is far more negative, averaging around –14% for the past decade. Thus, the influence of employment in state government is to compress earnings, with the relative earnings of state workers slightly higher at the bottom of the distribution and substantially smaller at the top of the distribution.

The pattern for the local differential is shown in Figure 10, and it is broadly similar. At the 10th percentile, the differential is routinely positive and is even above 5% at the very end of the time series. On the other hand, the differential at the median is typically negative and usually around –6% over the past decade. The differential at the 90th percentile is routinely large and negative, averaging just over –12% over the past decade. Again, the pattern of employment compensation in government is one of compression. The lowest paid are not as lowly paid, while the highest paid are not as highly paid as in the private sector.

Indeed, additional estimates with larger ranges of quantiles make clear that the differential is in favor of public sector workers at the bottom and moves increasingly in favor of private sector workers as one moves up the earnings distribution. Viewed this way, the average differential presented earlier (and which is the focus of much of the debate) misses a critical point. The biggest problem regarding the comparability of state and local earnings may be the structure and pattern of those earnings rather than how close the adjusted average differential is to zero. An average differential of zero, in which half the public sector is overpaid and half is underpaid, can hardly be called comparable to the private sector. This point fits interestingly with attempts to privatize public services and the implications of doing so on the average differential. We note that if states and localities privatize by contracting out jobs at the bottom of the earnings distribution, they will be eliminating those jobs with comparable or more than comparable earnings. This necessarily causes the measured average differential to indicate greater relative underpayment for the public sector workers that remain. Obviously, the reverse holds as well. If the public sector were to contract out jobs in the upper portion of the distribution, the workers that remain in the public sector would cause the measured average differential to indicate less relative underpayment or even overpayment. This discussion is not about the wisdom of contracting out, only about how the consequences of doing so could alter the average measure of comparability in an environment in which the distribution of earnings is so very different between the public and private sectors.

Conclusions

We implemented a very standard comparability exercise using 30 years of the CPS. We presented a variety of estimates to reflect possible choices that researchers have made and which reflect the heart of the discipline. Our results—that the earnings of state and local workers are less comparable—are not new. They were already evident in the work of others by the year 2000 and have remained evident in subsequent work. While a comparison of unadjusted average earnings will show wages are higher in state and local government, this difference results because the workers in those sectors have more education. If one holds education and other earnings determinants the same, the typical state and local worker earns less.

We used aggregate data on fringe benefits to adjust the earnings differentials we estimated. Workers in the state and local sector get a slightly larger share of their compensation in fringe benefits, but it is not dramatically larger. We showed that when we account for this difference, most of the estimates remain negative or essentially zero, suggesting, if anything, slightly lower average total compensation in the state and local sector after accounting for worker and job characteristics. Critically, we suggested that an important source of the larger share spent on fringe benefits by the public sector is the difference in the basic provision of key benefits such as health insurance and retirement. Many private sector firms, especially smaller ones, simply do not offer either benefit. Finally, our results showed the marked difference in the distribution of earnings between the public and private sectors, even after controlling for earnings determinants.

The implications of our exercise are severalfold. First, the compensation of state and local workers over the course of the past decade has not been excessive. Second, this remains true when including fringe benefits. Third, the pattern of results over the past 20 years has generally been one of declining relative compensation of state and local workers compared to those in the private sector.

These implications might have suggested a policy prescription that now is not the time to advocate large-scale rollbacks in the compensation of state and local workers. Nonetheless, public officials, state legislatures, and governors have passed legislation based on the view that taxpayer dollars are typically wasted by overcompensating state and local workers. We suggest that some of this apparent disconnect can be explained by our work, and that of others, on the distributional aspect of comparability.

In short, it is the distributional aspect of earnings that has grown increasingly less comparable. While the average compensation differential is typically small and negative, it remains remarkably easy to find segments of the public sector that are overcompensated relative to their private sector comparables and to find segments that are significantly undercompensated relative to their private sector counterparts. More finely grained policy approaches than simply changing the average level of public sector compensation are required to move public and private wage distributions toward comparability.

Acknowledgments

The authors thank the National Institute on Retirement Security for financial support for the closely related work, *Out of Balance: Comparing Public and Private Compensation over 20 Years*. The authors also thank Ilana Boivie and Dan Mitchell for useful comments on earlier drafts and thank Dale Belman and Robert Elliott for thoughtful discussions and productive joint work on related subjects.

Endnotes

[1] Each household spends four months being surveyed, is out of the survey for the next eight months, and then re-enters for four more months before finally exiting the survey sample.

[2] Modifications of this definition, 40 hours or 30 hours, do not alter the general pattern of results.

[3] As an illustration, if state and local workers are disproportionately located in higher-earnings states, failure to include the indicators would bias the estimates. Indeed, Borjas (1986) showed that changes of earnings of state employees do reflect changes in the wealth of their state, as well as a variety of other economic and political determinants. The indicator in the CPS is the state in which the worker resides, not the state in which the worker is employed. The latter is not available in the CPS.

[4] The regression coefficient β is converted to the percentage effect by $e^\beta - 1$.

[5] This can be driven home in simple fashion by temporarily ignoring the full comparability exercise and simply presenting the raw averages among the college educated. Bender and Heywood (2010) showed that in 2008, among the nation's college educated, those in state government earned 13% less than those in the private sector, while those in the local government earned 11% less than those in the private sector.

[6] See Bender and Elliott (2002) for an attempt to introduce very detailed job attributes and working conditions into public sector earnings estimates.

[7] We have also estimated each year's state and local differentials using the Oaxaca (1973) decomposition technique. In this technique, we estimated the private sector earnings regime (assuming that it represented market returns) and projected the earnings of each state and local worker, assuming their characteristics were rewarded in the same fashion. The resulting percentage difference remains always negative and, over the years 2000 to 2008, is actually a couple of percentage points below those shown in Figure 2. These estimates are available from the authors.

[8] In one critical respect, this represents a conservative methodology because it is generally recognized that workers with greater earnings (thus facing higher marginal tax rates) prefer to receive a larger share of their earnings in fringe benefits (see as one example Royalty 2000). Recognizing this and that public sector workers earn more because of their greater education, one might start with a prior assumption that under comparability, benefits as a share of total compensation should be larger in the public sector.

[9] Of course, costs may be lower for reasons other than efficiency. For example, there is substantial evidence that a number of state and local government defined benefit pensions are underfunded. Yet Munnell, Aubry, and Quinby (2010) claim that the sum of underfunding amounts to 2% of payroll over the next 30 years. This is hardly enough to influence the general flavor of the results but should be kept in mind.

[10] The ratio of state to local earnings can be written as (E^L/E^P), while the shares of earnings to total compensation are $\beta^L = (E^L/T^L)$ and $\beta^P = (E^P/T^P)$. Thus, $(E^l/E^P)(\beta^P/\beta^L) = T^L/T^P$, which is the ratio of total compensation for local workers to that for private workers.

[11] It is also worth noting that while many private sector workers receive a pension and Social Security, a variety of states use their pensions to replace Social Security. States in which workers neither contribute to nor draw Social Security make pension comparisons difficult.

[12] For example, Piketty and Saez (2003) used income tax returns to show that the top of the U.S. earnings distribution experienced enormous relative gains over the past 25 years of the previous century, while Blank (2002) noted a rise in the working poor well before the current Great Recession.

References

Asher, Martin, and Joel Popkin. 1984. "The Effect of Gender and Race Differentials on Public–Private Wage Comparisons: A Study of Postal Workers." *Industrial and Labor Relations Review*, Vol. 38, pp. 16–25.

Ballard, Charles L., and Nicole S. Funari. 2009. *The Retrenchment of the State Employee Workforce in Michigan.* Working paper, Department of Economics, Michigan State University.

Belman, Dale, Thomas Franklin, and John S. Heywood. 1994. "Comparing Public and Private Earnings Using State Wage Surveys." *Journal of Economic and Social Measurement*, Vol. 20, pp. 79–94.

Belman, Dale, and John S. Heywood. 1988. "Public Wage Differentials and the Public Administration 'Industry.'" *Industrial Relations*, Vol. 27, pp. 385–93.

Belman, Dale, and John S. Heywood. 1990. "The Effect of Establishment and Firm Size Public Wage Differentials." *Public Finance Quarterly*, Vol. 18, pp. 221–35.

Belman, Dale, and John S. Heywood. 1993. "Job Attributes and Federal Wage Differentials." *Industrial Relations*, Vol. 32, pp. 148–57.

Belman, Dale, and John S. Heywood. 1995. "State and Local Government Wage Differentials: An Intrastate Analysis." *Journal of Labor Research*, Vol. 16, pp. 187–201.

Belman, Dale, and John S. Heywood. 1996. "The Structure of Compensation in the Public Sector." In Dale Belman, Morely Gunderson, and Douglas Hyatt, eds., *Public Sector Employment in a Time of Transition*. Madison WI: Industrial Relations Research Association.

Belman, Dale, and John S. Heywood. 2004a. "Public Wage Differentials and the Treatment of Occupational Differences." *Policy Analysis and Management*, Vol. 23, pp. 135–52.

Belman, Dale, and John S. Heywood. 2004b. "Public Sector Wage Comparability: The Role of Earnings Dispersion." *Public Finance Review*, Vol. 32, pp. 567–87.

Bender, Keith A. 1998. "The Central Government–Private Sector Wage Differential." *Journal of Economic Surveys*, Vol. 12, pp. 177–220.

Bender, Keith A. 2003. "Examining Equality between Public and Private Sector Wage Distributions." *Economic Inquiry*, Vol. 41, pp. 62–79.

Bender, Keith A., and Robert F. Elliott. 2002. "The Role of Job Attributes in Understanding the Public–Private Sector Wage Differential." *Industrial Relations*, Vol. 41, pp. 407–21.

Bender, Keith A., and John S. Heywood. 2010. *Out of Balance: Comparing Public and Private Compensation over 20 years*. Washington, DC: National Institute for Retirement Security.

Blackburn, McKinley L. 2007. "Estimating Wage Differentials without Logarithms." *Labour Economics*, Vol. 14, pp. 73–98.

Blank, Rebecca. 2002. "Evaluating Welfare Reform in the United States." *Journal of Economic Literature*, Vol. 40, pp. 1105–66.

Borjas, George J. 1986. "The Earnings of State Government Employees in the United States." *Journal of Urban Economics*, Vol. 19, pp. 156–73.

Borjas, George J. 2003. "The Wage Structures and Sorting of Workers into the Public Sectors." In John D. Donahue and Joseph S. Nye, eds., *For the People: Can We Fix Public Service?* Washington, DC: Brookings Institution, pp. 29–54.

Cauchon, Dennis. 2009 (Apr. 10). "Benefits Widen Public, Private Workers' Pay Gap." *USA Today*.

Duncan, Greg J., and Frank P. Stafford. 1980. "Do Union Members Receive Compensating Wage Differentials?" *American Economic Review*, Vol. 70, pp. 355–71.

Freeman, Richard B. 1987. "How Do Public Sector Wages and Employment Respond to Economic Conditions?" In David A. Wise, ed., *Public Sector Payrolls*. Chicago: National Bureau of Economic Research for University of Chicago Press.

Heywood, John S. 1989. "Wage Discrimination by Race and Gender in the Public and Private Sectors." *Economic Letters*, Vol. 29, pp. 99–102.

Hill, Marvin, and Emily DeLacenserie. 1991. "Interest Criteria in Fact-Finding and Arbitration." *Marquette Law Review*, Vol. 74, pp. 399–49.

Hirsch, Barry T., and Edward Schumacher. 2004. "Match Bias in Wage Gap Estimates Due to Earnings Imputation." *Journal of Labor Economics*, Vol. 22, pp. 689–722.

Hoffnar, Emily, and Michael Greene. 1996. "Gender Discrimination in the Public and Private Sectors: A Sample Selectivity Approach." *Journal of Socio-Economics*, Vol. 25, pp. 105–14.

Idson, Todd L. 1990. "Establishment Size, Job Satisfaction and the Structure of Work." *Applied Economics*, Vol. 22, pp. 1007–18.

Kearney, Richard C., and David G. Carnevale. 2001. *Labor Relations in the Public Sector* (3rd ed.). New York: Marcel Dekker.

Kertscher, T. 2009 (Oct. 12). "Firstwatch: F is for Furlough." *Milwaukee Wisconsin Journal Sentinel*.

Jones, Tim. 2011 (Mar. 3). "For Governors, Public Sector Unions Are the Enemy." *Bloomberg Businessweek*. <http://www.businessweek.com/magazine/content/11_11/b4219029449383.htm>. [March 22, 2011].

Lee, Sang-Hyop. 2004. "A Reexamination of Public Sector Wage Differentials in the United States: Evidence from the NLSY with Geocode." *Industrial Relations*, Vol. 43, pp. 448–72.

Lewis, Gregory B., and Sue A. Frank. 2002. "Who Wants to Work for the Government?" *Public Administration Review*, Vol. 62, pp. 395–404.

Lewis, Gregory B., and Chester S. Galloway. 2011. *A National Analysis of Public/Private Wage Differentials at the State and Local Levels by Race and Gender*. Georgia State University, Andrew Young School of Policy Studies Research Paper Series No. 11–10.

Linneman, Peter D., and Michael L. Wachter. 1990. "The Economics of Federal Compensation." *Industrial Relations*, Vol. 29, pp. 58–76.

Miller, Michael A. 1996. "The Public–Private Pay Debate: What Do the Data Show?" *Monthly Labor Review*, Vol. 119, no. 5, pp. 18–29.

Munnell, Alicia H., Jean-Pierre Aubry, and Laura Quinby. 2010. *The Funding of State and Local Pensions: 2009–2013*. Brief #10, Center for Retirement Research, Boston College.

National Conference of State Legislatures. 2009. *Actions and Proposals to Balance the FY 2010 Budget: State Employee Actions, Furloughs and Layoffs*. <http://www.ncsl.org/?tabid=17244>. [March 15, 2011].

Oaxaca, Ronald. 1973. "Male–Female Wage Differentials in Urban Labor Markets." *International Economic Review*, Vol. 14, pp. 693–709.

Piketty, Thomas, and Emmanuel Saez. 2003. "Income Inequality in the United States, 1913–1998." *Quarterly Journal of Economics*, Vol. 118, pp. 1–39.

Poterba, James M., and Kim S. Rueben. 1994. *The Distribution of Public Sector Wage Premia: New Evidence Using Quantile Regression Methods*. Working Paper No. 4734, National Bureau of Economic Research, New York, NY.

Royalty, Anne B. 2000. "Tax Preferences for Fringe Benefits and Worker Eligibility for Health Insurance." *Journal of Public Economics*, Vol. 75, pp. 209–77.

Schmidt, Chrisoph M., and Klaus F. Zimmermann. 1991. "Work Characteristics, Firm Size and Wages." *Review of Economics and Statistics*, Vol. 73, pp. 705–10.

Smith, Sharon P. 1976. "Government Wage Differentials by Sex." *Journal of Human Resources*, Vol. 11, pp. 185–99.

Smith, Sharon P. 1987. "Wages in the Public and Private Sector: Comment." In David Wise, ed., *Public Sector Payrolls*. Chicago: University of Chicago Press.

Snell, Ronald K. 2011. *Pensions and Retirement Plan Enactments in 2011 State Legislatures as of June 30, 2011*. National Conference of State Legislatures, Washington, DC.

Sun Journal (Editorial Board). 2009 (Oct. 1). "Squealing About the Income Gap." *Sun Journal* (Lewiston, Maine).

CHAPTER 7

The Fiscal Crisis, Public Pensions, and Labor and Employment Relations

ILANA BOIVIE

Communications Workers of America

AND

CHRISTIAN E. WELLER

University of Massachusetts–Boston

Introduction

The states' fiscal crisis, which started in 2008, has focused attention on their tax and spending priorities. Pensions for firefighters, police officers, and teachers, among others, have particularly come under scrutiny because states often have had to raise the employer contribution to their pension plans. The additional employer contributions have had to compensate for pension fund losses from the financial market drop in 2007 and 2008.

Some observers have argued that states should view the crisis as an opportunity to alter their retirement benefits. Some have specifically proposed changing the nature of public sector employee retirement benefits by switching from existing defined benefit (DB) pension plans to defined contribution (DC) retirement savings plans or to cash balance plans—a mixture of DB and DC plans.

There have been several assertions made in favor of such a change in public employee retirement benefits, one of which is of particular relevance here. First, proponents have asserted that alternative retirement benefits will provide incentives for more effective public employees to join the public labor force, thus raising overall public sector productivity. Defined contribution and cash balance plans supposedly increase employee mobility, which may make it easier for states to attract highly skilled employees and to let ineffective employees go.

In the private sector, moving from DB pensions to alternative benefits has gone along with increased labor force mobility. The argument that increased mobility leads to a more effective workforce, though, ignores that public and private employers typically need to offer some form of deferred compensation to attract and retain highly skilled employees. Many private firms, for instance, use stock options and stock grants instead of DB pensions to attract and retain skilled employees.

Public employers, who cannot issue stock options, may therefore end up with higher employee turnover. When highly skilled employees do not stay long, they are less likely to make a substantial contribution to public sector productivity. The result of a switch from DB pensions to alternative retirement benefits may in fact reduce public employee productivity since public employers may hire more inexperienced employees and face additional costs to greater recruitment and training efforts, following increased employee turnover.

When faced with financial challenges from 2001 to 2010, states in fact stayed with their DB pensions, even though most states changed their retirement plans during this time. This chapter suggests that states value many features of DB pensions, including their efficiency, which in part stems from their effectiveness as a recruitment and retention tool.

Our chapter proceeds as follows. We will first present some background on retirement systems and then present a summary of the evidence on DB pensions as recruitment and retention tools, especially in the public sector, in the second section. To put any changes into context, the third section offers a brief discussion of the financial and political pressures that states and localities faced with respect to their DB pensions during and after 2007–2009. The fourth section briefly summarizes what states have done to respond to the crisis, highlighting that most states chose to stay with their DB pensions in the face of financial and political pressures and suggesting that states value the efficiencies of their DB pensions. In the fifth section, we briefly discuss arguments in favor of alternative retirement benefits that differ from a labor management point of view to provide a more complete picture of the debate over public employee retirement benefits. The sixth presents our conclusions.

Defined Benefit Pensions and Labor Management

Retirement benefits are a critical part of public employee compensation. John Schmitt (2010) reports that total public sector benefits amounted to 31.5% of total compensation in December 2009. Bender and Heywood (2010) show that benefits amounted to an average of 32.7% for the public sector between 2004 and 2008 and that 6.5% of compensation is retirement benefits.

Public employees are typically covered by DB pensions. Employees receive lifetime retirement benefits based on years of service, age, and final earnings. They often have to work for at least five or more years before they become vested—that is, before they earn a nonforfeitable and generally constitutionally protected right to their benefits (National Education Association 2010). Future benefits are financed by employee and employer contributions in addition to investment earnings on accumulated assets.

Employee contributions are made at a fixed rate, regardless of whether the pension plan is underfunded or overfunded. Employers bear the risk if plans have too few assets to pay all promised benefits and more contributions become necessary. They have substantial discretion, however, with regard to the timing and amount of funding.

Public employee benefits make up a smaller share of total compensation earlier in employees' careers than later (Cahill and Soto 2003; Clark and Schieber 2000; Johnson and Uccello 2001; Weller 2005). Figure 1 is an illustrative example of the annual benefit accrual under a typical teacher DB pension. The x axis shows the years of service, and the y axis shows the annual amount of retirement benefits relative to the annual salary that a teacher earns under a DB pension, cash balance plan, or DC plan.[1] Employees earn an increasing amount of retirement benefits relative to earnings until they reach early retirement (e.g., after 35 years of service). Teachers still earn additional benefits after the early retirement incentive expires, but the annual accrual is less than during the years leading up to the early retirement age. A teacher, for instance, may work for 35 years in a school until she reaches age 58, assuming she started when she was 23 years of age, and she may earn 2% of her final salary annually as a benefit. If she retired at age 58 after 35 years of service with a final salary of

FIGURE 1

Annual Wealth Changes for Teacher Entering in 2011 Relative to Earnings, Under DB Plan, Cash Balance Plan, and DC Plan, Constant Normal Cost

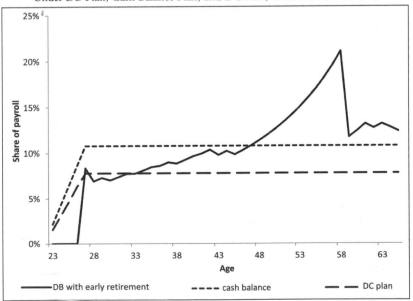

$90,000, she would receive an annual DB pension until her death of $63,000 (equal to 35 times 2.0% times $90,000).

It should be noted that as many as 30% of all state and local employees are not covered under Social Security, with the degree of coverage varying widely by state and by occupation (U.S. GAO 2007). For employees not covered by Social Security, their DB pension benefit may be all the more important, as it is likely their only source of guaranteed income in retirement. As a result, DB pension benefits tend to be more generous for public employees who do not have Social Security coverage than for those who do (Brainard 2010).

Proposed Changes in Retirement Benefit Design for Public Employees

Although DB pensions remain prominent in the public sector, there are several proposals to replace DB pensions with DC or cash balance plans (Barro and Buck 2010; Hansen 2010; Costrell and Podgursky 2009). Table 1 summarizes the characteristics of each retirement benefit type. Defined contribution plans are retirement savings plans, which are more common in the private sector than in the public sector as the primary retirement benefit. Under a typical private sector DC plan, employees and employers contribute a fixed percentage of earnings each year. The money is allocated to an individual account, with employees deciding on the investments and shouldering the risks associated with these decisions.

There is greater risk exposure under DC plans than under DB plans, which is intentional. The economic logic originally went that more risk poses a cost to individuals, who generally do not like risk. Individuals should consequently save more to compensate for the greater risk (see Browning and Lusardi [1996] for a summary of the related literature). More recent research in behavioral economics has shown that this logic has its limits since it makes unrealistic behavioral assumptions about individual decisions (see DellaVigna [2009] for a review of the relevant literature). The economic logic assumes that individuals fully understand complex risks, completely understand how to protect themselves from these risks, and will follow this knowledge. Others argue that humans generally do not have a full appreciation of all of the complexities and even when they do, they do not necessarily act on that knowledge. Greater risk exposure has resulted in more savings but not enough to compensate for the full increase in individual risk exposure (Weller 2010).

Cash balance plans, an additional proposal, are still DB pensions but resemble DC plans in key aspects. Each employee receives a notional (hypothetical) account, even though all funds are invested as one large pension pool, as is the case with a DB pension. The notional account makes the cash balance plan look like a DC plan to the employee since

TABLE 1

Characteristics of Typical Pension Plans, by Plan Type

Characteristic	Defined benefit plan		Defined contribution plan
Plan type	Traditional	Cash balance	403(b) plans
Participation	Automatic	Automatic	Voluntary
Contribution	Employer and employee	Employer and employee	Employee with occasional employer matches
Investments	Determined by employer	Determined by employer	Typically determined by employee
Withdrawals	Annuity	Annuity or lump sum	Lump sum
Rollovers before age 65	Not permitted	Permitted if lump sum option exists	Permitted
Benefit guarantee	Often constitutionally guaranteed	Often constitutionally guaranteed	None
Early retirement benefits	Common	Uncommon	Unavailable
Vesting	Up to a decade or more	Typically shorter than in traditional pension plans	Typically immediate for employee contributions and often immediate for employer contributions

Notes: Cash balance plans typically do not exist in the public sector. The description thus relies on typical characteristics of private sector cash balance plans. Also, defined contribution plans are generally supplemental retirement savings plans in the public sector and thus tend to be voluntary.

the employee sees an account balance that changes from year to year, but the cash balance plan looks like a DB pension to the employer, who is responsible for investing the money and making sure that the amount promised to the employee will be available upon retirement. An employee's notional pension account is credited with an amount equal to a fixed share of an employee's earnings each year, and the account balance increases annually at a predetermined interest rate or credit. The contribution and the interest rate are pre-determined, suggesting that the employer is responsible for investing the pension plan assets to generate at least this rate of return; otherwise, the employer will have to make additional contributions, as in a traditional DB pension. The plan is financed by employer and employee contributions and investment earnings. Employers again bear the risk of too low assets. Notional account balances can be rolled over into other retirement plans when an employee switches jobs (Cahill and Soto 2003; Clark and Schieber 2000; Johnson and Uccello 2001; Weller 2005).

The annual benefit earned with a cash balance or DC plan typically equals a fixed earnings share, which is usually higher during earlier years of employment and lower during later years of employment than under a DB plan (Figure 1). Defined contribution and cash balance plans hence may change the recruitment and retention incentives compared to the effects of the DB pension plan.

Defined Benefit Pensions, Labor Management, and Labor Productivity

Defined benefit pensions serve as an effective human resource management tool, largely because of their employee recruitment and retention effects. Employers in all sectors have used DB pension plans to reduce attrition of skilled employees.

Employers have been rewarded by easier employee recruitment and retention (Friedberg and Owyang 2005; Gustman, Mitchell, and Steinmeier 1994; Ippolito 1997; Nalebluff and Zeckhauser 1984). Ippolito (1997), for instance, found that employees seem to value pensions so highly that they would willingly forgo higher wages for guaranteed retirement income, possibly reducing the costs of recruiting skilled employees. Watson Wyatt (2005) found that employees of firms with DB pensions had twice the probability of citing the retirement plan as an important factor in choosing their employer compared to employees at firms with only DC plans and that employees of firms with DB pensions placed a much greater importance on both attraction and retention at their current employer than employees at firms with DC plans. MetLife (2008) similarly found that 72% of employees cited retirement benefits as an important factor in their loyalty to their employer. And a survey of employers from Diversified Investment Advisors (2004) found that 84% of DB pension sponsors—typically employers—believed that their DB pension has some impact on employee retention, with 31% stating that the impact is major. The survey further found that 58% of plan sponsors with more than 25,000 employees believe that their DB pension has a major impact on employee retention. The value that employees put on DB pensions allows employers to recruit and retain skilled employees.

The retention effect of DB pensions shows up in economic research as lower employee turnover. Allen, Clark, and McDermed (1993) offered evidence that employee tenure is greater at firms that offer DB pensions than at firms that do not. Even and MacPherson (1996) similarly concluded that firms without DB pensions experience substantially higher turnover rates, ranging from an increase of about 20% in employee turnover to more than 200%. The effect of DB pensions on employee turnover tends to be greater at smaller firms than at larger ones. Munnell, Haverstick, and Sanzenbacher (2006) quantified the reduced attrition associated with

DB pensions, suggesting that lower DB pension coverage and higher DC plan coverage beginning in the 1990s correlated with higher turnover rates. Defined benefit pension coverage increases tenure with a single employer by four years compared to having no retirement system in place, while DB coverage increases tenure with an employer by 1.3 years compared to DC plan coverage, and the combination of a DB pension and DC plan increases tenure by 3.1 years, relative to only DC plan coverage.

Employers with DB pensions may also be able to better attract desirable skilled employees due to a self-selection effect. Employees who are more likely to stick with a job also tend to be more apt to accept employment that offers a DB pension in the first place (Nyce 2007). Munnell, Haverstick, and Soto (2007) found that, because DB pensions tend to favor long-term service, public employees' relatively longer tenure than that of their private sector counterparts led to an employee preference for DB pensions over DC plans. Similarly, Dulebohn, Murray, and Sun (2000) found that longer-term employees tend to prefer DB pensions to DC and cash balance plans. This could be because employees who are looking for a career instead of a short-term job seek out employers who offer DB pensions. Ippolito (1997), for example, focused on the attraction effect of DB pensions and considered how employers use retirement plans to attract employees interested in making a long-term commitment to their employers. Employees who delay gratification and are less focused on immediate rewards are more attractive employees for these employers. Defined benefit pensions, which offer larger compensation to employees with greater tenure, are more attractive to these employees than to those who are more focused on current rewards. Employers with DB pensions may thus use retirement benefits to select employees who best fit their needs.[2] In the same vein, Nyce (2007) found that DB pensions had a much larger retention effect than DC plans and that DB pension plans raised employees' commitment to their employer, while no such effect existed for DC plans. These results were strongest among younger employees, suggesting that DB pensions can play a crucial role in retaining employees who are willing to make a long-term contribution to their employer's success.

Better recruitment of targeted employees, increased retention of skilled employees, and greater commitment to the employer translate into higher productivity with DB pensions. Dorsey (1995), for example, found that some labor productivity gains can be attributed to DB pension coverage. More recently, Hall (2006) found that firms moving from a DB to a DC plan between 1995 and 2000 experienced loss of productivity relative to firms that retained their DB pensions. This loss of productivity may be due to greater turnover after the switch to a DC plan. More experienced and more skilled employees leave more quickly and are replaced with less experienced, less skilled employees, thus reducing average labor productivity growth below its previous trend.

Additionally, employees' decisions on when to retire offer additional productivity benefits to employers with DB pensions. Defined benefit pensions can encourage "efficient retirement," such that employees withdraw from the labor force when their productivity decreases. Lazear (1983), for instance, argued that DB pensions can function similarly to severance pay in encouraging efficient retirement as employees age and their productivity starts to level off or even decrease. Nalebluff and Zeckhauser (1984) studied the effect that DB pensions have on individuals' retirement decisions and found that the features of most U.S. defined benefit pensions can be designed to facilitate appropriate and optimal retirement decisions among employees. Luchak, Pohler, and Gellatly (2008) found that employees with a DB pension were more likely to retire later when they experience higher levels of affective commitment to their employer. Employees with high affective commitment plan to retire, on average, about two years later than employees with low levels of affective commitment. Defined benefits hence often target an average age when employee productivity starts to soften, to set as an early retirement age.

The ability of DB pensions to encourage efficient retirement is especially crucial during financial and economic crises (Weller 2006; Weller and Wenger 2009). Employers can reasonably predict whether employees will leave during a crisis based on their DB pension. Employers with DC plans, in comparison, encounter a phenomenon known as job lock, whereby employees become more likely to stay on the job as a financial crisis and economic recession unfolds. Financial markets generally decline in tandem with deteriorating economic conditions. Employees who might have been inclined to consider retirement before a crisis may decide to work longer to make up for losses in their DC plans. Financial market losses also systematically correlate with high unemployment rates; thus, finding another job becomes more difficult at the same time labor demand decreases. Employees who want to work longer in this circumstance will have to try to stay with their existing employer (Weller and Wenger 2009). This problem is further exacerbated by the fact that employers tend to lower contributions to their employees' DC plans during an economic downturn (Munnell and Sunden 2004). In a 2008 survey of recent retirees, 76% indeed reported that their ability to afford retirement was an extremely or very important factor in their decision to retire, and 81% of those with a DB pension reported that the DB benefit itself was either extremely or very important in determining retirement affordability (Helman, Copeland, VanDerhei, and Salisbury 2008). This also implies an opposite logic during an economic expansion, when skilled employees become more likely to retire exactly when employers need them. Defined contribution plans can thus exacerbate labor market swings, while DB pensions tend to generate more stable employment relations over the course of the business cycle. Employers may consequently incur larger employment-related costs to manage their workforce with DC plans than with DB pensions.

The Role of DB Pensions in the Public Sector

Many of the effects of DB pensions show up especially in the public sector, where DB pensions are the primary and occasionally the only retirement system available to public employees. Munnell, Haverstick, and Soto (2007) found that public employees largely prefer DB pensions to other forms of retirement income. Similarly, public employees consistently express strong preferences in favor of DB pensions, according to national public opinion polls (Matthew Greenwald & Associates 2004). Several states offer employees a choice between DB pensions and DC plans, and Olleman and Boivie (2011) found that when public employees are given such a choice, they overwhelmingly choose the DB pension. For example, in 2010, a mere 4% of employees in the Ohio Public Employee Retirement System (PERS) elected the DC plan over the DB pension when offered (Olleman and Boivie 2011), a result that has been consistent since the option was put in place in 2004. Additionally, between 2002 and 2011, 68% of Washington PERS members chose an all-DB pension over the default of a combined DB pension and DC plan (Olleman and Boivie 2011). Finally, Consolidated Public Retirement Board & Buck Consultants, LLC (2008) studied the unique case of West Virginia, where the Teachers Retirement System (TRS), a DB pension, was frozen—new hires were no longer admitted into the DB pension—in 1991. All newly hired teachers after 1991 were put into the Teachers Defined Contribution Retirement System (TDC). The TDC was closed in 2005 by the state, and all newly hired teachers were switched back into TRS. The teachers who had been enrolled in the TDC between 1991 and 2005 were given the option of choosing which plan they would prefer. On July 1, 2008, the state legislature certified a teachers' vote in which 78% of teachers voted in favor of having the option to switch back into the DB pension. The Charleston Gazette reported that an overwhelming number of younger teachers, more than 75%, decided to make the switch back to the TRS (Kabler 2008).

Defined benefit pensions have proved to be substantial recruitment and retention tools for public employers. Gabriel, Roeder, Smith and Company (GRS) (2005) found that DB pensions boosted state and local governments' ability to recruit highly qualified and skilled employees and to retain them throughout their career.

Public employment is indeed more stable than employment in the private sector. Greenfield (2007) found that layoffs and resignations in the private sector were three to four times higher than in the public sector. Public employees tend to be more attached than private sector employees to their jobs. In fact, Munnell, Haverstick, and Soto (2007) found that the tenure of public employees increased between 1973 and 2004, while that of private sector employees decreased. The median job tenure was 7.7 years for public employees by 2004 compared to 5.0 years for private employees. Additionally, public sector employees tend to be older than private sector employees.

The longer tenure tends to go along with other employee features that likely raise public employee productivity. Public employees, for instance, are more likely than private sector employees to value their work, suggesting that DB pensions may serve as a device for employers to select employees who are a good fit for them. Houston (2000) showed that public employees are more likely than private employees to place a higher value on the intrinsic reward of important work that provides a feeling of accomplishment. Private sector employees, in comparison, place a higher value on pay and on working fewer hours. Wright (2001) similarly found that public sector employees valued their work more than private sector employees because of the inherent nature of public sector organizations that address complex social functions—supplying goods and services that cannot necessarily be bought and sold in a private market. Those who enter public service may place a higher value on carrying out acts for the good of their community and the resulting internal satisfaction that these acts provide than their private sector counterparts. Defined benefit pensions again may serve as a tool for employers to select these employees.

Public employees tend to invest more in their skills than private sector employees, possibly because of the long-term economic commitment function of DB pensions. Defined benefit pensions may provide incentives for highly skilled employees such as researchers, computer programmers, and lawyers to stick with public service instead of seeking better-paid positions in the private sector. Moreover, because many occupations in the public sector have few private sector counterparts (e.g., public safety, criminal justice), DB pensions provide incentives for employees to seek nontransferable skills and apply them over long periods to public service careers. In the teaching profession, for example, public school teachers who work under strict certification requirements (Cannata 2008) also tend to turn over far less frequently than their private sector counterparts (Cannata 2008; Guarino, Santibañez, and Daley 2006). Defined benefit pensions can thus raise public sector efficiency.

A move to DC plans from DB pensions could therefore make it more difficult for public sector human resource managers to recruit, retain, and manage skilled employees. The Center for State and Local Government Excellence (2011b) surveyed government hiring managers in 2011 and found strong indications that even in the weak labor market that prevailed at that time, state and local government employers struggled to fill vacancies for highly skilled occupations such as engineering, environmental sciences, information technology, and health care professionals. These difficulties likely stem from a persistent pay gap between public and private employment (Bender and Heywood 2010; Schmitt 2010).[3] Compensation is necessarily different since governments do not have the same tools at their disposal as private employers, such as performance bonuses, stock options, or other profit-sharing plans (MuniNetGuide 2008). Defined benefit pensions offer public employers a way to remain competitive in the market for skilled employees. State and local governments without DB pensions may find it even more difficult to attract skilled employees. In a cost–benefit analysis of a switch from a DB pension to a DC plan for the state of New Mexico, the actuarial consulting firm GRS (2005) concluded that such a change would either result in a decrease in retirement benefits, an increase in total costs, or some combination of these. In turn, the switch could severely hinder state and local governments' ability to recruit and retain a qualified workforce. The result could be higher turnover, labor shortages, greater training costs due to higher turnover, and lower productivity caused by a larger share of inexperienced employees than would be the case under a DB pension (GRS 2005).

The Economics and Politics of Public Pensions After the Great Recession

The literature suggests that DB pensions efficiently meet the labor and employment needs of public sector employers. States and localities have had to address a variety of financial challenges in the wake of the financial and economic crisis of 2007–2009, however, including increased demands from public DB pensions. This debate was not only influenced by states' and localities' fiscal constraints but also by the politics surrounding public employees, their pay, and their benefits. The combination of economic and political challenges thus influenced the design of retirement benefits for public employees, possibly reducing the benefits' efficiency as a public sector labor management tool.

States' Budgetary Challenges

States faced large general budgetary constraints in the wake of the 2007–2009 crisis. The economy remained relatively weak after 2009, and states continued to struggle. The National Conference of State Legislatures (NCSL 2010a) concluded that states had a cumulative budget gap of $145.9 billion in their 2010 budgets. States implemented various changes to balance their budgets throughout this period, including furloughs and layoffs for state employees. The Center on Budget and Policy Priorities, for example, estimated that states cut $425 billion from their budgets between December 2007 and January 2011, followed by even more severe cuts for 2012 (Johnson, Oliff, and Williams 2011).

The budgetary constraints were met with increasing demands from public DB pension plans. The stock market decline of 2008 and 2009 hit investors of all stripes, and public pension plans were not immune. The U.S. Government Accountability Office (2008) concluded that most experts believe a funding level of 80% or more—the ratio of a DB pension plan's assets relative to its liabilities, or promised benefits—is adequate for most public DB pension plans. Brainard (2010) found that the aggregate funding ratio of the nation's largest public pension plans fell from 85% in 2008 to 80% in 2009. The funding ratio of public pension plans likely decreased further after 2009 because financial market losses can linger on the books of DB pension plans using an actuarial practice called asset smoothing. Researchers at Boston College's Center for Retirement Research estimated that public pension plans held 77% of their future promised benefits in assets in 2010 and that this ratio could drop to 72% by 2013 (Munnell, Aubry, and Quinby 2010a). Others put public employee underfunding at even higher levels, based on more adverse economic assumptions (Novy-Marx and Rauh 2011).

The additional contributions necessary to cover the estimated underfunding tend to be nontrivial but manageable. Munnell, Aubry, and Quinby (2010a) estimated that an additional 2.2% of payroll over 30 years will cover the estimated underfunding. Munnell, Aubry, and Quinby (2010b) showed that while there is substantial variation in funding and contribution levels among states, the required contributions to address the underfunding remain manageable for most states.

States began addressing the pension underfunding in the middle of several years of severe budget shortfalls. Between 2000 and 2010, for example, 39 states either increased contributions or lowered benefits under the DB pensions (Pew Center on the States, n.d.), as we discuss in greater detail.

The Political Environment for Public Pension Changes

The political environment presents additional challenges to public DB pensions since states face pressures from interest groups to change their retirement benefits from DB pensions to DC plans or cash balance plans at the same time as they are trying to manage the existing underfunding. Madland (2007) concluded that ideological orientation rather than party affiliation leads individuals to support DC plans over DB pensions, while

Munnell and colleagues (2008) demonstrated that states with Republican governorships and Republican-dominated legislatures were more likely to introduce DC plans in addition to or instead of DB pensions.

National and state interest groups have become key players challenging the continuation of public DB pensions in recent decades, with the primary goal of terminating state and local DB pensions. Although many of these groups believe that there will be cost savings associated with such a switch, public employees will likely receive some form of alternative compensation as a replacement for the DB pension. For example, in 2005, the state of Alaska froze its DB pension plan, but new hires are still offered DC accounts in lieu of the old DB pension (Snell 2010b).

Almeida, Kenneally, and Madland (2009) found that these groups often did not consider the economic efficiency of DB pensions and instead based their challenges on ideological positions of general opposition to public social insurance arrangements. Several anti-tax movements have recently gained popularity nationwide, according to *The New York Times*, which could further increase opposition to public DB pensions (Barstow 2010).

The tea party movement—a comparatively large but disparate anti-tax movement—has typically called for drastic cuts in public spending. It lists among its "non-negotiable core beliefs" that "government must be downsized," "reduce[d] personal income taxes [are] a must," and "intrusive government [must be] stopped" (Tea Party, n.d.).[4] A recent *Washington Post* survey found that 24% of local tea party group members said they were motivated by concern over government spending and the deficit— together the single largest motivating factor—followed by another 20% who were motivated by the size of government and 4% by taxes. Almost half of tea party members listed public operations as their primary concern (Thompson 2010).

Regional tea party groups consequently have targeted local issues, including public pensions. A spokesman for one tea party affiliate in Pennsylvania, the York 912 Patriots, told the *Wall Street Journal* in 2010, "A lot of our members are upset that we have to pay for raises and fund pensions for teachers" (Levitz 2010). And the Troy (Michigan) Area Tea Party proposed to cut municipal employee compensation—pay and benefits—to address the city's budget challenges (Levitz 2010).

Other anti-tax groups have championed the cause of lower benefits in the public sector. The Free Enterprise Nation, a self-proclaimed "voice of the private sector," took out full-page advertisements in 2009 in national media outlets such as the *Wall Street Journal* specifically criticizing public pension benefits as overly generous compared to private sector retirement benefits (Free Enterprise Nation 2010). California Pension Reform, a state-level group specifically targeting DB pensions in California, published an online database of individual retired California public employees and their annual pension benefits in 2009, and they continue to update the data (California Pension Reform, n.d.).

The agenda pursued by these groups is perhaps best summed up by Americans for Tax Reform's (ATR) Grover Norquist (Dreyfuss 2001). Norquist said of public DB pension plans in 2001 that "just 115 people control $1 trillion in these funds. We want to take that power and destroy it" (Dreyfuss 2001:16). Norquist and others attacking public DB pensions actively planned and supported state-by-state campaigns to dismantle public DB pensions from 2005 through 2011. For example, ATR was a supporter of former California Governor Schwarzenegger's 2005 push to move that state's public employees into a DC plan (Angelides 2005). In 2010, Norquist issued a press statement urging federal legislation that would "unburden" employees with DB pensions by replacing those benefits with DC plans (ATR 2010). ATR is also an official member of Floridians for Sustainable Pensions, a coalition whose stated goal is to replace public employee DB pensions with DC plans (Floridians for Sustainable Pensions, n.d.).

Alongside tea party growth, there is also some evidence that the growth of the Republican Party at the state and federal levels through successes in the 2010 elections raised political pressures at the state level to alter retirement benefits. The Republican Party gained 61 seats in the U.S. House of Representatives and six seats in the U.S. Senate, while it netted seven new governorships and achieved more majorities in state legislatures than at any time since 1928 (NCSL 2010b). *The New York Times* reported that many analysts attributed the Republican Party's successes in the 2010 election to the influence of the tea party and other anti-tax groups, bringing both ideological motivation and party affiliation together (Zernike 2010).

The combination of the ideological motivation of anti-tax groups and the increased political power of the Republican Party raises the pressure on states to alter their retirement benefits from DB pensions to alternative benefits. *Stateline* reported, for example, that six newly elected Republican governors came out in favor of moving all public employees out of DB pension plans and into DC retirement accounts after their election (Fehr 2010).

In addition to these political challenges, public DB pensions for teachers in particular have come under attack from some education policy experts who proposed to replace DB pensions for teachers with alternative retirement benefits.

Robert M. Costrell, an education economist at the University of Arkansas, and Michael Podgursky, an education economist at the University of Missouri at Columbia, have published several papers since 2008 (Costrell and Podgursky 2008, 2009, 2010). They assert that DB pensions create adverse economic incentives for ineffective teachers to stay on the job too long and for effective teachers to leave earlier than they would under other retirement systems. It is important to note that the opposite logic also holds (i.e., that DB pensions create incentives for effective teachers to stay longer on the job than they otherwise would and for ineffective teachers to leave earlier—typically upon reaching early retirement age—than they otherwise would).[5]

The National Council on Teacher Quality (NCTQ 2010), an education reform advocacy group, similarly proposed their preferred ways to retain effective teachers. Their recommendations include replacing DB pensions with DC or cash balance plans for public school teachers. NCTQ based its recommendation on the assertion that young teachers do not appreciate DB pensions, but Almeida and Boivie (2009) reported that young employees value DB pensions as much as, if not more than, their older peers. That teachers in particular highly value DB pensions is borne out by actual experience in systems where teachers are given the option of choosing the type of plan they prefer and overwhelmingly chose DB pensions.

The momentum at the state level to change retirement benefits has been further enhanced by federal legislative efforts in the Republican-dominated U.S. House of Representatives. Representatives Devin Nunes (R-CA), Paul Ryan (R-WI), and Darrell Issa (R-CA) introduced the Public Employee Pension Transparency Act of 2010. The act "provides enhanced transparency for state and local pensions, [and] also establishes a clear federal prohibition on any future public pension bailouts by the federal government" (Committee on Oversight & Government Reform 2010), with the intention of bringing greater attention to proposals to replace DB pensions with alternative benefits. Analyses of the legislation found that the disclosure requirements of the bill would present a distorted picture of public pension funding; these distortions would confuse policy makers and would offer a more negative view of public DB pensions. Finally, this confusion could well lead to abandonment of DB pensions in the public sector (Lav 2011; Zorn 2011).

Government Responses to Fiscal and Political Challenges

The environment faced by public DB pensions has been both financially and politically challenging. Many states have taken steps to change the retirement benefits for their employees, even as they continue to make progress toward funding their pensions.

The Pew Center on the States (2011) estimated that the funded level of state DB pension plans fell from 84% in 2008 to 78% in 2009 for a cumulative unfunded pension liability of $660 billion in 2009. Munnell and colleagues (2011) projected more current funding levels for the 126 state and local plans and estimated that the aggregate funded level fell to 77% in 2010.[6]

By the end of 2010, however, state and local DB pensions also saw their cumulative assets increase to $2.93 trillion, a gain of 25% since June 2009, largely due to investment gains; the median investment return for large public pension plans in 2010 was 13.1% (National Association of State Retirement Administrators 2011b). In addition, public plan sponsors in aggregate paid 88% of the annual required contribution (ARC) in 2009, a level consistent with the amount paid over the previous six years (Brainard 2010). The general revenue that states collect from income, sales, and property taxes, meanwhile, declined by $54 billion and $70 billion in 2009 and 2010, respectively (National Association of State Budget Officers 2010). While facing both a short-term cash flow deficit in revenues and higher recommended contributions to fund long-term pension obligations, states in aggregate still contributed $73 billion to pension trusts in 2009, an increase of $1 billion from 2008 (Pew Center on the States 2011).

While the percentage of plans receiving 90% or more of their ARC has fallen since 2000, six in ten plans received 90% or more of their ARC in 2009 (Brainard 2010). Since 2001, in fact, a substantial portion of ARCs were consistently paid despite two economic downturns; on average, 91% of ARCs were paid between 2001 and 2010 (Brainard 2010).

In terms of changing retirement benefits, Brainard (2009) argued that the uniqueness in plan design, benefit levels including Social Security coverage, funding levels, and pension plan governance may dictate different responses across states and localities. Many states, though, have implemented some form of lower benefits and higher contributions for their DB pension plans since 2001 (Pew Center on the States, n.d.; Snell 2010a, 2010b). According to the National Conference on State Legislatures, the actions taken by states to ensure their pensions' long-term sustainability have been quite substantive and varied—and many reforms began well before the stock market drop in 2008 (Snell 2010b). Reforms have included increased employee contribution rates, reduced benefits for new employees, and greater restrictions on early retirement and on retirees returning to service.

In all, 25 states enacted significant pension reforms in 2011, and 19 enacted reforms in 2010 (Snell 2011). For instance, 25 states increased employee contribution rates in 2010 and 2011 (Snell 2011). Colorado, Iowa, Minnesota, Mississippi, Vermont, and Wyoming increased contribution rates for both active and new employees, while Louisiana, Missouri, Utah, and Virginia imposed contribution increases on new hires only (Snell 2010a). Missouri, Utah, Virginia, and Wyoming had previously been noncontributory, but they required employee contributions for the first time after the crisis. And 23 states increased the retirement age and service requirements for full benefits, reduced early retirement benefits, and imposed greater restrictions on return to covered service in 2010 and 2011 (Snell 2011). A total of 17 states reduced post-retirement benefit increases, 13 imposed a longer period for calculation of final average salary, and 12 increased vesting requirements, delaying the period until public employees may receive any benefits (Snell 2011).

Thus continues a trend as 29 states enacted major retirement benefit changes since 2005 (Snell 2010a), primarily to DB pensions. Between 2005 and 2009, for example, 12 increased employee contributions to their pension funds, 11 changed the benefit multiplier or final average pay calculation, 10 increased the age and service requirements, 7 implemented anti-spiking provisions, 9 changed post-retirement increases, and 6 increased the vesting time period (Snell 2010b).

Benefits promised under public DB plans are considered highly protected because under the laws of most states, the sponsor cannot close down the plan for current participants. In many states, employees hired under a particular benefit have the right to continue earning that benefit for the length of their employment (Munnell, Aubry, and Quinby 2010b). The legal and regulatory protections of public pension benefits, however, vary widely by state (Monahan 2010).

For that reason, it has conventionally been seen as much easier to reduce the benefits of newly hired workers than to do so for current employees or active retirees; however, pension reforms of 2010 and 2011 proved otherwise. For example, the increases in employee contribution rates previously noted, while not a direct benefit cut, do represent a decrease in total compensation to fund the pension benefit. Additionally, legislation was adopted in Colorado, South Carolina, and Minnesota to reduce cost-of-living adjustments for current retirees (Snell 2011). Although states loosened constitutional protections moving forward in this way, there is no evidence that they have ever defaulted on their past pension obligations to employees.

A small number of states, such as Michigan and Utah, moved to restructure retirement benefits entirely. The Michigan School Employees Retirement System replaced the DB pension with a hybrid plan for all new employees hired after July 2010. The hybrid plan includes both a DB pension and a DC plan. The DB portion includes higher age and service requirements, a lower final average salary calculation, and a lower pension benefit than the previous DB pension system. Also, the DB component does not include any post-retirement cost-of-living adjustments (Michigan House Fiscal Agency 2010). Employer contribution rates to DC plans will be negotiable within limits by individual school districts. Employer contributions vest after four years, and participants have an opt-out option—that is, they do not have to contribute to their DC plan (Snell 2010a).

Employer costs under Michigan's new plan are expected to decline because the hybrid plan offers a less generous benefit than the DB pension (Center for State and Local Government Excellence [CSLGE] 2011a). Initial analyses of Michigan's switch estimated that the hybrid will save the public school system between $2 and $4 million in 2011 and between $200 and $400 million over ten years (Neumann 2011). Initial estimates projected that as many as 17,000 newly hired teachers would be covered under the new hybrid plan by the end of 2011; however, due to an early retirement incentive that was offered to older teachers (Williamson 2010), as of February 2011, slightly more than 11,600 teachers were yet covered by the hybrid plan (CSLGE 2011a). As the plan remains in effect in years to come, the full effects of the switch on both employer costs and recruitment and retention concerns can be more fully examined.

Furthermore, employees hired in Utah after January 2011 have an option of either a hybrid plan, with both a DB pension and a DC plan, or only a DC plan. Employers will contribute 10% of salary for the DB pension of the hybrid plan, and employees will have to make up the difference if that contribution is insufficient to fully fund the benefits. The excess is deposited into employee DC plans, however, if the DB pension is overfunded. Employees can also voluntarily contribute more to their DC plan under the hybrid plan. Alternatively, employers will contribute 10% of salary to the employees' DC plan if they choose the DC-only plan (Utah Retirement Systems, n.d.; Snell 2010a).

The Utah design gives employees a unique decision: to get the advantages of a DB pension—including a guaranteed benefit for life, professional investment management, and the larger benefits provided by longevity pooling—they must also take on the investment risk. If the employee chooses the DC plan, the employer will contribute 10% of pay to the DC account. If the employee chooses the hybrid plan, the employer will contribute 10% of pay. Thus, regardless of each employee's decision and investment returns, the employer contribution remains a flat 10% of pay (Olleman and Boivie 2011).

This survey of the widespread efforts that states undertook to address financial challenges and to operate within the confines of emerging political pressures shows that states decided to keep their DB pensions as the only or at least one of the primary retirement benefits for their employees. Although several states and municipalities conducted feasibility studies of switching from the DB pension to a DC plan, those studies found that the move would save little to no money in the long term and could actually increase retirement plan costs in the near term (Cavanaugh 2010; GRS 2005, 2007; Kansas Public Employees Retirement System 2009; The Segal Group 2010; Wojcik 2008). The Segal Group, an actuarial consulting firm, conducted individual feasibility studies for the city of Los Angeles and the state of Nevada in 2010. In Los Angeles, Segal found that a lower DB benefit would bring significantly more cost savings than would a DC or hybrid switch (Cavanaugh 2010); in Nevada, Segal concluded that if the DB pension were frozen in favor of a DC plan, DB costs would increase dramatically (The Segal Group 2010). In 2009, the Kansas Public Employee Retirement System (2009) found that of three different DC options, none would save money compared to the baseline DB pension—and in fact, one would be more expensive. Perhaps not surprisingly, none of these states or municipalities has opted in favor of the DC switch. It is possible that this decision to stay with DB pensions reflects an employer appreciation for the efficiency of DB pensions, particularly because states faced increasing political pressures to change their retirement systems.

Other Rationales for Changing Retirement Benefits

Labor–management arguments are not the only ones surrounding public employee retirement benefits. Two additional arguments that have been made in favor of switching from DB pensions to DC plans deserve further consideration. It has been argued that DC plans are fairer than DB pensions to a more mobile workforce (Costrell and Podgursky 2009) and that the demands of DC plans are easier than DB pensions to manage for employers (Rauh and Stefanescu 2009).

The assertion that DC plans are fairer than DB pensions depends on a limited definition of fairness. Public employees who leave public service quickly presumably lose some of their compensation because they are not vested in a DB pension, which makes the entire DB pension, in this view, unfair to short-term employees because it creates an unequal wealth distribution on an annual basis that favors long-term employees over shorter-term ones.

The opposite conclusion emerges when a lifetime wealth distribution, rather than an annual compensation wealth effect, is considered. A longer-term view to evaluate the distributional effects of DB pensions seems especially appropriate in this context since DB pensions are primarily retirement benefits. Porell and Almeida (2009) found that DB pensions in fact reduced the chance of experiencing economic hardships in retirement, particularly for groups of employees such as nonwhites, who are typically disadvantaged in their wealth distribution. Defined benefit pensions in other words helped somewhat to equalize retirement income inequities that otherwise would exist. Wolff (2002) similarly showed that DB pensions and Social Security, another retirement benefit that offers lifetime income, equalized retirement wealth by race, education, and marital status but that this effect wore off over time as DC plans increasingly took the place of DB pensions. A lifetime view of the retirement wealth effect of

DB pensions shows more of an equalizing effect than a snapshot of annual compensation does, and a longer-term view seems appropriate given the retirement income security functions of retirement savings.

The fairness argument also overstates its case. Most public DB pension systems are contributory—that is, employees contribute a share of their earnings (Brainard 2010). Employees are generally allowed to withdraw those funds, plus some nominal interest earned on the funds, when they leave service, although employer contributions stay with the DB pension plan (NASRA 2011a). Shorter vesting periods could overcome any remaining potential adverse distributional effects because short-term employees could more quickly gain a right to retirement benefits than they otherwise would. Shortening vesting periods would have to be weighed against the potential adverse consequences for labor–management practices because shorter vesting could lead to increased turnover. States could address any adverse short-run distributional effects in the DB pension context if they wanted to.

The second argument in favor of DC plans as a replacement to DB pensions is more straightforward. The costs of DC plans are by definition more predictable because the employer promises to contribute only a fixed share of earnings annually—a contemporaneous increase in compensation—compared to a promised amount of benefits in the future under a DB pension, which can carry unpredictable employer contributions in the present.

There are ways to make the employer costs of DB pensions more predictable. One policy tool would be to set a contribution floor so that employer contributions could not drop during good economic times when asset values are high due to good financial market performance (Weller, Price, and Margolies 2006). This would necessitate that policy makers set a maximum funding ratio since states could otherwise potentially contribute more than necessary, resulting in too many public funds being tied up in public DB pension plans. Weller and Baker (2005) suggested a funding ratio of 120% for private sector plans. States could also change the actuarial valuation of their DB pension plans such that their funding ratios would fluctuate less and employers would have to contribute more during good economic times and less during bad economic times than is currently the case, as discussed by Weller, Price, and Margolies (2006). States that are worried about the unpredictability of the employer contribution to DB pension plans can take reasonable steps to make the contributions more predictable.

Conclusion

The financial crisis of 2008–2009 presented financial challenges to state and local DB pensions. They were hurt in the stock market crash because large shares of DB pension assets are typically invested in the stock market. This led to a drop in plans' funded ratios and an increase in governments' unfunded pension liabilities and costs (Brainard 2010).

Some observers argued that states should alter their retirement benefits by switching from DB pension plans to DC or cash balance plans. We reviewed the evidence on the labor relations effects of existing DB pension plans to see what the likely effects of such a switch would be. The literature and the empirical evidence are unambiguous on a number of key effects. First, public employers would attract a different labor force if they switched retirement benefits away from DB pensions. Public employees would become less committed to their employers and thus invest less in nontransferable skills that are critical to effective government. Second, employee turnover would increase under alternative benefits. Alternative benefits no longer defer compensation into the future and thus offer fewer economic incentives for employees to stay with public employers. Third, public employers would face higher costs, both as a result of ending the existing DB pensions and because of higher investment and administrative costs for alternative retirement plans.

The value of DB pensions in the public sector is probably best illustrated by the fact that when faced with a choice, employers and employees overwhelmingly choose to stay with DB pensions rather than move to alternative benefits. The majority of states made revisions to their DB pensions between 2001 and 2011 but none abandoned the DB pension model for its employees.

DB pension plans have a track record of simultaneously meeting the goals of employers due to the plans' recruitment and retention effects and the goals of employees due to the economic security they offer.

The Great Recession presented some funding challenges to public pensions. States and localities are willing to address these challenges so they can effectively compete for skilled employees in the future.

Endnotes

[1] The lower accumulation rate under a DC plan than under a cash balance plan fully compensates for the greater risk exposure, so the total costs of both plans are the same.

[2] It also could be that employers who offer DB pensions are more careful in their hiring decisions because of the long-term commitment involved in offering a DB pension as a retirement benefit.

[3] Raw data from the U.S. Bureau of Labor Statistics (BLS) offer misleading comparisons of public and private sector compensation because these data ignore the difference in composition of the private and public sectors. The BLS 2011 data release states, "Compensation cost levels in state and local government should not be directly compared with levels in private industry. Differences between these sectors stem from factors such as variation in work activities and occupational structures. Manufacturing and sales, for example, make up a large part of private industry work activities but are rare in state and local government. Professional and administrative support occupations (including teachers) account for two-thirds of the state and local government workforce, compared with one-half of private industry" (BLS 2011:4). Regression-based analyses such as those cited here are thus more accurate.

[4] "Non-negotiable core beliefs" are listed at http://www.teaparty.org/about.php.

[5] Costrell and Podgursky (2008) originally advocated for a switch from DB pensions to DC plans for teachers. More recently, they supported a move to a cash balance plan, a type of DB pension in which benefits are stated as a hypothetical account balance for each employee. Under a cash balance design, benefits are usually accrued in a more linear fashion than under the traditional DB pension.

[6] Properly measuring funding levels in public pension plans has been the subject of academic debate, with several voices advocating for public plans to discount pension liabilities using a risk-free rate of return. After reviewing public pension accounting standards over several years, the U.S. Governmental Accounting Standards Board (GASB), the body charged with setting accounting standards for public pension plans, signaled that it will not adopt mark-to-market accounting for public plans (GASB 2011).

References

Allen, S.G., R.L., Clark, and A. McDermed. 1993. "Pensions, Bonding, and Lifetime Jobs." *Journal of Human Resources*, Vol. 28, no. 3, pp. 463–81.

Almeida, B., and I. Boivie. 2009. The Staying Power of Pensions in the Public Sector. *CPER Journal*, Vol. 195, pp. 5–11.

Almeida, B., K. Kenneally, and D. Madland. 2009. "The New Intersection on the Road to Retirement: Public Pensions, Economics, Perceptions, Politics, and Interest Groups." In O.S. Mitchell and G. Anderson, eds., *The Future of Public Employee Retirement Systems*. New York: Oxford University Press.

Americans for Tax Reform (ATR). 2010 (May 27). "Diverse National Coalition Opposes Congressional Pension Bailout Bills." Press release. <http://www.atr.org/diverse-national-coalition-opposes-congressional-pension-a4996>. [May 20, 2011].

Angelides, P. 2005 (Feb. 7). The Right's Attack on Public Pensions. *LA Times*.

Barro, J., and S. Buck. 2010 (Apr. 6). *Underfunded Teacher Pension Plans: It's Worse Than You Think*. Civic report. New York: Manhattan Institute and The Foundation for Educational Choice.

Barstow, D. 2010 (Feb. 15). "Tea Party Lights Fuse for Rebellion on Right." *New York Times*.

Bender, K.A., and J.S. Heywood. 2010. *Out of Balance? Comparing Public and Private Sector Compensation Over Twenty Years*. Washington, DC: Center for State and Local Government Excellence and National Institute on Retirement Security.

Brainard, K. 2009. *Public Fund Survey Summary of Findings for 2008*. Essex, CT: National Association of State Retirement Administrators.

Brainard, K. 2010. *Public Fund Survey Summary of Findings for 2009*. Essex, CT: National Association of State Retirement Administrators.

Browning, M., and A. Lusardi. 1996. "Household Saving: Micro Theories and Micro Facts." *Journal of Economic Literature*, Vol. 34, no. 4, pp. 1797–855.

Cahill, K., and M. Soto. 2003. *How Do Cash Balance Plans Affect the Pension Landscape? An Issue in Brief*. No. 14. Chestnut Hill, MA: Center for Retirement Research at Boston College.

California Pension Reform. No date. *100K Pension Club*. <http://www.californiansfor pensionreform.com/database.asp?vttable=calpers>. [May 18, 2011].

Cannata, M. 2008. *Teacher Qualifications and Work Environments across School Types*. Policy brief. Arizona State University and University of Colorado at Boulder.

Cavanaugh, K. 2010 (Oct. 20). "The Answer to Retiree Mess? Not 401(k)s." *Los Angeles Daily News*.

Center for State and Local Government Excellence (CSLGE). 2011a. *Fact Sheets on States with Defined Contribution Pension Plans, 2011: Michigan School Employees*. Washington, DC: CSLGE.

Center for State and Local Government Excellence (CSLGE). 2011b. *State and Local Government Workforce: 2011 Realities*. Washington, DC: CSLGE.

Clark, R., and S. Schieber. 2000. An Empirical Analysis of the Transition to Hybrid Pension Plans in the United States. Paper presented at the conference on Public Policies and Private Pensions, Washington, DC, September 2. <http://www.brookings.edu/es/ events/pension/01clark_schieb.pdf>. [January 12, 2011].

Committee on Oversight & Government Reform. 2010. "Public Employee Pension Transparency Needed." <http://oversight.house.gov/release/public-employee-pension-transparency-needed>. [July 4, 2012].

Consolidated Public Retirement Board & Buck Consultants, LLC. 2008. *Individual Voluntary Option for Members of the Teachers' Defined Contribution (DC) Retirement System to Transfer to the Teachers' Retirement System (TRS)*. Retirement Choice Decision Guide, Consolidated Public Retirement Board.

Costrell, R., and M. Podgursky. 2008. "Peaks, Cliffs, and Valleys: The Peculiar Incentives of Teacher Pension Systems." *Education Next*, Vol. 8, no. 1, pp. 22–8.

Costrell, R., and M. Podgursky. 2009. "Peaks, Cliffs, and Valleys: The Peculiar Incentives in Teacher Retirement Systems and Their Consequences for School Staffing." *Education Finance and Policy*, Vol. 4, no. 2, pp. 175–211.

Costrell, R., and M. Podgursky. 2010. "Distribution of Benefits in Teacher Retirement Systems and Their Implications for Mobility." *Education Finance and Policy*, Vol. 5, no. 4, pp. 519–57.

DellaVigna, S. 2009. "Psychology and Economics: Evidence from the Field." *Journal of Economic Literature*, Vol. 47, no. 2, pp. 315–72.

Diversified Investment Advisors. 2004. *Diversified Investment Advisors Report on Retirement Plans*. Purchase, NY: Diversified Investment Advisors.

Dorsey, S. 1995. "Pension Portability and Labor Market Efficiency: A Survey of the Literature." *Industrial and Labor Relations Review*, Vol. 48, no. 2, 276–92.

Dreyfuss, R. 2001. "Grover Norquist: 'Field Marshal' of the Bush Plan." *The Nation*, Vol. 272, no. 18, 11–6.

Dulebohn, J.H., B. Murray, and M. Sun. 2000. "Selection Among Employer-Sponsored Pension Plans: The Role of Individual Differences." *Personnel Psychology*, Vol. 53, pp. 405–32.

Even, W.E., and D.A. MacPherson. 1996. "Employer Size and Labor Turnover: The Role of Pensions." *Industrial and Labor Relations Review*, Vol. 49, no. 4, pp. 707–28.

Fehr, S.C. 2010 (Nov. 4). "Election Adds Pressure to Change Public Pensions." *Stateline*.

Floridians for Sustainable Pensions. No date. *About*. <http://sustainablepensions.com/about/coalition-overview>. [May 18, 2011].

Free Enterprise Nation. 2010. "FEN: One Year of Influencing National Dialogue." Free Enterprise Nation blog. <http://www.thefreeenterprisenation.org/blog/FEN-Blog.aspx?tagid=345>. [May 18, 2011].

Friedberg, L., and M.T. Owyang. 2005. *Explaining the Evolution of Pension Structure and Job Tenure*. Working paper. St. Louis, MO: Federal Reserve Bank of St. Louis.

Gabriel, Roeder, Smith and Company (GRS). 2005. *New Mexico Educational Retirement Board: Defined Contribution Retirement Plan Study*. Dallas, TX: Gabriel, Roeder, Smith and Company.

Gabriel, Roeder, Smith and Company (GRS). 2007. *Projections of ERSRI with Frozen Participation*. Irving, TX: Gabriel, Roeder, Smith and Company.

Greenfield, S. 2007. *Public Sector Employment: The Current Situation*. Washington, DC: The Center for State and Local Government Excellence.

Guarino, C.M., L. Santibañez, and G.A. Daley. 2006. "Teacher Recruitment and Retention: A Review of the Recent Empirical Literature." *Review of Educational Research*, Vol. 76, no. 2, pp. 173–208.

Gustman, A.L., O.S. Mitchell, and T.L Steinmeier. 1994. The Role of Pensions in the Labor Market: A Survey of the Literature. *Industrial and Labor Relations Review*, Vol. 47, no. 3, pp. 417–38.

Hall, T. 2006. "An Empirical Analysis of Pensions for the Labor Market." Paper presented at the Society of Labor Economics Eleventh Annual Meetings, Cambridge, MA, May 5–6.

Hansen, J. 2010. "An Introduction to Teacher Retirement Benefits." *Education Finance and Policy*, Vol. 5, no. 4, pp. 402–37.

Helman, R., C. Copeland, J. VanDerhei, and D. Salisbury. 2008. *EBRI 2008 Recent Retirees Survey: Report of Findings*. Issue Brief No. 319. Washington, DC: Employee Benefits Research Institute.

Houston, D.J. 2000. "Public Service Motivation: A Multivariate Test." *Journal of Public Administration Research and Theory*, Vol. 10, no. 4, pp. 713–28.

Ippolito, R.A. 1997. *Pension Plans and Employee Performance: Evidence, Analysis, and Policy*. Chicago: University of Chicago Press.

Johnson, N., P. Oliff, and E. Williams. 2011. *An Update on State Budget Cuts: At Least 46 States Have Imposed Cuts That Hurt Vulnerable Residents and the Economy*. Washington, DC: Center on Budget and Policy Priorities.

Johnson, R., and C. Uccello. 2001. *The Potential Effects of Cash Balance Plans on the Distribution of Pension Wealth in Midlife*. Final report to the Pension and Welfare Administration, U.S. Department of Labor. Washington, DC: Urban Institute.

Kabler, P. 2008 (Aug. 26). "State to Save $22 Million in Teacher Pension Switch." *Charleston Gazette.*

Kansas Public Employees Retirement System. 2009. *KPERS Long-Term Funding: Defined Contribution Options.* KPERS Joint Committee on Pensions, Investments and Benefits.

Lav, I. 2011. *Proposed Public Employee Pension Reporting Requirements Are Unnecessary: Rules Would Create Confusion and Could Roil Markets.* Washington, DC: Center on Budget and Policy Priorities.

Lazear, Edward P. 1983. "Pensions as Severance Pay." In Z. Bodie and J.B. Shoven, eds., *Financial Aspects of the United States Pension System.* Chicago: University of Chicago Press.

Levitz, J. 2010 (Nov. 23). "Tea Parties Turn to Local Issues." *Wall Street Journal.*

Luchak, A.A., D.M. Pohler, and I.R. Gellatly. 2008. "When Do Committed Employees Retire? The Effects of Organizational Commitment on Retirement Plans under a Defined-Benefit Pension Plan." *Human Resource Management,* Vol. 47, no. 3, pp. 581–99.

Madland, D. 2007. The Politics of Pension Cuts. In T. Ghilarducci and C. Weller, eds., *Employee Pensions: Policies, Problems, and Possibilities.* Ithaca, NY: Cornell University Press.

Matthew Greenwald & Associates, Inc. 2004. *Retirement Plan Preferences Survey: Report of Findings.* Schaumburg, IL: Society of Actuaries.

MetLife. 2008. *Sixth Annual Study of Employee Benefits Trends. Findings from the National Survey of Employers and Employees.* New York: MetLife, Inc.

Michigan House Fiscal Agency. 2010. *Legislative Analysis: A Summary of Senate Bill 1227 as Enacted.* Michigan House Fiscal Agency.

Monahan, A.B. 2010. *Public Pension Plan Reform: The Legal Framework.* Legal Studies Research Paper Series. No. 10-13. Minneapolis: University of Minnesota Law School.

MuniNetGuide. 2008 (Apr. 7). *Public Sector Offers Attractive Employee Compensation Benefits Packages.* <http://www.muninetguide.com/articles/Public-Sector-Offers-Attractive--266.php>. [April 13, 2012].

Munnell, A.H., J.P. Aubry, J. Hurwitz, M. Medenica, and L. Quinby. 2011. *The Funding of State and Local Pensions in 2010.* SLP #17. Chestnut Hill, MA: Center for Retirement Research at Boston College.

Munnell, A.H., J.P. Aubry, and L. Quinby. 2010a. *The Funding of State and Local Pensions: 2009–2013.* SLP #10. Chestnut Hill, MA: Center for Retirement Research at Boston College.

Munnell, A.H., Aubry, J.P., and L. Quinby. 2010b. *The Impact of Public Pensions on State and Local Budgets.* SLP #13. Chestnut Hill, MA: Center for Retirement Research at Boston College.

Munnell, A.H., A. Golub-Sass, K. Haverstick, M. Soto, and G. Wiles. 2008. *Why Have Some States Introduced Defined Contribution Plans?* SLP #3. Chestnut Hill, MA: Center for Retirement Research at Boston College.

Munnell, A.H., K. Haverstick, and G. Sanzenbacher. 2006. *Job Tenure and Pension Coverage.* CRR Working Paper 2006-18. Chestnut Hill, MA: Center for Retirement Research at Boston College.

Munnell, A.H., K. Haverstick, and M. Soto. 2007. *Why Have Defined Benefit Plans Survived in the Public Sector?* SLP #2. Chestnut Hill, MA: Center for Retirement Research at Boston College.

Munnell, A.H., and A. Sunden. 2004. *Coming Up Short: The Challenge of 401(k) Plans.* Washington, DC: Brookings Institution.

Nalebluff, B., and R. Zeckhauser. 1984. *Pensions and the Retirement Decision.* NBER Working Paper No. 1285. Cambridge, MA: National Bureau of Economic Research.

National Association of State Budget Officers (NASBO). 2010. *Preliminary Summary: NGA/NASBO Fall 2010 Fiscal Survey of States.* Washington, DC: NASBO.

National Association of State Retirement Administrators (NASRA). 2011a. *Responses to Questions Regarding Interest Rates Applied Service Purchase and Member Account Balances.* Essex, CT: NASRA.

National Association of State Retirement Administrators (NASRA). 2011b. *Strong Investment Gains and Legislative Changes Speeding Public Pension Recovery.* Essex, CT: NASRA.

National Conference of State Legislatures (NCSL). 2010a. *Actions & Proposals to Balance the FY 2010 Budget: State Employee Actions, Furloughs and Layoffs.* Washington, DC: NCSL.

National Conference of State Legislatures (NCSL). 2010b. *Map of Post-Election Partisan Composition of State Legislatures.* Washington, DC: NCSL.

National Council on Teacher Quality (NCTQ). 2010. *2010 State Teacher Policy Yearbook: Blueprint for Change: National Summary.* Washington, DC: NCTQ.

National Education Association (NEA). 2010. *Characteristics of Large Public Education Pension Plans.* Washington, DC: NEA.

Neumann, J. 2011 (Mar. 1). "States Mull Shift in Worker Pensions." *Wall Street Journal.*

Novy-Marx, R., and J. Rauh. 2011. "Public Pension Promises: How Big Are They and What Are They Worth?" *Journal of Finance,* Vol. 66, no. 4, pp. 1211–49.

Nyce, Steven. 2007. "Behavioral Effects of Employer-Sponsored Retirement Plans." *Journal of Pension Economics and Finance,* Vol. 6, no. 3, pp. 251–85.

Olleman, M.C., and I. Boivie. 2011. *Decisions, Decisions: Retirement Plan Choices for Public Employees and Employers.* Washington, DC: National Institute on Retirement Security and Milliman, Inc.

Pew Center on the States. No date. *Pension and Retiree Health Care Reform in the States.* <http://www.pewcenteronthestates.org/initiatives_detail.aspx?initiativeID=61599>. [April 22, 2011].

Pew Center on the States. 2011. *The Widening Gap: The Great Recession's Impact on State Pension and Retiree Health Care Costs.* Washington, DC: Pew Center on the States.

Porell, F., and B. Almeida. 2009. *The Pension Factor: Assessing the Role of Defined Benefit Plans in Reducing Elder Hardships.* Washington, DC: National Institute on Retirement Security.

Rauh, J., and I. Stefanescu. 2009. "Why Are Firms in the United States Abandoning Defined Benefit Plans?" *Rotman International Journal of Pension Management,* Vol. 2, no. 2, pp. 18–25.

Schmitt, J. 2010. *The Benefits of State and Local Government Employees.* CEPR Issue Brief, Washington, DC: Center for Economic and Policy Research.

The Segal Group. 2010. *Public Employees' Retirement System of the State of Nevada: Analysis and Comparison of Defined Benefit and Defined Contribution Retirement Plans.* Greenwood Village, CO: The Segal Group.

Snell, R. 2010a. *Pensions and Retirement Plan Enactments in 2010 State Legislatures.* Washington, DC: National Conference of State Legislatures.

Snell, R. 2010b. *Sustaining State Retirement Benefits: Recent State Legislation Affecting Public Retirement Plans, 2005–2009.* Washington, DC: National Conference on State Legislatures.

Snell, R. 2011. *State Retirement Legislation in 2010 and 2011.* Washington, DC: National Conference of State Legislatures.

Tea Party. No date. *Non Negotiable Core Beliefs.* <http://www.teaparty.org/about.php>. [May 4, 2011].

Thompson, K. 2010 (Nov. 14). "Tea Party Groups Divided on How to Use Newly Won Clout." *Washington Post.*

U.S. Bureau of Labor Statistics (BLS). 2011. *Employer Costs for Employee Compensation, June 2011.* Washington, DC: BLS.

U.S. Government Accountability Office (GAO). 2007. *State and Local Government Retiree Benefits: Current Status of Benefit Structures, Protections, and Fiscal Outlook for Funding Future Costs.* GAO-07-1156. Washington, DC: GAO.

U.S. Government Accountability Office (GAO). 2008. *State and Local Government Retiree Benefits: Current Funded Status of Pension and Health Benefits.* GAO 08-223. Washington, DC: GAO.

U.S. Governmental Accounting Standards Board (GASB). 2011. *Exposure Draft: Reporting Items Previously Recognized as Assets and Liabilities.* Washington, DC: GASB.

Utah Retirement Systems. No date. *URS Senate Bills.* <https://www.urs.org/Pages/SenateBills.aspx>. [May 20, 2011].

Watson Wyatt. 2005 (Apr.). "How Do Retirement Plans Affect Employee Behavior?" *Watson Wyatt Insider.*

Weller, C. 2005. *Ensuring Retirement Security with Cash Balance Plans.* Washington, DC: Center for American Progress.

Weller, C. 2006. "The Recent Stock Market Fluctuations and Retirement Income Adequacy." *Eastern Economic Journal,* Vol. 32, no. 1, pp. 67–81.

Weller, Christian E. 2010. "Did Retirees Save Enough to Compensate for the Increase in Individual Risk Exposure?" *Journal of Aging and Social Policy,* Vol. 22, no. 2, pp. 152–71.

Weller, C., and D. Baker. 2005. "Smoothing the Waves of Pension Funding: Could Changes in Funding Rules Help Avoid Cyclical Under-Funding?" *Journal of Policy Reform,* Vol. 8, no. 2, pp. 131–51.

Weller, C., M. Price, and D. Margolies. 2006. *Rewarding Hard Work: Give Pennsylvania Families a Shot at Middle Class Retirement Benefits.* CAP Economic Policy Report. Washington, DC: Center for American Progress.

Weller, C., and J. Wenger. 2009. "Integrated Labor and Financial Market Risks: Implications for Individual Accounts for Retirement." *Journal of Aging and Social Policy,* Vol. 21, no. 2, pp. 256–76.

Williamson, C. 2010 (Oct. 4). "Michigan System Gets Hybrid Plan Up and Running." *Pensions and Investments.*

Wojcik, J. 2008 (Aug. 11). "Public Entities Generally Keep Traditional Pension Plans." *Business Insurance.*

Wolff, E. 2002. *Has the Equalizing Effect of Retirement Wealth Worn Off?* Working paper. Department of Economics, New York University.

Wright, B.E. 2001. "Public Sector Work Motivation: A Review of the Current Literature and a Revised Conceptual Model." *Journal of Public Administration Research and Theory*, Vol. 11, no. 4, pp. 559–86.

Zernike, K. 2010 (Nov. 2). "Tea Party Comes to Power on an Unclear Mandate." *New York Times*.

Zorn, P. 2011. *Research Memorandum: The Public Employee Pension Transparency Act.* Dallas, TX: Gabriel, Roeder, Smith and Company.

CHAPTER 8

California's Public Sector Adapts to the Great Recession

DANIEL J.B. MITCHELL

University of California, Los Angeles

California, the most populous state in the United States, constitutes just under one eighth of the nation's population and a similar portion of its economic activity. In many respects, the state mirrors the adjustment of the public sector nationally in its regional response to the Great Recession. But California does deviate from the median state in a variety of ways apart from size. Its politics have been characterized (some would say dominated) by direct democracy: the initiative, referendum, and recall. And its unionization rate is somewhat higher than the national average, in large part due to higher public sector unionization.

While all state and local governments have experienced difficulties adapting their public sectors to the Great Recession and its resultant squeeze on tax revenue, California began the episode with an underlying structural deficit rooted two decades earlier. That shaky starting point complicated its adjustment. It did not help that California was very much the heartland of the housing and mortgage bubble whose collapse triggered the Great Recession. Thus, its labor market was more heavily affected than most other states. These themes are developed in this chapter.

Brief Political History

California attained statehood in 1850, but its economic linkage to the rest of the United States once the Gold Rush subsided was the Transcontinental Railroad, which was not completed until 1869. That crucial rail link evolved into the Southern Pacific Railroad during the latter part of the 19th century. Because of the railroad's near monopoly on trade and travel, its wealthy owners—the so-called Big 4—were perceived as squeezing state farms and businesses, dominating state politics, and corrupting the legislature.[1]

Progressives of the early 20th century, who were largely Republicans, rebelled against the influence of the railroad and saw direct democracy as the obvious counterweight to political corruption. In 1910, they succeeded in electing Hiram Johnson as governor. Johnson's administration the following year brought with it the initiative, referendum, and recall—along with women's suffrage and workers compensation insurance.

Progressivism in its early 20th century form continues to influence the state. As a doctrine it emphasizes an equation of good government with nonpartisanship. Since legislation—including constitutional amendments—can be enacted by voters, this substitute channel of authority weakens the role of the legislature and other elected officials. Even laws passed by the legislature and signed by the governor can be reversed through referenda. So-called ballot box budgeting can require spending by formula or obligation (in the case of bond authorizations), even when revenue is not provided, thereby leaving the legislature constrained in dealing with budget crises.

By some measures, California voters over the century since the advent of direct democracy have grown more progressive in a way that would be familiar to Hiram Johnson (i.e., constraining elected officials). They imposed tight term limits on members of the state legislature in 1990. As the 2010 U.S. Census loomed, they created an independent tribunal to draw legislative and congressional districts to prevent legislative gerrymandering.[2] Voters have expanded nonpartisan top-two primaries, in which candidates run as individuals in a single primary—not in primaries by party—and the general election consists of a runoff between the top two primary vote getters. Perhaps, more tellingly, the most rapidly growing political party among registered voters is no party. Although Democrats have a plurality in voter registration, more than a fifth of voters are not affiliated with Democrats, Republicans, or third parties. They are called "decline to state" voters, and their proportion of the electorate has steadily grown.

Some Underlying Economics

It is tempting to pin the blame for fiscal dysfunction in California on its direct democracy because these arrangements look different from those found in many other states. A lengthy section of the April 23, 2011, edition of *The Economist* magazine was devoted to just that premise. But there are reasons not to dwell entirely on direct democracy as *the* cause of the dysfunction. After all, in the years after World War II California was often looked to as a model for good governance, although it had direct democracy at the time. Its approach to freeway building pre-dated, and set the pattern for, the later federal interstate highway system.[3] It developed large and complex water supply systems. Its public schools were considered first rank. And at the higher education level, its 1960 Master Plan for Higher Education developed a framework for its community colleges, state colleges, and the University of California and presaged substantial expansion of all three systems.[4]

At the same time, California attracted an influx of people from other states (and later abroad) through growing job opportunities and affordable housing. Having Hollywood as a de facto public relations agent for the California lifestyle simply added to the attraction. In a sense, too much success and the consequent population in-migration led to an early glimmer of problems to come. In the late 1970s, a complicated stew of anti-growth sentiment and the economic impact of infill from an expanding population led to rising property values, which sparked a housing boom and commensurate jumps in property taxes. The result was the passage of Proposition 13 in 1978, an initiative that drastically cut and capped property taxes and led to the ongoing fiscal complications in California that are discussed in this chapter.[5]

It is noteworthy that Proposition 13 is often seen as sparking the national taxpayer revolt reflected in related developments in other states. Moreover, the taxpayer revolt tended to pull national politics rightward, notably with the election of Ronald Reagan (a former California governor) as president. The national uptake of a California phenomenon suggests that there is more to the California story than direct democracy. In recent years, California dysfunction has also been mirrored at the federal level. The same inability to enact budgets on time has been seen in Washington and Sacramento. Party polarization is a factor in both capitals. And there seems to be still another national–California connection with causation running from Washington to California.

As Figure 1 shows, there have been two major inflexion points in California history since statehood. As measured by population, California has a long history of growing faster than the rest of the United States. However, there is an upward tick in 1940, marking the expansion of federal military expenditures in the state during World War II, the Korean War, the Vietnam War, and the Cold War. The Cold War disappeared after 1990 with the end of the Soviet Union, and so did supernormal growth in California.

As Figure 2 shows, in employment terms, there has been a widening gap since 1990 between the old trend in jobs and the actual results in California. Even the California-centered dot-com boom of the late 1990s and the subsequent housing and mortgage boom of the mid-2000s did not prevent the gap between the old trend and the actual results from widening. The modern impression of California as a land of dysfunction thus has its roots in the 1990s. National attention in the 1990s often focused on visible symptoms such as the Los Angeles riots in 1992. The national obsession—once the dysfunction idea took hold—even included nonpolitical natural disasters such as the Northridge earthquake in 1994.[6]

FIGURE 1
California Population Relative to United States Population

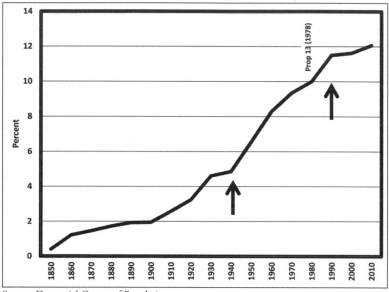

Source: Decennial Census of Population.

FIGURE 2
California Nonfarm Employment History and Forecast
Versus 2.3% Trend from 1990 (Third Quarter)

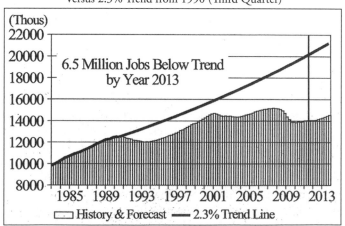

Source: UCLA Anderson Forecast (2011), p. California-91.

In short, California's polity has had a great deal of difficulty recognizing and adjusting to the underlying end of military-fueled prosperity, even apart from the stresses imposed by the Great Recession. California's peculiar direct democracy institutions worked well enough when the state was growing rapidly. They became stressed when the engine of rapid growth was removed. Those familiar with earlier California history will not be surprised. During the Great Depression, there was also government dysfunction, in part operating through direct democracy and ballot propositions. But when the money rolled in starting with World War II, the dysfunction faded.

California's Public Sector

In 2010, state and local employees in California accounted for 15.5% of the state's nonfarm workforce. For the United States as a whole, state and local workers are about 15% of nonfarm employment. Thus, California appears to be about average by that measure. The unionization rate in the public sector in California in 2010 was high: 56.6% on a membership basis, 59.6% in terms of coverage. Comparable figures for the United States were 36.2% and 40%, respectively.[7] As Table 1 shows, the combination of high unionization in the public sector and declining unionization in the private sector means that more than half of union members in California are now in government positions. That shift helps

TABLE 1
California Union Membership Trend Unionization Rates

| | Unionization rates | |
| | Public sector union membership as a percentage of total membership | Membership basis | |
		Public	Private
Troy–Sheflin data			
1975	22.1%	35.8%	34.1%
1982	22.9	32.9	25.4
Hirsch–Macpherson data			
1983	27.7	43.4	17.7
1990	40.8	46.7	13.0
2000	48.5	50.3	10.7
2010	56.0	56.6	9.3

Note: Troy–Sheflin membership data are based on reports of labor organizations. Hirsch–Macpherson data are based on the Current Population Survey.
Source: Troy and Sheflin (1995). Hirsch–Macpherson data are from http://www.unionstats.com.

foster the idea of unions as a narrow special interest group representing just government workers at the expense of everyone else—and special interest labels are particularly anathema to California's progressive tradition.

State Regulation of Public Sector Collective Bargaining

California adopted a series of statutes regulating public sector collective bargaining using a model largely copied from the federal private sector regulatory framework.[8] Enactment of such statutes began in the early 1960s with a limited law covering local government. Major legislation followed in the 1970s, starting with a law for public schools. Similar statutes were later enacted for state workers other than university employees, with a separate statute applying to employees of the University of California and the California State University systems. In addition, there are specialized statutes for certain other groups. A state Public Employment Relations Board is the main administrative tribunal for much of the public sector. Although California law is silent on the right to strike of government workers, that silence has been judicially interpreted to mean that the right to strike exists in the public sector, with exceptions for certain public safety workers.

Data do not exist on small public sector strikes. However, the U.S. Bureau of Labor Statistics does keep track of major work stoppages involving 1,000 or more workers. There are at most a handful of such events in any given year in California, and they tend to be of short duration, often lasting only a day or so. At the peak of the business cycle in 2006, four stoppages occurred: three in various county governments and one in the City of Los Angeles. In 2007, there were only two: one in a school district and another in a transit district. The Great Recession seemed to repress such conflicts; there were no major California stoppages in either 2008 or 2009. With some degree of economic recovery under way, stoppages occurred in two school districts in 2010.[9]

At the state level, there were threats of job actions of various types up to and including strikes. The issue of furloughs was contentious but largely fought through litigation, with most decisions ultimately favoring the governor. At one point, there was a dispute over whether Columbus Day would remain a paid holiday, even though Governor Schwarzenegger had ordered state employees to work. Some individual workers indicated they would stay home on that day, but the issue seemed to peter out. Given the budgetary climate, union officials at the state level seemed to conclude that using the political route was the main practical path to influence.

Unions and State Politics

While unions played a role in state politics before the 1970s, the combination of general growth in the public sector and a widening public sector union presence was reflected in a major battle over a ballot initiative pushed by then-Governor Ronald Reagan. The initiative—Proposition 1 of 1973—would have capped state spending and a complicated formula would have ratcheted down the cap over time. It was seen at the time as a state version of similar approaches that conservatives were hoping to write into the federal constitution. Part of the opposition campaign focused on the complicated formula, which had been developed by academic economists and which the governor himself could not explain.[10]

Proposition 1 was defeated, only to be followed in 1979 by Proposition 4—the so-called Gann Limit spending cap—which was enacted in the anti-tax fervor after 1978's Proposition 13 (property taxes).[11] Public sector unions played important roles in the opposition to both Propositions 13 (in 1978) and 4 (in 1979) but evidently could not stem the popular tide of that era. However, when the Gann limit was reached in the late 1980s and produced tax rebates, teachers' unions and the broader educational establishment then successfully promoted Proposition 98 (and later Proposition 111), with formulas for state spending on K–14 education that effectively gutted the Gann limit.[12]

Table 2 uses contract data to show the key California unions in the public sector. The data, from a file maintained by the U.S. Department of Labor, refer to union contracts covering 1,000 or more workers.[13] It is apparent that in terms of union coverage, the dominant union is the Service Employees International Union (SEIU). Other important players are the unions representing teachers (especially the California Teachers Association), AFSCME, and the independent union representing prison guards (CCPOA). Some of the smaller unions are essentially local and may play significant roles in the politics of certain jurisdictions. Public sector unions have mainly been supporters of Democrats but, particularly in the case of the prison guards, can be pragmatic and may lend support to candidates of either party if they seem friendly to union positions.

It might be expected in a system of direct democracy that unions—as large membership organizations—would be at the forefront of using ballot propositions to further their goals. Initiatives, whether at the state or local level, require gathering signatures and then campaigning and voting drives. Large membership organizations would seem to have advantages in such efforts. However, with some notable exceptions such as Proposition 98

TABLE 2
Major California Public Sector Unions (Percentage of Workers)

Union	Percentage of Workers
Service Employees International Union	42.5%
California Teachers Association (NEA affiliation)	8.2%
American Federation of State, County and Municipal Employees	5.8%
United Teachers Los Angeles (CTA/NEA and AFT/CFT affiliation)	4.2%
California Federation of Teachers (AFT affiliation)	4.1%
California Correctional Peace Officers Association	3.7%
Communications Workers of America	2.9%
Coalition of University Employees	2.6%
Statewide Law Enforcement Association	2.0%
San Bernardino Public Employees Association	1.8%
International Union of Operating Engineers	1.7%
International Association of Fire Fighters	1.4%
Association for Los Angeles Deputy Sheriffs	1.3%
Professional Employees in California Government	1.3%
International Union of Police Associations	1.1%
Los Angeles Police Protective League	1.1%
Orange County Employees Association	1.0%
Amalgamated Transit Union	0.9%
Laborers International Union of North America	0.9%
California Association of Highway Patrolmen	0.8%
California Association of Psychiatric Technicians	0.8%
International Brotherhood of Electrical Workers	0.7%
Engineers and Architects Association (AFT affiliation)	0.6%
International Association of Machinists and Aerospace Workers	0.6%
Municipal Employees Association (San Diego)	0.6%
United Transportation Union	0.6%
All Others	6.8%

Source: U.S. Department of Labor major contract files available at http://www.dol.gov/olms/regs/compliance/cba/index.htm.

described previously, unions have not been enthusiastic users of direct democracy.[14] They have tended to operate in a defensive mode when propositions they do not like appear on a ballot—for example, defeating so-called paycheck protection initiatives in 1998 and 2005.[15]

In 2011, they persuaded Governor Jerry Brown to sign a law moving ballot propositions to the November 2012 general election and removing them from the presidential primary (which would be dominated by Republicans). Part of the motivation was to shift the odds against voter approval of a spending cap ballot proposition and a paycheck protection measure.[16] In effect, unions were using the legislative route to constrain direct democracy.

One result of union aversion to proactive direct democracy has been that the most enthusiastic supporters of the system of ballot propositions tend to be on the populist–right end of the political spectrum. Of course, both public and private unions have reasons to want to influence government action. But unions tend to focus on promoting and supporting candidates and on traditional lobbying. For example, various Hollywood unions successfully pushed for tax breaks at the state level to counteract similar breaks and subsidies for movie and TV producers offered in other states and countries. At the local level, unions have also pushed living wage ordinances for private providers to governments.[17]

Construction unions have particular interests in local development projects that are given public support through tax-increment financing and other devices. A state attempt to take some of the local funding by redevelopment agencies from property tax-increment financing and use it instead for the state's general-fund projects became a major battle in the 2011–2012 budget, as noted later in this chapter. Construction unions also seek to have local governments use project labor agreements, which indirectly favor union workers, when those governments fund infrastructure projects.[18] Obviously, public sector unions have a more direct interest in government spending programs that pay for the wages and benefits of their members. That interest comes into sharp focus when budget crises occur.

Unions, public and private, can be fractious. Hollywood unions, especially those representing above-the-line professionals (actors and writers), are known for internecine internal disputes and wide variations in the degree to which they cooperate with one another in negotiations. The SEIU, which has both public and private sector membership, has been distracted by a breakaway health care local. Purely public sector unions have their ups and downs in terms of influence. The CCPOA, which represents prison guards, was seen at one time as very influential in Sacramento. But expensive litigation with past union officials, combined with the budgetary impact of the Great Recession and court decisions demanding a downsizing of the state prisoner population, put the CCPOA largely on the defensive. There is a sense that politics is local with regard to organized labor in California. National divisions, such as the split between the AFL-CIO and the Change to Win Federation, do not seem to have had much effect on local activity. At the state level, unions have worked together, or not, depending on their perceived interests and not on their affiliation.

Public Versus Private Employment Response to Economic Downturns
Although economic downturns reduce tax revenue, the public sector in California reacts with a lag to downturns compared to the private sector. Figures 3, 4, and 5 illustrate the response of private employment and public employment (state and local) to the recession of the early 1990s (end of Cold War), the dot-com bust, and the housing bust. Each chart is indexed so that the year containing the start of the downturn is set to 100 for nonfarm private employment, state employment, and local employment. In each case, private sector employment declines quickly, but there is a lag in the public sector response—and the percentage decline when it occurs is generally less than in private employment.

FIGURE 3
California Nonfarm Employment Trend 1990–2001:
Private, State, and Local (1990 = 100)

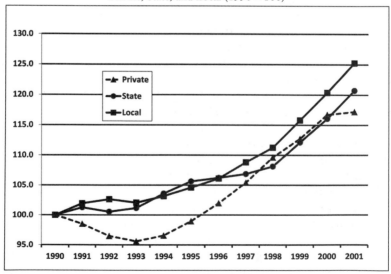

Source: U.S. Bureau of Labor Statistics. State data available at http://data.bls.gov/cgi-bin/surveymost?la.

FIGURE 4
California Nonfarm Employment Trend 2001–2007:
Private, State, and Local (2001 = 100)

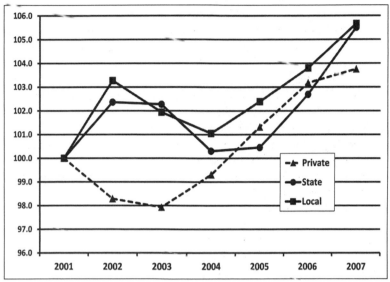

Source: U.S. Bureau of Labor Statistics. State data available at http://data.bls.gov/cgi-bin/surveymost?la.

FIGURE 5
California Nonfarm Employment Trend 2007–2010:
Private, State, and Local (2007 = 100)

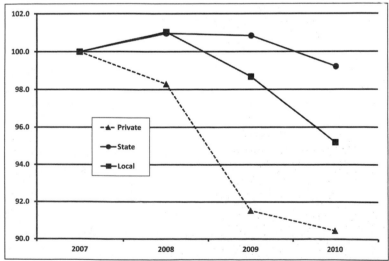

Source: U.S. Bureau of Labor Statistics. State data available at http://data.bls.gov/cgi-bin/surveymost?la.

The lag occurs because much of government production (services such as police, fire, and education) is not directly linked to the business cycle and in some areas (e.g., social services) demand for government production increases during periods of economic distress. In addition, government entities can run down past reserves to finance continued services and employment and, within limits, use debt finance. Finally, some funding for public employment at the state and local level comes from federal sources.

In the aftermath of the Great Recession, stimulus funding from the federal government helped delay and mitigate state and local job reductions in California until the money ran out. Federal money came with various strings attached. There were maintenance-of-effort requirements so that recipient governments would not simply shift regular expenses to support by the federal subsidy. The object of the stimulus program was to increase government activity beyond the baseline, not just support the baseline level. In the case of state-funded home care aides in California, federal rules—after litigation—blocked wage cuts the state attempted to impose.

California is not unique in exhibiting a public sector employment lag when the economy turns down. As Figure 6 indicates, during the Great Recession, California's public sector was arguably more responsive than the U.S. norm, perhaps because California was harder hit than most states. However, even that observation requires some qualification. As Figure 7 shows, at the peak of the housing boom, California's unemployment rates were low and in line with the national average across various state regions. The one exception was the state's Central Valley (represented by Fresno County on the chart), a rural area with a great deal of poverty and chronically high unemployment.

As the Great Recession took hold, unemployment rose in all regions, but the dispersion among regions increased. The Inland Empire region in Southern California had been a center of outlying housing construction, and with the housing and mortgage bust, its unemployment rate shot up.[19] The high-tech Silicon Valley was less affected than the rest of the state because its key industry is geared to the global economy much more than to local developments. As a result, the public versus private employment trend deviation played out differently in the two areas. In the Silicon Valley (Figure 8), private sector employment declined but by *less* than in the public sector. In the Inland Empire (Figure 9), the pattern was reversed.

Part of the story behind this mirror-image effect is linked to California's fiscal arrangements. Especially after Proposition 13 drastically cut local

FIGURE 6
U.S. Nonfarm Employment Trend 2007–2010:
Private, State, and Local (2007 = 100)

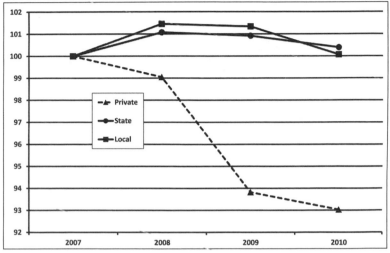

Source: U.S. Bureau of Labor Statistics. National data available at http://data.bls.gov/cgi-bin/
surveymost?ce.

FIGURE 7
Unemployment Rates by Area: 2006–2010

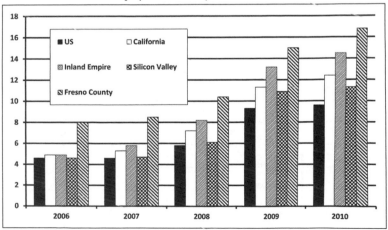

Source: California Employment Development Department. Local area data available at http://
www.labormarketinfo.edd.ca.gov.

FIGURE 8
Silicon Valley Nonfarm Employment Trend 2007–2010:
Private, State, and Local (2007 = 100)

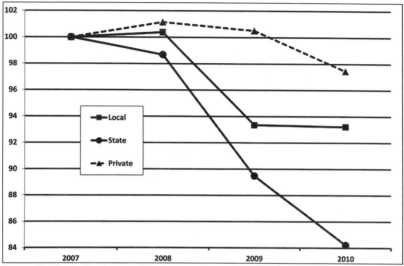

Source: California Employment Development Department. Local area data available at http://www.labormarketinfo.edd.ca.gov.

FIGURE 9
Inland Empire Nonfarm Employment Trend 2007–2010:
Private, State, and Local (2007 = 100)

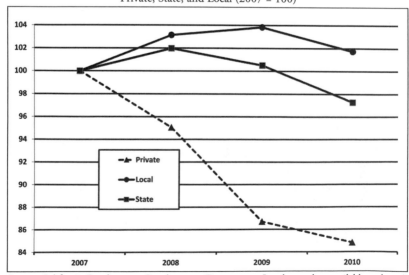

Source: California Employment Development Department. Local area data available at http://www.labormarketinfo.edd.ca.gov.

property taxes, local governments, particularly school districts, became heavily dependent on state financing. Thus, whether a school district is in the affluent Silicon Valley or the depressed Inland Empire, its budget reflects the broader state budget and economy. State finance therefore can be, at least in relative terms, either a cushion against or an exaggerator of the business cycle; it tends to spread booms and busts in local areas statewide. For example, in the post–Cold War recession of the early 1990s, the declining aerospace industry was largely located in Southern California. But because the decline affected an important region of the larger state economy, school districts and other local jurisdictions in Northern California were affected by the general adverse impact on the state's overall budget.

Despite these regional variations, a general perception that the public sector is not doing its share can easily develop due to the public–private deviation in job trends. There can be political tensions and resentment as a result of the public–private contrast. Because of the overall relatively liberal–centrist political orientation of California, however, there was no overt Wisconsin-type political reaction in the state.[20] There were no serious proposals at the state level in California to end public sector collective bargaining, but there were moves in some conservative jurisdictions in that direction. Most notable was the affluent City of Costa Mesa in Southern California, whose city council went on an aggressive campaign of outsourcing and thereby stirred up an outsized controversy that attracted statewide and national interest.[21]

Retirement Benefits

In other jurisdictions and at the state level, there was a battle about government collective bargaining on the public pension issue, which served as a proxy for the larger issue of public unions and bargaining. Even in left-leaning San Francisco there were ballot initiatives and agitation about public pensions that extended to some prominent Democrats.[22] City of Los Angeles voters approved various constraints on police and fire pensions and retiree health care in March 2011.

At the state level, California has three major pension systems. CalPERS (California Public Employment Retirement System) is the largest of the three, with $236 billion in assets as of mid-2011. It covers state employees, except the University of California, plus employees of various localities that use its coverage. CalSTRS (California State Teachers Retirement System) has about $147 billion and covers schools. Finally, there is UCRP, the University of California Retirement Plan, with about $42 billion.

All three are significantly underfunded, and thus each poses long-run challenges to the state. However, it is not the case that there is a liberal–

conservative divide in terms of pension underfunding in California. The City of San Diego, a conservative Republican jurisdiction, became something of a poster child for poor pension management of its municipal plan even before the Great Recession. As the issue became apparent, it roiled San Diego politics. There were analogous developments in conservative Orange County, including a political battle over whether the county should be spending its money on litigation to undo past pension promises.

Accrued pension benefits in California are vested rights. However, the mix of employer and employee contributions and the level of those contributions are not fixed. Pension fixes at the state and local levels have generally involved increasing employee contributions and in some cases creating a lower tier of benefits for new hires. Public sector unions have been on the defensive with regard to retirement benefits because of the decline in the private sector of defined benefit (DB) plans, which are the norm in government. In the private sector, defined contribution (DC) plans have become the norm.

Defined benefit plans guarantee benefits by a formula typically based on years of service, age, and earnings history in the period prior to retirement. Retirees are thus shielded from the risk of the financial marketplace. The private sector now much more commonly uses DC plans, such as 401(k)s, which put the risk of investment performance on the employee. As in the case of employment trends, the public–private contrast in retirement programs has tended to put public sector unions in California on the defensive.

In terms of immediate budget impact, however, DB plans by their nature had only a minor role in state fiscal affairs. The large absolute amounts in the plans mean that remedies for underfunding can be deferred. For example, the plan for the University of California—even if there were no future contributions and the existing assets earned only a modest return—would likely be able to continue payouts for perhaps two decades.

To be sure, that approach (i.e., deliberate underfunding until the plan assets were dissipated) would not be good pension management policy or good fiscal policy. From the employee perspective, a fully funded pension trust fund is a guarantee that promises made will be kept. From a fiscal viewpoint, funding today's pension promises today is in keeping with the view that current expenses should not be charged to future taxpayers. But the fact that a defined benefit plan allows deferral of the funding of current promises illustrates that pension modifications can be deferred during budget crises. Some local jurisdictions, toying with the idea of switching to defined contribution to improve their budget positions, seemed surprised by the discovery that the C in DC stood for "contribution." In a defined contribution world, by definition you have to make the contribution—it is not deferrable.

Apart from the structure of retirement benefits, it is bad economics to single out particular portions of an employee benefit package without looking at the entire package. There are many complicated elements in comparing the value of benefits, which will vary with the career history of individual employees. However, to the extent that standardization is possible, it appears that California public employees earn pay packages roughly comparable to those in the private sector once adjustments for individual characteristics are made. Even a study commissioned by a group pushing for pension cutbacks did not find major overall discrepancies.[23]

Average results, however, do not mean that particular groups are not out of line, either on the positive or negative side. There is considerable heterogeneity among California employees. Some are covered by Social Security, for example, while others are not. Generally, safety workers such as first responders have the most generous pensions—perhaps because of positive public attitudes toward police and firefighters. And even when total compensation is in line with the private sector, there can be underfunding. Employees are paid in part with retirement promises. Whether those promises are being properly funded is another matter.

Complicating the pension issue in California has been the question of governance. In some cases, there have been conflicts of interest and scandals regarding pension administrators and those seeking investment business from the funds, particularly at CalPERS. There have also been issues of large pension payouts to individuals where pension spiking or inappropriately high salaries have been paid. These instances— particularly a salary/pension scandal in the small Southern California city of Bell that left the city teetering on insolvency—received wide public attention in the news media. The result has been a miasma of pension problems—some administrative, some corrupt, some regarding adequate funding, and some regarding individual pension abuse.

The public does not necessarily segregate one pension issue from another. What results is an overall, but vague, impression of a pension problem. That is, at the level of the general public—as opposed to politicians and policy wonks—it is not clear that there is a deep sense of a pension problem, absent someone pushing the issue. When the California Field Poll questioned voters about their attitudes toward public pensions in 2009 and 2011, more respondents thought that public pension entitlements were either about right or not generous enough than thought them excessive. Yet when the pollsters went on to suggest remedies such as pension reductions for a problem many respondents evidently thought did not exist, there was generally support for remedies. Presumably, if a pollster suggests a remedy, respondents suspect there must be a problem that requires a remedy.[24]

Table 3 summarizes data from the two Field pension polls. The polls in 2009 and 2011 were separated by the 2010 gubernatorial election in which the pension issue was highlighted as a problem. Thus, there was a shift in the direction of regarding public pensions as too generous. Even in 2011, as already noted, more respondents thought pensions were about right or not generous enough than thought them too generous. Yet in 2009—the year in which the poll response was more favorable to public pensions—when pollsters suggested a cap on pensions, majorities favored them (except for those voters who characterized themselves as liberal).

It may not be surprising that conservatives have less favorable attitudes than liberals about public pensions. But the age effect is interesting. Older voters are more likely than younger voters to view public pensions as too generous, a finding that suggests seniors who worked in the private sector are comparing their actual or impending retirement income with their perceptions of public pensions. It might be noted that the pollsters did not attempt to measure in any kind of dollar format what voters thought public pensions were. Similarly, issues of funding were not explored. A pension could be too generous and yet adequately funded. Or it could be too stingy but underfunded. It could be well managed or poorly managed. None of these distinctions were explored by the pollsters, and they also tend to be lost in public forums.

Governor Jerry Brown introduced a 12-point plan for public pensions (state and local) in late October 2011. Many of the details were not fleshed out. In broad terms, the proposal involved a two-tier approach, with new employees in a hybrid plan that would be part defined benefit and part defined contribution. As initially posed, parts of the Brown plan would require a vote of the electorate that could occur only if the legislature placed the plan on the ballot or the plan was put on the ballot via an initiative. The former route would require bipartisan support, and the latter would need $1 to $2 million for payments to signature-gathering firms to accomplish. Hence, the fate of the plan at this writing is unclear. Democrats in the legislature provided a cautious response. Republican responses ranged from "does not go far enough" to expressing encouragement. The largest state union, SEIU Local 1000, issued a statement that was intentionally noncommittal and nonconfrontational, indicating the governor should be thanked for providing "a good starting point."[25]

TABLE 3
California Field Poll on Registered Voter Attitudes Toward Public Pensions

	Too Generous*	Favor Cap**
All Respondents	32% [42%]***	59%
Male	40 [52]	60
Female	24 [34]	59
Political Viewpoint		
Strongly conservative	9 [55]	72
Moderately conservative	35 [56]	64
Middle of the road	31 [40]	62
Moderately liberal	20 [39]	47
Strongly liberal	14 [22]	42
Age		
18–29 years	14 [28]	72
30–39 years	26 [40]	53
40–49 years	30 [42]	56
50–64 years	42 [47]	58
65 and older	38 [52]	59
Union Status		
Yes, any	24 [30]	60
No	34 [47]	59

*Do you think that the pension benefits that most state and local government workers in California currently receive at retirement are too generous, about right, or not generous enough?

**I am going to read some proposals to change the benefits paid to newly hired state and local government workers at retirement. For each, please tell me whether you favor or oppose this proposal: Set an upper limit on the total amount that a newly hired government worker can receive in pension benefits at retirement. Do you favor or oppose this proposal?

***Numbers in brackets are from the 2011 poll (conducted February 28–March 14, 2011); other numbers are from the 2009 poll (con-ducted September 18–October 6, 2009).

Source: The California Field Poll makes special tabulations available through the *Sacramento Bee*. The 2011 results are at http://media. sacbee.commedia/2011/03/16/14/316tabs.source.prod_affiliate.4.pdf. The 2009 special tabulation results, dated October 16, 2009, are no longer online. Less extensive results for both dates directly from Field are at http://field.com/fieldpollonline/subscribers/Rls2369.pdf and http://field.com/field pollonline/subscribers/Rls2318.pdf.

As in the case of pension reforms aimed at unfunded liabilities, immediate budget savings are limited when the policy change focuses on new hires. However, the Brown plan involved a requirement that *current* employees contribute to their pension programs on a 50/50 basis. In most California plans, the employee share of contributions is below 50%— sometimes well below. For example, CalPERS reports an average one-third/two-thirds ratio for the employee versus employer share. The issue of pensions and the budget will be discussed again after a review of budget accounting.

Budget Accounting

It may seem odd to devote space to budget accounting methodology. In a sense, a public budget's condition is what it is, regardless of the accounting. However, accounting methodology is used by policy makers to judge budgetary health, or lack thereof, and to determine remedies for perceived fiscal problems. California is not unique in its budgetary accounting, but its experience indicates that the way the budget is depicted pushes policy in particular directions. Generally, a legislator told that his or her jurisdiction is running a surplus will think that there is no problem to fix. Alternatively, if the situation is described as a deficit, the reverse will be perceived.

Two important features of state and local accounting are not widely understood. The first is that terms such as *surplus* and *deficit* do not—or need not—mean what they do at the federal level. The second is that although state and local accounting is subject to rules promulgated by the Governmental Accounting Standards Board (GASB), those standards do not apply to the budgets legislators see and approve. Instead they apply to the information provided to potential investors in prospectuses when securities are issued. Given the second point, as sovereign entities, state and local governments are free to use whatever accounting they like for their own internal planning and legislative purposes.

To understand the problem, note that at the state and local levels there are typically various funds kept separately and treated in a way that loosely corresponds to a household checking account. The common practice is to have a general fund that covers the ongoing operations of the jurisdiction. Usually when terms such as *surplus* or *deficit* are applied, they refer just to the general fund. But there are also special funds for particular purposes. For example, as is the case in California, the gasoline tax and certain other motor vehicle–related taxes and fees go into a special fund for transportation expenses such as road maintenance and construction. But, again as in California, there can be hundreds of other funds, some quite small, earmarked for particular purposes.

Special funds often do not have a clear time dimension. For example, constructing a road may take several years. A public authority will approve the project and then expend funds as needed. Revenues will arrive to fund the project or, particularly for a capital project, there may be borrowing to support it. The controlling authority needs to be sure that, whether from a net revenue inflow or from borrowed money, there is a sufficient reserve to pay ongoing bills. In short, the key indicator for the controlling authority to watch is the reserve—a stock measure. Like a household managing its checkbook, the controlling authority must avoid overdrawing its account (having a negative reserve).

The general fund, because it finances ongoing expenses, is typically enacted on a fiscal year basis (although some jurisdictions use two years as the relevant period). Most of what flows into the general fund is tax and fee revenue for that year. Most of what flows out is the ongoing expenses for the year such as salaries of teachers, police, and other public employees; transfer payments to individuals (welfare); payments to providers with whom the jurisdiction contracts; and transfers to lower levels of government.

There are three components of the budget process: two flow measures (the inflows and outflows) and one stock measure (the reserve) to be forecast and budgeted. The projected reserve in the fund at the end of the fiscal year is determined by the reserve at the start of the year plus the *net* inflow (which can be positive or negative). There is a mix, therefore, of flow and stock measures that gives rise to a confusion in terminology, which then affects fiscal policy.

At the federal level, there is no reserve. When the federal deficit (or surplus—there have been some!) is discussed, the concept is unambiguously a flow concept. A deficit means less is flowing in than is flowing out. A surplus is the reverse. At the state and local levels, however, and particularly in California, the flow and stock distinction tends to be lost. A situation in which inflows are less than outflows might be referred to as a surplus or balanced as long as the reserve remains positive. (The reserve will be falling in such a situation but may not be less than zero at the end of the period.) Similarly, if inflows exceed outflows but the reserve is projected to be negative at the end of the period, the budget might be described as in deficit or unbalanced. (If the reserve is negative at the beginning of the period and inflows exceed outflow, it will be less negative but not necessarily positive at the end of the period.)

The flow–stock confusion at the state and local levels can affect policy. For example, in the 2000–2001 fiscal year, California had a significant reserve that had built up during the dot-com boom. But the economy was turning down, and the state was running a small deficit in the federal sense (outflow greater than inflow). At the time, however, state officials were insisting that they would deal with the consequences of a disastrous electricity deregulation plan by spending money from the perceived surplus on electricity. A colleague and I warned in an editorial that if California ran a deficit at the peak of the cycle, it would likely face a budget crisis as the economy worsened.[26] Then-Governor Davis's finance director replied that there was no problem and that we were in error—the state was actually in surplus. What he meant was that there was still a positive reserve. The ultimate consequence of this confusion was the predicted budget crisis and, ultimately, the recall of the governor.

Similar confusion has characterized the periods leading up to and in the aftermath of the Great Recession. Even before the Great Recession officially began, California was running a deficit in the federal sense, but the budget was described as balanced until the inevitable budget crisis occurred. Attempts to remedy the crisis have also been colored by accounting methodology. Once the reserve was negative, any budget that did not lead to a projected positive reserve at the end of the fiscal year was described as a deficit or unbalanced. That approach effectively means that fiscal policy must aim at correcting the negative reserve within a fiscal year period; it rules out the possibility of an alternative policy to consider a multi-year workout plan.

Apart from its influence on fiscal policy, the stock–flow confusion at the state and local level may be part of the story behind the lag in public employment response to economic downturns. The confusion during the downturn tends to mask the fiscal problem since the terminology can indicate budgets are in balance until the last penny of the reserve is gone. That impression delays the urgency of a response until there is a full-blown crisis when the reserve goes negative and cash flow problems begin to be felt. When there is a crisis, the stock–flow confusion suggests that there must be a very fast resolution of the crisis—which can lead to layoffs even in the face of steady budgetary improvements. If a budget already is in a negative reserve position, the description of it as being in deficit even when there is a surplus in the federal sense of the word takes the option of a multi-year solution off the table.

Finally, note that the call for legally binding rainy day funds is partly a by-product of current state and local accounting practices. Efforts to create such rainy day funds have been a feature of California state politics over the years, particularly during the governorship of Arnold Schwarzenegger (2003–2011). In effect, the formulas proposed for rainy day funds divert some of the inflow that otherwise would fatten the reserve during good times into a separate pot. They seek to avert legislators' eyes from the growing reserve. Assuming a separate rainy day reserve is built, flow from the rainy day reserve into the regular reserve during hard times might allow a multi-year workout for a fiscal problem rather than a one-year resolution. But the formula budget or rainy day approach might not be needed if state and local governments carefully distinguished stocks from flows.

California's Fiscal Adjustment to the Great Recession

Figure 10 depicts the cash flows into and out of the California general fund and the reserve in the fund. Except for fiscal year 2011–2012, the data are actual results after the fact.[27] The data for fiscal 2011–2012 are the official estimates for the budget enacted in June 2011.[28] After-the-fact data do not reflect the original budget proposals, which are made by the governor in early January before the start of the fiscal year. The original budget proposal is typically modified in May by the governor—the "May revise"—to reflect updated figures on revenues and spending as well as political feasibility. Once a budget is enacted, however, what happens after the fact may not be what was planned. In short, Figure 10 omits the *Sturm und Drang* that ultimately led to the actual results. But it does provide some insight into the degree of fiscal adaptation to the Great Recession and its aftermath.

Some key points can be seen on the chart. First, California found itself in deficit as early as the 2006–2007 fiscal year (i.e., *before* the Great Recession). That fact is a reflection of the underlying problem of a structural deficit—a deficit that is not corrected by good economic times, which, as noted earlier, developed in California in the early 1990s. Second,

FIGURE 10
General Fund Cash Flows and Reserve ($ Billions)

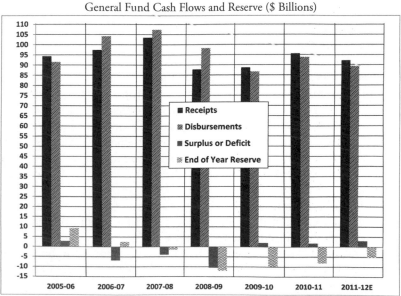

E = Estimate
Source: California State Controller; California Department of Finance. See endnotes 27 and 28.

the positive reserve in the general fund shown on the chart in the earlier years was present only because incoming Governor Schwarzenegger borrowed his way out of the budget crisis left by his predecessor. So, even at the business cycle peak with an ostensibly positive reserve, the state was living off borrowed funds.

Third, the state did make a major fiscal correction in response to the Great Recession. Revenue fell very sharply during fiscal year 2008–2009, producing a large deficit. But by the following year and in the year after that, the state ran budget surpluses on a cash flow basis, thanks to temporary tax increases and spending cuts. There were budget tricks of various types in that period, but these measures worked well enough. There was a cash flow crisis in summer 2009, which led to the state issuing IOUs for some expenses and for tax refunds, but those IOUs were paid off within a few months.

Fourth, the budget projection for fiscal year 2011–2012 shows a drop in revenue because the temporary tax increases enacted during the 2008–2009 fiscal year expired. Even so, the state planned to run a budget surplus. Because the governor would do the accounting, the fiscal objective, driven by the budget accounting methodology described in the previous section, was to end with a positive reserve. On a projected cash basis, however, the reserve will not end in positive territory at the close of fiscal 2011–2012, despite what would then be three years of budget surpluses.

Fiscal and Labor Adjustments

Officially, the Great Recession began in late 2007. Its downward pace was greatly accelerated by the financial crisis in mid-to-late 2008. Thus, much of the budgetary impact was felt during the governorship of Republican Arnold Schwarzenegger, who took office in October 2003 in a recall election, was re-elected in 2006, and left office in January 2011, succeeded by Democrat Jerry Brown. Schwarzenegger's success in the 2003 recall was largely the result of his predecessor's budget crisis. What Schwarzenegger inherited from his predecessor, Democrat Gray Davis, was a fiscal workout plan.

By the time of the recall, the United States and California economies had been recovering, and the state budget situation was improving. But there was a large overhang in the form of a big negative reserve in the general fund. This overhang was being financed by short-term borrowing from external and internal markets. Internal borrowing essentially means that the general fund borrows from other state funds. To the extent that the internal option is exhausted and external borrowing is needed, the state becomes subject to financial market forces.

At the end of fiscal year 2003–2004—which would have been Governor Davis's responsibility had it not been for the recall, the state would have needed to roll over its short-term external debt. It could have done so but only at increasingly punitive interest rates. Therefore, Davis had developed a complicated plan to refinance on a long-term basis. The complication was the state's constitution, which requires a vote of the people for issuance of long-term debt and bans long-term borrowing to fund ongoing operating expenses. Long-term borrowing is seen as appropriate for long-term capital projects as long as the electorate approves.

To get around the constitution's two hurdles, Davis proposed an elaborate scheme known as the triple flip, whose details are unimportant. What is important is that any attempt to avoid constitutional strictures was bound to be legally questionable, and taxpayer lawsuits were a certainty. Thus, although there was a Davis plan for long-term refinance—essentially a multi-year workout approach—it is doubtful that the bonds underlying that plan could have been sold. Investors would have had to take the risk that a court decision would declare the bond flotation unconstitutional, potentially making their bonds worthless.

A New Governor and a Year of Good Feeling

Incoming Governor Schwarzenegger inherited the Davis plan but capitalized on his initial popularity to enlarge the Davis plan (raising the proposed borrowing from about $10 billion to $15 billion) and to legalize it by taking it to the electorate in a special election. Two related propositions (Propositions 57 and 58) were approved by voters in 2004, which modified the state constitution. They allowed long-term financing for ongoing operations on a one-time basis and added loose provisions for dealing with future budgetary emergencies.

The legislature had approved placing the two propositions on the ballot as part of a bipartisan compromise on their terms. Then the governor and most of the other state officials (Democrats) sold the plan as a one-shot remedy after which the state would supposedly "throw away the credit card." Public sector unions that might otherwise have faced member layoffs endorsed the plan. Thus, calendar year 2004 was an era of good feeling with high popularity ratings for the governor. The budget crisis seemed to end, and the public was treated to a bipartisan deal.

Labor Confrontation

The era of good feeling came to a screeching halt in 2005, dubbed the "Year of Reform" by the new governor.[29] Governor Schwarzenegger harbored the notion that the main problem in state politics was the influence of special interests, a view much in line with California's historic progressivism. To him, however, the key special interest was public sector labor unions, which he saw as pushing for state spending and making the state prone to budget crises. Through the initiative process, he ultimately put four propositions on the ballot in a special election called for November 2005.

Only one of four dealt with the budget directly. Proposition 76, written by the heads of the state Chamber of Commerce and the California Business Roundtable, would have diverted revenue surges (as had occurred during the dot-com boom) into a rainy day fund and would have given the governor emergency powers to cut the budget if the legislature failed to act. It would have overridden features of Proposition 98, heavily supported by the California Teachers Association (CTA), that earmark funding by formula for K–14 education.

Also on the ballot was a paycheck protection initiative, Proposition 75, which was aimed at public sector unions. Proposition 74 increased the amount of time schoolteachers needed to work to earn tenure from two to five years. It was clearly aimed at the CTA. Finally, Proposition 77 took redistricting out of the hands of the legislature and put it into the hands of a panel of retired judges.[30] Early polling suggested that the budget and the redistricting initiatives were dead on arrival. The other two might have had a chance, but the massive opposition campaign mounted largely by unions sank all four. It appears that both sides, pro and con, spent a total of about $150 million on the campaign. One residue of the 2005 episode was that there was little trust left between public sector unions or their allies (the Democratic majority in the legislature) and the governor.

The Interregnum

With hindsight, the period 2006 and 2007 can be viewed as an inter-regnum between the governor's political crisis of 2005, which tanked his popularity, and the renewed budget crisis that the Great Recession brought. In early 2006, with his popularity much diminished, Governor Schwarzenegger faced uncertain re-election prospects. Given California's electoral makeup, he would need to win back the support of Democrats and independents. In his State of the State speech in January 2006, he apologized for having called the special election and then put forward a plan to renew the state's infrastructure (to be financed by borrowing). Infrastructure construction, particularly with no immediate cost, was appealing to the electorate. The bonds needed were approved by voters in the general election of November 2006, which also gave the governor a second term.

Increased infrastructure spending was something unions could support, especially in the building trades but also in the public sector.

And in 2007, the governor pushed yet another Big Idea—a universal health care plan for California modeled after the Massachusetts plan. Like the Massachusetts plan (and later the Obama plan), the Schwarzenegger plan featured various employer mandates and an individual mandate for coverage.[31]

Various factors contributed to the ultimate defeat of the governor's health plan. But before it died, the plan was strongly endorsed by the national SEIU. Other unions, which initially wanted just an employer mandate, were eventually persuaded by the SEIU to be neutral. Only the California Nurses Association, which insisted on a single-payer approach, was strongly opposed as the plan evolved. The health plan did pass the state assembly but died in the state senate in early 2008, with the key opposition argument being the oncoming state budget crisis. As Figure 10 shows, the state budget was already in deficit at the time and was running down the reserve that the Schwarzenegger 2004 borrowing plan had restocked.

Renewed Crisis: 2008–2009

Elsewhere, I described in detail the ongoing budget deterioration that followed the health plan failure in California and the complicated role of organized labor as the budget crisis unfolded.[32] There was an extended period during summer 2008 when the governor and the legislature were unable to enact a budget and no budget was in place. Partly as a way of pressuring state unions to in turn put pressure on legislative Democrats, the governor ordered that state workers should be paid only the minimum wage (to comply with labor law), with the remainder of their pay to be forthcoming only when a budget was enacted.

The state controller (who is the state's paymaster) refused the order. Litigation that was resolved only after a budget was in place generally favored the governor's position. However, no one was paid the minimum wage because of the litigation delay. And the final court decision left open a path for a future refusal by the controller, an argument that the state's antiquated computers could not be programmed to pay the minimum wage. (That opening was in fact revisited during a similar dispute in 2010.)

As the stalemate proceeded during summer 2008, the governor eventually gave ground and agreed to consider a sales tax increase. But legislative Republicans would not agree. In the eventual deal, no tax increase was provided. All parties to the deal understood that the budget accord would have to be reopened midyear, and it was.

The 2008 budget deal was reopened in early 2009 as part of a package proposed by the governor intended to cover the remainder of fiscal year 2008–2009 and the coming fiscal year 2009–2010. The governor imposed

furloughs on state workers. There was litigation over whether such furloughs could be ordered for the staffs of other elected officials, such as the
state controller and the treasurer, or in programs not funded by the state.
That issue was not finally decided by the courts until after Governor
Schwarzenegger left office. (It was decided in favor of the governor.)

What finally emerged in February 2009, after a few necessary Republican
legislative votes were negotiated, was a set of temporary tax increases.
These increases were to expire in 2011, but the February deal put further
extensions of the increases beyond 2011 on the ballot in a special election
scheduled for May 2009. Other propositions placed on that ballot were
to facilitate borrowing against the state lottery and diversion of taxes earmarked for child welfare and mental health to the general fund.

The February 2009 deal had several effects that went beyond the
immediate budget concerns. Included among the tax extension propositions was a state spending cap determined by a formula—something
Republicans generally have supported and Democrats have not. Also
included was an agreement to put a proposition on the ballot to change
the primary system so that legislative candidates would run in top-two
nonpartisan primaries.[33] Proponents argued that such a system would
favor more centrist candidates who would be less likely to produce stale-
mates over budgetary and other matters.

As a consequence of the February 2009 deal, the few Republicans who
went along with the accord were punished. The Republican legislative
leaders in both houses lost their positions, decreasing the chance of any
future bipartisan accord in future budget negotiations. The top-two
primary system was eventually approved by voters, thus changing the
electoral system. As the May 2009 special election on extending the temporary tax increases approached, the labor movement was split. On one
hand, there was a chance for more state revenue. On the other hand, there
was the disliked spending cap. As a result of the split, the pro-extension
campaign was offset by a strong opposition effort, and the tax extensions
failed. Given the rejection of the extensions, the outcome of the May 2009
election set calendar year 2011—when a new governor would take office—
as a likely year for strife over the state budget.

IOU Season, the Post-May 2009 Budget Crisis, and Arnold's Last Stand

More immediately, however, the voter rejection of the substantive
propositions in May 2009 was taken by Governor Schwarzenegger as a
sign that the electorate would support deep cuts in the budget.[34] He produced a new budget proposal that included such drastic measures as an
end to the Healthy Families program (health insurance for children of

the working poor). Not surprisingly, the result was a stalemate in the legislature and the issuance of IOUs by the state for certain tax refunds and vendor payments during summer 2009.

Technically, however, there was a budget in place as a result of the February 2009 multi-year deal, so the earlier question of paying state workers only the minimum wage, absent a budget, did not come up in summer 2009. Eventually, a budget revision was enacted with more cuts and layoffs. The governor imposed further cuts via line item vetoes that were challenged in court unsuccessfully.[35] And the stage was set for yet another budget battle when the governor, leaving office in January 2011, issued his budget proposal for fiscal year 2010–2011.

The 2010–2011 budget process took place with a gubernatorial election in the background and a continuing budget crisis. Governor Schwarzenegger, a lame-duck governor increasingly disliked by members of his own party, sought to curry favor with the Obama administration from time to time, hoping for fiscal aid from Washington. But beyond the general stimulus funding that went to all states, special assistance to California never came. At the end of his second term, Governor Schwarzenegger left office in a position similar to his predecessor Gray Davis, who had been pushed out in the 2003 recall: Schwarzenegger was equally unpopular and left a legacy of accumulated debt.[36]

As has been noted earlier, the 2009–2010 and 2010–2011 budgets were in official surplus, but past debt and the problem of temporary taxes slated to expire in 2011 needed to be resolved. Thus, Schwarzenegger and his successor needed large budget surpluses—bigger than those actually achieved—to undo the legacy. And any quick resolution of the debt legacy was made difficult by a sluggish recovery in the aftermath of the housing bust which, like the earlier dot-com bust, disproportionately affected the state's economy.

Not surprisingly, when July 1, 2010, came, there was no state budget enacted or even in sight. The upshot was more furloughs and a resurrection of the minimum wage issue. By that time, the state controller had only one path of resistance against the governor's order to pay state workers the minimum wage. Litigation in prior episodes had left open only the argument that state computers were unable to make the change in a manner consistent with labor law. Even though no budget was enacted until October 2010, that tactic proved successful in stalling any actual minimum wage payments.

The minimum wage demand of the governor was mainly a device to push state unions to pressure the Democratic majority in the legislature and to obtain concessions from those unions. Although the savings tended to be less than advertised, unions that signed concessionary deals with the governor could ask for contractual terms that shielded them from future minimum wage payment threats.[37] And they did.

Voters Sample Whitman but Go for Brown

Until shortly before the November 2010 gubernatorial election, unions faced a significant risk that the new governor would be Republican Meg Whitman, a former eBay CEO who was willing to expend vast sums of her personal fortune on the campaign. Whitman called for an end to defined benefit pensions except for public safety workers. Generally, she made it clear that she would be tough on public sector unions.

Most unions, with the exception of some in public safety (given Whitman's pension exception), backed Democrat Jerry Brown even though he was slow to declare his candidacy officially.[38] Brown was vague about what he might do on pensions. He had been governor in the late 1970s and early 1980s and was famously mercurial in that era—and not always perceived as a friend to labor. Despite his slow start in the 2010 campaign and Whitman's supersized campaign spending, Brown had the advantage of a Democratic-leaning state and voter disenchantment with the idea that an outsider such as Whitman could solve the state's fiscal problems.

Now unpopular, Schwarzenegger had portrayed himself as an outsider in the 2003 recall, and the Democrats played up the similarities of Schwarzenegger and Whitman. As a result, Whitman distanced herself from Schwarzenegger to the point that he never endorsed her candidacy. Whitman also had to take stands, particularly on immigration, to appeal to the Republican right in the June primary, and her attempts to backtrack in the general election angered her base.

Nonetheless, opinion polls put Brown and Whitman in a virtual tie in September 2010. What seemed to turn the electorate against Whitman was the "Housekeeper-Gate" scandal. Whitman had employed a maid who turned out to be an illegal immigrant. She fired the woman, allegedly made the kind of remarks a billionaire should not make to a low-paid housekeeper, and was sued for back wages. In a TV interview, Whitman said that her former maid should be deported. The spectacle of a billionaire mistreating the help turned the polls against Whitman, and she lost badly given the money she had spent on the campaign: 54% to 41% (with the balance of votes going to minor party candidates). Indeed, Whitman received fewer votes than a proposition also on the November 2010 ballot to legalize marijuana (which also lost).[39]

There were other ballot propositions in November 2010 that were to have an impact on subsequent budgetary developments. Proposition 21 would have provided for an added motor vehicle fee of $18 per annum earmarked for state parks, some of which were threatened with closure.

California motorists would have been able to enter the parks for free had it passed. But it failed, and the result was taken as a sign that voters were not receptive to tax increases.

Proposition 22 was designed to restrict the state from raiding local government funding. Among the seemingly protected local entities were community redevelopment agencies. Such agencies rely on tax increment financing and other sources for local construction and infrastructure projects. This proposition passed but proved to have an unintended consequence, discussed later.

Proposition 25 also passed. It changed a Great Depression era requirement that state budgets had to be passed by a two-thirds' majority. Henceforth, the requirement would be only a simple majority. However, the requirement that tax increases could be enacted only by a two-thirds' legislative vote remained. Indeed, voters enacted Proposition 26, which tightened the tax versus fee distinction to prevent the legislature from relabeling taxes as fees in order to escape the two-thirds rule.

Proposition 25 contained a kicker to enhance its appeal to voters that would play a role in the drama of enacting a budget for 2011–2012. The legislature could pass a budget by majority vote as long as there were no tax increases, and it was "balanced" by some definition. But if they failed to pass a balanced budget, there was also a punishment. Legislators would lose a day's pay for each day beyond June 15, the constitutional deadline, that they failed to pass a budget.

How Now Brown?

As a gubernatorial candidate, Jerry Brown never said he wouldn't raise taxes.[40] But his campaign was based on a pledge that there would be no new taxes (or implicitly no extension of the expiring temporary tax increases) without a vote of the people. When he took office in January 2011 and presented his budget proposal for fiscal year 2011–2012, Brown did propose extending the expiring temporary taxes via a vote of the people. However, there were only two routes to such a vote. The legislature could put the tax extensions on the ballot or it could be done by initiative. Either way, it seemed important, at least initially, for the vote to occur before June 30, 2011. After that date, the tax extensions would become tax increases—and polling suggested these would be less likely to be approved.

Forgoing the Initiative Option

If it could be accomplished, the legislative route would avoid the cost of gathering signatures but would require a two-thirds' majority vote, which meant a few Republicans would have to go along. If a few Republicans could be persuaded to cooperate, Brown would have the advantage of billing his proposal as bipartisan. But that seeming advantage was questionable. At most, Brown might have obtained a few Republicans who would support having a vote but who would themselves urge voting no.

Either the legislative or initiative route would have to be completed in about three months to allow time for the administrative process to arrange a special election before June 30, 2011. Brown could have tried both routes simultaneously so that at least one might succeed. But he made a fateful decision to go only the legislative route despite Republican indications that either no deal was possible or would involve terms on a host of issues that Brown could not accept.

Forgoing a Budget from Hell

Brown could have provided two budgets: one assuming success in having a vote of the people on tax extensions and the other assuming a "budget from Hell" if the extensions were rejected. But there were fears that if a "budget from Hell" were made public, Democrats and public sector unions might defect and/or voters might feel the governor was threatening them. So Brown presented only a budget based on winning tax extensions and painted only a loose verbal picture of what an alternate "budget from Hell" might entail.

Forgoing a Multi-Year Approach

The final major choice Brown made was that he would define a deficit as anything that did not produce a positive reserve by June 30, 2012. As noted earlier, this common state and local fiscal approach means that even a surplus budget in the common English usage of that term (inflow greater than outflow) can be termed a deficit if it is not a big enough surplus to end with a positive reserve. As noted, this definition effectively takes a multi-year solution option off the table, although such an option might at least be considered. The Legislative Analyst's Office did point to the multi-year option and even provided some guidance as to how the approach might be undertaken.[41] But the governor did not go that route.

Realignment

Given his projected revenue needs, even assuming the tax extensions, Governor Brown looked for all sources he could find. One element of the budget was realignment, for instance, which meant pushing certain responsibilities to local government. The most controversial element was moving state prisoners guilty of certain nonviolent offenses to county-operated jails. Apart from dealing with the litigation on prison overcrowding that was forcing the issue, realignment had the benefit of making the state budget smaller and thus reducing funding guarantees to K–14 education under Proposition 98. Realignment was rationalized, however, on the basis of the benefits of local control and discretion. Helping realignment's prospect was the general weakening of the influence of the prison guards' union.

Picking a Fight over Redevelopment

Proposition 22, passed in 2010, made raiding local governments for revenue more difficult. In particular, it was harder to pull funds away from local community redevelopment agencies. So what Brown proposed was to abolish such agencies totally; the notion was that if they did not exist, the state could take their funds. The abolition was justified on the grounds that the job creation attributed to the agencies was dubious. However, local municipalities that had created such agencies did not see the issue that way nor did building trades unions. An eventual compromise was reached whereby the agencies could stay in operation as long as they paid the state for the privilege. The agencies took the issue, however, to the state supreme court.[42]

Dropping the Timetable

Brown appeared to believe that the Republicans would ultimately compromise and allow at least a vote on tax extensions by the end of June, but they did not. He did not have a budget enacted within his original time frame nor within any time frame that would allow a vote on tax extensions by June. That development meant he had to follow standard practice and produce a second modified budget proposal, the May revise.

He also had to either abandon the tax extensions or try to negotiate for enough Republican votes to put them on the ballot sometime after June. By that point, however, the extensions would be increases and unlikely to pass.[43] Nonetheless, Brown continued to negotiate with legislative Republicans into June, while giving continued assurances to Democrats that he could reach a deal. Brown did produce a May revise, and legislative leaders eventually pushed through a majority vote budget with no tax increases or extensions. But the story did not end with that vote.

Two Heroes

As the June 15 constitutional deadline approached, the Democratic majority in the legislature seemed to panic. Governor Brown's dealings with legislative Republicans seemed to be going nowhere. The Democrats quickly put together a budget that could be passed in time to avoid losing pay under the stricture of Proposition 25. In theory, the legislature could put together a budget that ostensibly was balanced by simply assuming sufficient revenue and including unspecified cuts. However, even a fanciful budget has to comply with the formula rules.

Although no complete package had ever been vetoed, Brown almost immediately vetoed the entire budget package, producing a drama that made him a media hero. Legislative leaders were miffed but noted that because they had passed a budget by June 15, their pay should not be cut under Proposition 25. They had complied with Proposition 25 even if the budget was not in effect due to the veto. At that point, state controller John Chiang stepped forward.

The controller declared that the legislature had not really passed a budget because, in his analysis, the legislators had in their haste not properly complied with required formulas and other technical elements. What he was saying was that to count as a true budget enacted by June 15, the plan had to be correct and that, in this case, the legislature had not done its sums correctly. There would be no pay until a correctly done budget was passed (even if it were fanciful). Chiang emerged as a second media hero for denying the legislators their daily bread. The fact that, in his analysis, any fanciful budget with the sums done correctly would pass muster was lost in the general celebratory atmosphere.

Final Enactment

On June 27, 2011, a deal was announced between Democratic legislative leaders and the governor. There would be an all-cuts budget that could be passed by majority vote. It would assume $4 billion in unspecified revenues beyond prior projections. In the past, there had been budgets that relied on forecasts of revenue that seemed dubious, but the supposed revenue was always allocated among the various taxes the state collects. In this case, however, the revenue was just an add-on above the regular projections and not added through any specific taxes.

In effect, the legislature was saying that it expected extra revenue to appear although it could not say from what source. However, the enacted budget provided a trigger mechanism that would mechanically cut the budget should total revenues fall short of assumptions by various amounts. Brown signed the budget, incorporating some line item vetoes, and Controller Chiang deemed it to be a real budget. The controller's decision thus made legislators eligible to be paid (although not for the interim between June 15 and passage of the second budget).[44]

The new budget was enacted in time to avoid any crises that might result from having no budget in place. But there were loose ends. Litigation continued under Proposition 22 over the compromise redevelopment plan that allowed community redevelopment agencies to operate if they agreed to pay the state for the privilege. The outcome of realignment as applied to state prisoners remained unclear. There was no certainty about revenues, including the added-on $4 billion. And whether the trigger would be pulled if revenues fell sufficiently short of projections was also unclear. What the legislature enacted in June—including the trigger—it could revise any time thereafter.

As Figure 10 indicates, on a cash basis, that the budget enacted for 2011–2012 would still leave the reserve in negative territory at the end of the fiscal year, even though receipts would exceed expenditures—that is, the budget would be in sufficient surplus to reduce the negative reserve but not to end it. On the accrual basis used by the governor, the reserve would end up positive but only by a little more than a billion dollars, a razor-thin amount in a budget of more than $88 billion. And if the $4 billion failed to appear and if the trigger were pulled, there could still be a negative reserve at the end of the year, depending on expenditures.

The Pension–Budget Link

In the months following budget enactment, the governor hinted that he would be making proposals to modify state and local public pensions. Indeed, some of his failed budget negotiations with legislative Republicans involved the pension issue. As noted earlier, Brown eventually did produce the outlines of a pension proposal in late October 2011 involving increased employee contributions for active workers and a two-tier hybrid approach for new hires that included a mix of defined benefit and defined contribution.[45]

Brown indicated he wanted a ballot proposition to approve his pension plan—presumably a proposition put on the ballot by the legislature. It is possible at this writing, however, that there could be competing propositions placed on the ballot by initiative, and it is likely that the pension proposals will become intertwined with negotiations over the budget for 2012–2013. Public sector unions might go along with some modified version of the Brown pension proposal, but only if they were to find the threat of alternatives to be an even less desirable outcome.[46] In contrast to the tax issue, which was so prominent in the 2011–2012 budget negotiations, some Republicans might go along with Brown on pensions. But he would still need a mix of Republican and Democratic votes to use the legislature as the route to the ballot. Brown could take the initiative route but would need funding for gathering signatures—and presumably not much funding would come from unions to take that route.

Conclusions

In a sense, there is no conclusion to California's fiscal drama. Year after year, new budgets must be enacted. Economic and political developments from outside the state have tended to be the ultimate driver of state fiscal affairs. At this writing, there is much uncertainty about the larger economic and political outlook. But there do seem to be some lessons from the California experience.

California's processes of direct democracy—as well as other institutional features of its internal polity—are clearly part of the mix of influences on the state's fiscal and labor responses to the Great Recession. Voters have enacted some reforms related to redistricting and to the format of primaries intended to lessen legislative partisanship and polarization. Various groups are touting other ballot initiatives to reform state government. Nonetheless, California has been operating with a structural budget problem going back to its insufficient adjustment to the impact of the end of the Cold War on federal military-related spending in the state.

The large geographic size of the state means that it is actually composed of regional economies. Thus, the decline in aerospace after the end of the Cold War was concentrated in Southern California. The dot-com boom and bust was largely a Bay Area phenomenon. Because much tax revenue is collected statewide and local government budgets are intertwined with the state budget, however, problems in one region are transmitted to others via the public sector.

The public sector response operates with a lag due to the ability of governments to pull down reserves and to borrow in various forms. In the Great Recession's aftermath, the lag was lengthened by the availability of federal stimulus funding, albeit with various limitations on that funding on state and local fiscal uses. Despite appeals for special assistance, Washington was reluctant to do any particular favors for California beyond the general aid available to all states.

Although public sector workers in California have the right to strike and collective bargaining is more prominent in California's public sector than in the average state, the strike weapon was not seen as effective by unions in most jurisdictions, given the impact of the Great Recession. Unions tended to use the political route to exercise whatever influence they could develop.

There were no serious moves to end collective bargaining in California along the lines found in Wisconsin and some other states. However, a proxy battle—yet to be resolved—was fought over the public pension issue. Early skirmishes over the pension issue tended to result in a two-tier approach of decreased benefits for new hires and increased employee contributions to pension funds. It is likely that the pension issue will heat up in 2012 with possible competing ballot propositions. There have already been some ballot skirmishes at the local level on pensions, and more seem to be on the way.

Despite seemingly unique features, California ultimately mirrors the national debate over the size and purpose of the public sector. At the national level, the Great Recession heightened tensions surrounding that grand debate. What emerges in California is likely to be more a reflection of the larger national conflict than that of strictly intrastate trends and developments.

Endnotes

[1] There have been more nuanced views since of the railroad and its impact on California's economic growth (Orsi 2007). Even as it squeezed local businesses through freight tariffs, the railroad's ultimate interest was a healthy state economy. The Big 4 were Leland Stanford, Mark Hopkins, Charles Crocker, and Collis Huntington, whose names remain on various contemporary San Francisco Bay Area institutions and locations (Rayner 2008).

[2] Republican governors—from Deukmejian in the 1980s to Wilson in the 1990s to Schwarzenegger in the 2000s—have long sought to take redistricting out of the hands of the Democratic-dominated legislature. When Republicans finally succeeded through a ballot proposition in winning such a procedure for the post-2010 U.S. Census redistricting, they subsequently became the procedure's most vociferous critics and filed referenda and litigation to overturn the outcome. The nonlegislative tribunal set up to do the redistricting, which consisted of citizens selected through a complex process, produced district maps that appeared to weaken Republican influence. The challenges were mounted against the state senate and congressional proposed districts. State assembly districts were not (at this writing) challenged.

[3] The California freeway system, established in 1947 under Governor Earl Warren, featured an earmarked gasoline tax and trust fund, the model later followed at the federal level (Mitchell 2006a).

[4] Kevin Starr (2009) describes the development of California in the post–World War II period.

[5] Proposition 13 was the result of a confluence of forces. There was a busing controversy in Los Angeles. Busing tended to disconnect white home owners in the San Fernando Valley, where much of the Proposition 13 agitation developed, from neighborhood schools—and schools and property taxes were linked. In addition, a series of court decisions had pushed for equalization of school finance across school districts. Thus, increased property taxes did not necessarily go to local schools because the state effectively rechanneled revenue to equalize per student funding.

[6] On the post-1990 period, see Starr (2004).

[7] Unionization data are from http://www.unionstats.com.

[8] A summary of California law regulating collective bargaining in the public sector can be found in Edelman and Mitchell (2004).

[9] The 2006 county stoppages took place in Santa Cruz, Sacramento, and Contra Costa (in addition to the City of Los Angeles stoppage mentioned in the text). The 2007 stoppages were in the transit district covering Orange County and the Hayward school district. Finally, the 2010 stoppages occurred in the Capistrano and Oakland school districts (http://www.bls.gov/wsp/#news).

[10] At the time, Governor Reagan was a potential candidate for the 1976 Republican presidential nomination, a goal he failed to achieve in 1976 but succeeded in attaining in 1980. Proposition 1 had it passed, would have been a political asset for Reagan in his 1976 effort (Mitchell 2007).

[11] The Gann limit was much simpler and less restrictive than Governor Reagan's Proposition 1.

[12] It appears that even the gutted Gann limit was actually reached at the peak of the tax revenues from the dot-com boom. But estimates of revenue at the time fell under the limit, so no action was taken.

[13] The files were downloaded from the U.S. Department of Labor website in August 2011. They are available online at http://www.dol.gov/olms/regs/compliance/cba/index. htm. Because the files refer only to contracts covering 1,000 or more workers, they may understate the importance of unions representing smaller units.

[14] For discussion, see Mitchell (2008b). Union officials sometimes explain the aversion to the ballot initiative approach by citing the costs involved compared to more traditional legislative lobbying.

[15] Paycheck protection measures require unions to obtain support from individual members before using dues money for political purposes. The 2005 version applied only to public sector unions, although it was unclear whether it would have affected union members in the private sector who also represented public workers. The 1998 measure applied to both sectors (Clark 1999). At this writing, it appears there will be another paycheck protection measure on the 2012 ballot.

[16] The spending cap was delayed to a later year.

[17] A union representing hotel workers succeeded in having the Los Angeles city council enact a living wage ordinance for hotels near the Los Angeles airport on the grounds that the hotels—while not providing services to the local government—were economically linked to the municipal airport.

[18] Conservative jurisdictions tended to enact blanket bans on project labor agreements. However, the legislature enacted a ban on enactment of local blanket bans. Thus, while local jurisdictions are not forced to use project labor agreements, they must make the decision on a case-by-case basis.

[19] The Inland Empire is generally considered the area east of Los Angeles, centered in Riverside and San Bernardino Counties.

[20] In Wisconsin, the Republican governor and legislature essentially ended collective bargaining as it had previously been practiced. A similar move occurred in Ohio, but voters reversed it in a referendum in November 2011.

[21] The fact that one Costa Mesa employee committed suicide by jumping off the roof of city hall especially attracted media attention.

[22] Among the San Francisco Democrats who were particularly active in pushing pension cutbacks were former mayor and speaker of the state assembly Willie Brown and public defender Jeff Adachi (a declared candidate for mayor in 2011). Adachi put two measures on the municipal ballot restricting San Francisco pensions. Both lost, the most recent in November 2011. An alternative proposition on pensions in San Francisco—negotiated by the mayor with local unions—was approved by voters in November 2011.

[23] For the study and its methodology, see California Foundation for Fiscal Responsibility (2011).

²⁴ Journalistic accounts of the poll focused on support for the remedies and not the plurality of respondents who felt that pensions were about right or insufficient (DiCamillo and Field 2011).

²⁵ The statement was made by Local 1000 president Yvonne Walker (Ortiz 2011).

²⁶ The budget data cited in the editorial were readily available (at the time) online from the California Department of Finance (Hirsch and Mitchell 2001).

²⁷ The data for Figure 10 come from the June monthly statements of the California state controller, available at http://www.controller.ca.gov.

²⁸ The data for budget year 2011–2012 come from the California Department of Finance and are available at http://www.dof.ca.gov/reports_and_periodicals/documents/2011%20BA%20Cash%20Flow%20for%20Web.pdf.

²⁹ Details of this period are discussed in Mitchell (2006b).

³⁰ A public pension initiative was supposed to be part of the package but was dropped from the group due to drafting problems.

³¹ Details of this episode are described in Mitchell (2008a).

³² Initially, unions opposed Governor Schwarzenegger's budget plans. But as will be noted later in this chapter, as the budget problem evolved, some unions cooperated with the governor (Mitchell 2009).

³³ In a top-two primary, all candidates of all parties initially run against each other. The top two run against each other in the general election. There is no partisan primary. The top two might thus be from the same party. Such primaries are in wide use in local governments in California. The theory is that in the primary with multiple candidates competing, there will be an incentive to appeal to voters from the minority party in order to put together enough votes to make it into the runoff. In partisan primaries, in contrast, the appeal is only within the party; thus, in Republican or Democratic majority districts, only the majority party has any chance in the general election, and minority party voters are without any influence.

³⁴ This section is based heavily on Mitchell (2011).

³⁵ The governor has line item veto powers when a new budget is enacted. Plaintiffs argued unsuccessfully that the budget revision was not a new budget, just a modification of an old one; therefore, the line item power did not apply.

³⁶ At the end of his term, Governor Schwarzenegger's reputation was tarnished by a prison sentence reduction he gave to the son of a political ally. Shortly after leaving office, a sex scandal within his family further damaged his standing. However, before either of these problems arose, Schwarzenegger's poll ratings in 2010 were virtually tied with those of Davis at the time of the 2003 recall.

³⁷ Under the standard procedure for state union contracts, the Legislative Analyst's Office issues a report on the contract terms and whatever savings it estimates. Those estimates typically were below the levels that had been announced earlier when the negotiations concluded.

³⁸ Brown ran unsuccessfully for the U.S. Senate in 1982 and lost to Pete Wilson. He was out of office for a time but came back to elective office as mayor of Oakland and then state attorney general. Thus, his campaign focused on having had long experience in state and local government.

³⁹ Whitman officially spent $178 million on the campaign, of which $144 million came from her personal fortune (see http://www.followthemoney.org/database/StateGlance/

candidate.phtml?c=116698). Brown spent about $41 million (see http://www.follow themoney.org/database/StateGlance/candidate.phtml?c=116678). It is impossible to track union support for Brown in dollar terms because of independent committees and the passing through of money from one committee to another. However, construction trades were prominent among the unions listed as donors by the official Brown for Governor 2010 committee, as were the various public sector unions such as SEIU and AFSCME (see http://www.electiontrack.com/lookup.php?committee=1321867).

[40] I have reported on Governor Brown's budget during his first year in office in Mitchell (2012).

[41] A multi-year approach is described in a letter to State Senator Mark Leno by the California Legislative Analyst's Office (2011a).

[42] That decision proved to be a fateful mistake for the agencies. The end result of the litigation was their total abolition!

[43] Brown tried unsuccessfully to persuade Republicans to go along with a bridge tax that would extend some of the temporary taxes up to the election, but there were no GOP votes for that proposal.

[44] There was successful litigation challenging the controller's action in withholding pay and suggestions that he had undermined his future political career by angering the legislature. But the lost pay was never recouped.

[45] California Governor (2011). Not all elements of the plan are clear from the official document. A detailed analysis of the plan can be found at California Legislative Analyst's Office (2011b).

[46] As noted earlier, SEIU and other unions did not take an explicit opposing position on the Brown plan for pensions—instead treating it politely in public as a starting point for a discussion. A political consultant for a union-backed group dealing with the public pension issue made it clear that the likely strategy would not be to back the Brown plan as presented. See Maviglio (2011).

References

California Foundation for Fiscal Responsibility. 2011 (Jul.). "California Public Sector Retirement Programs and Compensation." <http://www.fixpensionsfirst.com/docs/Full_Report.pdf>. [November 10, 2011].

California Governor. 2011 (Oct. 27). "12-Point Proposal Raises Retirement Age for Public Employees; Ends System-Wide Abuses and Cuts Costs for Taxpayers by Billions." Media release. <http://www.gov.ca.gov/news.php?id=17296>. [November 10, 2011].

California Legislative Analyst's Office. 2011a (Feb. 10). "Letter to Senator Mark Leno." <http://blogs.sacbee.com/capitolalertlatest/LAOall.pdf>. [November 10, 2011].

California Legislative Analyst's Office. 2011b (Nov. 8). "Public Pension and Retiree Health Benefits: An Initial Response to the Governor's Proposal." <http:// lao.ca.gov/reports/2011/stadm/pension_proposal/pension_proposal_110811.pdf>. [November 10, 2011].

Clark, Paul E. 1999. "Using Members' Dues for Political Purposes: The 'Paycheck Protection' Movement." *Journal of Labor Research*, Vol. 20, no. 3, 329–42.

DiCamillo, Mark, and Mervin Field. 2011 (Mar. 17). "More California Voters Now View Public Pension Benefits as Too Generous; Narrowly Oppose Taking Away Collective Bargaining Rights of Public Sector Employees; Majority Support for a Number of

Pension Reform Proposals." Media release of California Field Poll. <http://field.com/fieldpollonline/subscribers/Rls2369.pdf>. [November 10, 2011].

Edelman, Edmund D., and Daniel J.B. Mitchell. 2004. "Dealing with Public-Sector Labor Disputes: An Alternative Approach for California." In Daniel J.B. Mitchell, ed., *California Policy Options 2004*. Los Angeles: UCLA School of Public Affairs, pp. 151–80.

Hirsch, Werner Z., and Daniel J.B. Mitchell. 2001 (Feb. 12). "Surplus? California Is Running a Deficit." *Los Angeles Times*, p. B7.

Maviglio, Steve. 2011 (Nov. 9). "Why Labor Should Resist Brown's Pension Envy." Calbuzz. com. <http://www.calbuzz.com/2011/11/why-labor-should-resist-gov-browns-pension-envy/>. [November 10, 2011].

Mitchell, Daniel J.B. 2006a. "Earl Warren's Fight for California's Freeways, Setting a Path for the Nation." *Southern California Quarterly*, Vol. 88 (Summer), pp. 205–38.

Mitchell, Daniel J.B. 2006b. "'They Want to Destroy Me': How a California's Fiscal Crisis Became a War on 'Big Government Unions.'" *WorkingUSA*, Vol. 9 (Mar.), pp. 99–121.

Mitchell, Daniel J.B. 2007. "Governor Reagan's Ballot Box Budgeting: One That Got Away." *Southern California Quarterly*, Vol. 89 (Summer), pp. 195–227.

Mitchell, Daniel J.B. 2008a. "Something Different in the Air? The Collapse of the Schwarzenegger Health Plan in California." *WorkingUSA*, Vol. 11 (Jun.), pp. 199–218.

Mitchell, Daniel J.B. 2008b. "Unions and Direct Democracy in California: A New Pattern Emerging?" In Daniel J.B. Mitchell, ed., *California Policy Options 2008*. Los Angeles, UCLA School of Public Affairs, pp. 197–221.

Mitchell, Daniel J.B. 2009. "Division of Labor: California's Renewed Budget Crisis Splits the Union Movement." *WorkingUSA*, Vol. 12 (Dec.), pp. 591–609.

Mitchell, Daniel J.B. 2011. "Government by (Hot) Checks and (Im)Balances: California's State Budget from the May 2009 Voter Rejection to the October 2010 Budget Deal." In Daniel J.B. Mitchell, ed., *California Policy Options 2011*. Los Angeles: UCLA School of Public Affairs, pp. 11–67.

Mitchell, Daniel J.B. 2012. "Really! No Mental Reservations: Jerry Brown Inherits California's Budget Crisis." In Daniel J.B. Mitchell, ed., *California Policy Options 2012*. Los Angeles: UCLA Luskin School of Public Affairs, pp. 26–74.

Orsi, Richard J. 2007. *Sunset Limited: The Southern Pacific Railroad and the Development of the American West, 1850–1930*. Berkeley: University of California Press.

Ortiz, Jon. 2011 (Oct. 27). "SEIU Local 1000: Pension Proposals a 'Good Starting Point.'" State Worker blog of the *Sacramento Bee*. <http://blogs.sacbee.com/the_state_worker/2011/10/seiu-local-1000-pension-proposals-a-good-starting-point.html>. [November 10, 2011].

Rayner, Richard. 2008. *The Associates: Four Capitalists Who Created California*. New York: Norton.

Starr, Kevin. 2004. *Coast of Dreams: California on the Edge, 1990–2003*. New York: Knopf.

Starr, Kevin. 2009. *Golden Dreams: California in an Age of Abundance, 1950–1963*. New York: Oxford University Press.

Troy, Leo, and Neil Sheflin. 1995. *U.S. Union Sourcebook* (1st ed.). West Orange, NJ: Industrial Relations Data and Information Services.

UCLA Anderson Forecast. 2011. The UCLA Anderson Forecast for the Nation and California, September 2011. Los Angeles: UCLA.

Chapter 9

Public Service Cost Containment in Trinidad and Tobago: Assessing the Impact of Contract Employment

Charlene M.L. Roach

and

Gloria Davis-Cooper

The University of the West Indies

Introduction

This chapter focuses on examining and assessing the impact of using alternative methods to recruitment, such as contract employment, to assist with staffing and maintaining the workforce needs of the public service of Trinidad and Tobago (TT). Our approach comes during the wave of global economic recessionary forces, which compel governments to seek out new ways to create cost containment processes that can transform their public service delivery systems. Additionally, administrative reform initiatives (e.g., new public management, or NPM) are being applied to the public service of TT to enhance government's performance by using private sector techniques. The TT government is seeking ways to "do more with less" and to make the public sector more responsive to the demands of the economic environment. It is also exploring methods of stream-lining and preparing the workforce for the nation's strategic plan, Vision 2020, which is intended to make TT a developed nation by the year 2020. The chapter will also examine the lessons for other governments from TT's experience with contract employment.

Contract employment is a strategic tool used by the government within the TT public service in an effort to staff and maintain the workforce in an era of reform and cost containment. Our chapter examines and evaluates the use of this approach in staffing and maintaining the workforce as one alternative in human resource management (HRM) to recruitment. Theoretically, contracting falls under administrative reform measures, such as NPM, that explore private sector methods in order to make government bureaucracies and their agencies more effective, productive, and efficient (Osborne and Gaebler 1992).

We first highlight and explain the NPM concept and its philosophical underpinnings, principles, values, and implications for public bureaucracies such as the TT public service. Second, we expand on workforce staffing and maintenance principles and their rationale in HRM practice. Third, we examine strategies for cost containment that organizations pursue as alternatives to recruitment. More specifically, we describe and evaluate contracting, a private sector technique implemented in the TT public service. Fourth, we assess the impact of contract employment on the TT public service and the implications for the government's strategic priorities. Finally, our chapter examines the lessons that can be applied to other governments based on TT's experience with contract employment.

Background: The New Public Management Reform Initiatives

The NPM doctrine can be described as an administrative reform initiative that seeks to use private sector techniques and approaches to improve the efficiency, productivity, work processes, structures, services, and organizational outcomes for public sector agencies (Garson and Overman 1983; Hernes 2005; Khademian 1998). NPM reforms across nations focus on governments' attempts to do more with less. They attempt to promote and transform public bureaucracies that are underperforming into ones that can be effective and efficient. Since the 1980s, this approach has been applied to public agencies with the intent of changing the culture and work climate of these organizations, especially in an era of global economic recessions and cost containment efforts (Lynn 1998, 1999).

The NPM doctrine for this sector can be defined as including practical public management; performance measurement standards; concentration on output impacts, accountability, and transparency; decentralization; emphasis on continuous improvement (to enhance competitiveness, creativity, and successful results); and use of business or private sector techniques and approaches (Hood 1991, 1998). As a corollary, its philosophical underpinnings enshrine principles grounded in cutback methods, business/managerial reforms, competition, decentralization, restructuring, and privatization (Weikart 2001). Thus, NPM doctrines underscore values and principles of customer/client responsiveness, responsibility and accountability, innovation, increasing productivity and organizational performance, and reorganization or de-bureaucratization (Leland and Smirnova 2009; Vigoda-Gadot and Meiri 2008). The implications of NPM doctrine, values, principles, and philosophical underpinnings are to transform public bureaucracies by relying heavily on a business or private sector style of management.

Application to Trinidad and Tobago

When applied to the TT public service, NPM reforms reflect the changes seen through the introduction of contract employment: an emphasis on being more responsive to citizens' needs, on using performance management indicators, on restructuring government ministries and agencies, and on circumventing bureaucratic red tape in recruitment and selection. Despite contradictory views over the use and impact of NPM reforms in the TT public service, it is a compelling administrative reform agenda and promises to transform and reinvent the old ways of serving in public agencies, moving to a new way of serving the public through this businesslike orientation to administration and management. Contract employment (or contracting)—as an alternative to recruitment under the staffing function of HRM—can be analyzed under the lens of this NPM doctrine. The following section expands on the staffing function as it relates to recruitment and selection.

Staffing and Maintaining the Workforce—An HRM Practice

Staffing and maintaining the workforce is an umbrella concept used in HRM to include activities focused on recruiting, selecting, promoting, testing, developing, and evaluating human resources. These functions are critical to helping organizations consolidate their human capital and equipping them with the right numbers of employees with the requisite knowledge, skills, abilities, and aptitudes (KSAAs) needed to keep them current, productive, and able to accomplish the organizations' goals and objectives. In essence, staffing and maintaining the workforce as an HRM concept can be described as the lifeblood of the HRM system.

Recruitment refers to the HRM activities that affect the number and types of prospective employees who apply for a job and their acceptance of job offers. Recruitment can be a time-consuming and costly activity for organizations. Many employers do not commit adequate time and resources to it.

Alternatives to Recruitment as an Organizational Strategy

For various reasons, organizations may seek out alternative techniques to supplement recruitment and to allow them to accomplish goals, objectives, and strategies in cost-effective ways. The rationale behind these alternatives is to provide organizations with short-term measures to meet staffing needs without the long-term commitment that recruitment implies. Main alternatives include using overtime, temporary employees, and contract employment. The motivation is to allow organizations to have the KSAAs required to perform jobs and to reduce expenditures by lowering sunk costs incurred through pensions, compensation, higher salaries, and other benefits of permanent positions.

Overtime Employment

When facing pressures from the external environment, both public and private organizations might require employees in some instances to work overtime instead of exploring recruitment of additional permanent employees. This alternative to recruitment provides benefits to existing employees, who can earn extra income. In fact, through this approach, employees can learn new skills, increase their responsibilities, and facilitate their job advancement, rotation, and enrichment opportunities. The extra pay supplements their incomes while at the same time helping the organization fulfill its mandates.

Overtime allows organizations to circumvent costs associated with recruitment. However, long-term use of this option may create problems such as stress, workload pressures, and fatigue, and can lead to increased accidents at the workplace. As a strategic tool, this alternative should be used on a short-term to medium-term basis but certainly not in the long term. In addition to the limitations mentioned, long-term use of overtime employment can actually increase labor costs and ultimately lower productivity and employee performance.

Temporary Employment

Temporary employment has become a hallmark of cost-cutting measures in the past two decades. This alternative is attractive, especially when labor shortages increase. Historically, temporary employees have tended to be lower skilled, such as clerical and administrative staff. They are sometimes known as "just in time" employees and in contemporary HRM practices can be used to staff and maintain a variety of jobs.

The major benefit of temporary employment to the public service is that it enables organizations to hire lower-skilled employees with little or no formal training on temporary or short-term contracts without long-term employment contracts. Use of temporary employees reduces the cost of fringe benefits, training and development, and career planning. Employers face fewer risks and can remain resilient to changes in their environment that may require cost containment, downsizing, and other cost-cutting responses.

For instance, temporary workers move in and out of their organizations, depending on organizational workload pressures. They perform critical tasks in jobs that become vacant. In the long term, organizations gain by having a constant supply of employees who perform duties and responsibilities of various jobs with reduced expenditure. However, one downside of using this arrangement is that such workers do not develop long-standing ties to employers or become familiar with their organizational cultures. Loyalty and commitment to organizational goals are reduced.

Contract Employment (Contracting)

Contracting falls under NPM strategies of outsourcing or staff sourcing that are used to increase efficiency and productivity for organizations in times of either economic constraints or labor shortages. The use of this peripheral human resource pool is becoming a popular NPM strategy in public and private employment.

Contract employment positions are in principle not intended to be permanent but, as with temporary employees, allow large bureaucracies such as the TT public service to hire workers for special needs, such as hiring contract workers with information technology (IT) skills to support the creation of agency websites and other IT functions. Contract workers may be used for peak times and during unexpected increases in demand (Chen and Brudney 2009). Further, they assist in circumventing ceilings on regular employment levels (Ban 1999).

Hiring contract employees can be a strategic approach to developing knowledge within organizations (Matusik and Hill 1998). For example, contract employees with good skills and knowledge can fill organizations' KSAA gaps. Using nonstandard or contract employees gives organizations time to develop the KSAAs possessed by contract employees in their current employees. Time to develop KSAAs provides flexibility and anticipated cost savings to organizations, especially for employees with high skills (e.g., IT skills) who may be potentially expensive permanent employees.

But there are potential limitations from an HRM perspective. Some drawbacks noted in the literature include threats to permanent employees' job security and their quality of life at work. Public service employees might view contract employment as a precursor to privatization. For example, fears of privatization developed in TT when the People's National Movement (PNM) government proposed a policy to privatize the Inland Revenue Division and to create a new entity called the Trinidad and Tobago Revenue Authority in 2010. This move was thwarted with PNM's losses in the 2010 general elections. However, it did create anxiety, fear, and stress in the workforce before the proposal died.

Contract employees do not have to be on the permanent payroll and do not enjoy the same permanent benefits that public servants enjoy. They can be alienated from the organizational culture, deemed powerless, less loyal, and less committed to organizational goals and objectives. In the long term, these effects can have negative outcomes on employment relationships (Chen and Brudney 2009).

Contract employment is one of the three alternatives to recruitment and can be a powerful organizational strategy. Theoretically, organizations can benefit because there is no permanent obligation to contracted employees beyond their employment agreements. The way contract employment was practiced in Trinidad and Tobago is the subject of the remainder of this chapter.

The Impact of Contract Employment in Public Service

In this section, we focus on the impact of contract employment in the TT public service. We begin with a brief discussion of the nature of contract employment used in the TT public service. We highlight the areas of public service impact, which include transfer of KSAA factors, economic feasibility and organizational structure, employees' morale, performance management, loyalty and commitment, and the industrial relations climate.

The Nature of Contract Employment in TT

The first wave of public service contract employment began in the 1960s and was supported by the Civil Service Regulations of 1967. These regulations made provision for the re-employment of former employees who retired from public service and for the hiring of people who were not citizens of TT (Marchack, n.d.). It was felt that retired employees possessed knowledge, skills, and experience that would assist the public service in the delivery of goods and services.

By 1989, the period in which the government commenced public sector reform, the second wave of contract employment was well under way. However, there was need for a revised policy to support a modern system of contract recruitment that would include selection and placement of IT personnel and HRM practitioners. These employees were needed to assist with procurement of goods and services from national and international enterprises.

The TT government formulated revised guidelines for contract employment in ministries, departments, and statutory authorities, which were made public on August 1, 2004. These guidelines neither changed nor nullified prior contractual agreements. Instead they identified a number of situations in which such recruitment was acceptable (Marchack, n.d.).

There were various reasons in the guidelines for recruiting employees to serve in contract positions in the TT public service. For example, workers were needed to serve in vacant positions where there were no tenured government employees with the skills and knowledge to support the implementation of strategic policies and programs. Second, there were cases where government agencies were contemplating the commencement of specific projects and programs sponsored by international development agencies. Additional employees were needed either to implement or monitor those projects. Finally, there were situations in which the government lacked the specialized expertise to provide advice that a consultant could provide on the feasibility of projects and could not wait to create and fill such positions. Contract employment was the preferred route of employment in those instances.

Taking the decision to employ non-national workers on contracts required much thought by the TT government. When contracted employees were recruited to fill senior positions in public service, the government not only had to address probing questions from citizens and Parliament, but it also had to show the benefits to be derived from using foreign contract workers.

Impact of Contract Employment on Public Service

The government of TT intended for contract employees first to assist in the timely delivery of public goods and services to the citizenry and second to transfer KSAAs to tenured public servants engaged in the socioeconomic development process of the economy. For example, the competencies required to perform complex assignments in information and communication technology (ICT), human capital management, and most recently in national security were initially obtained from contract employees. Thereafter, those functions were expected to be performed by tenured employees.

We conducted unstructured interviews with selected groups of public officials from January through June 2011. These officials reported that contract employment had an impact on the public service. The areas of most impact were (1) transfer of KSAAs, (2) economic feasibility and organizational structure, (3) employee morale, (4) performance management, (5) loyalty and commitment of employees, and (6) the industrial relations climate. Each area is further explored.

Transfer of KSAAs

The government's strategic plans for contract employment included the timely delivery of public goods and services and enhancement of public service employees' knowledge base through transfer of KSAAs. Contract employees responded effectively with on-time service delivery in specific areas. Their attitude about work and their skills seemed to enable superior performance.

The subsequent transfer of KSAAs to tenured employees also led to improved government performance. For example, the processing and delivery of marriage, birth, and death certificates; property deeds; and passports were sped up by the use of contract workers. Before the use of contract workers in the ministries of Legal Affairs and National Security, time to process the documents ranged from six weeks to two months.

With the use of contract workers, however, the documents now can be obtained in one to three weeks.

Improvements were also achieved in the delivery of health care services because of the contributions of contract employees. Some health care institutions were upgraded, while others were established through the devolution of authority to the Ministry of Health in 1994. Four regional health authorities were created and staffed with doctors and nurses contracted to operate these modern health facilities, which had been established to care for all emergencies and patients experiencing chronic, noncommunicable, and lifestyle diseases (Government of Trinidad and Tobago Ministry of Health, n.d.).

The main reason for introducing contract employees into the traditional public service was to assist in developing knowledge workers in areas lacking them. The TT government recognized that its traditionally tenured public servants did not possess the competencies required for strategic policy formulation, implementation, monitoring, and analysis. It believed that its only alternative was to hire a contingency workforce that possessed training in business management and administration.

Contract employment was not new to the TT public service. As noted earlier, a policy was established in the 1960s for recruiting such workers at both technical and professional levels to assist in nation building. But could TT's Vision 2020—an effort to plan for growth through 2020—produce a more inclusive policy for the recruitment, selection, and placement of contract workers? The new policy covered recruitment of workers in all job categories: manual, secretarial, clerical, administrative, technical, and professional. The government had even expressed its intention to open up contract positions at the highest public service level of permanent secretary. The person holding a permanent secretary position is considered the chief executive officer of the ministry or agency for which he or she is responsible.

By the year 2000, TT's ministries, departments, and agencies employed workers in various positions requiring competencies in computer programming, human resources (HR), and customer relations, based on advice from various government-appointed task forces and committees in the respective fields (Bissessar 2007). Government officials collaborated with teams of entrepreneurs, academics, and business leaders to develop final policies to improve public service.

Trinidad and Tobago's first development pillar in Vision 2020—"Developing Innovative People"—was designed in the context of expectations that TT advancement into the 21st century by the year 2020 could be achieved with the support of highly skilled employees who possessed KSAAs in science, technology, and business. However, migration of highly skilled native workers to other developing and industrialized countries left the TT government with only one option: recruitment of expatriates on work permits. Over the longer term, there were also efforts at upgrading the country's education curriculum and improving HR strategies to attract scholars to serve in the public service.

On the whole, the impacts of these short-term and longer-term strategies are difficult to gauge. They are still a work in progress, and we cannot offer a definitive evaluation of the effectiveness of transferring the KSAAs to the TT public service. There is a lack of empirical data on outcomes. Thus, we had to rely on perceptions and comments made by public employees about contract workers.

Economic Feasibility and Organizational Structural Impacts

Compensation above the average paid to tenured employees had always been an issue when contract workers were used. Professionals recruited from the Caribbean region or beyond received larger compensation packages than their resident counterparts. The use of contract workers thus cost the government more than the use of locals, assuming locals were available.

Additionally, employee representative associations and trade unions felt the effects of contract labor in the public service. Contracted employees were not usually members of trade unions, which meant a loss of membership and dues. It has been argued that use of contract labor will undercut public trade unionism, and there have been calls for the government to end the practice (Roget 2011).

Contract employment affected the structure and composition of the public service. Policy guidelines required that contractual positions not have the same titles as existing jobs on the ministries' list of so-called establishment positions (positions of regular employees). However, in some cases the only difference between the jobs performed by public service employees and contract workers was the job title; the duties and responsibilities were essentially the same. Public service workers perceived that they performed the same job as contract employees but received lower pay. This practice gave rise to feelings of inequity and morale issues in the workplace.

Government officials were heavily involved in the recruitment and selection of contract workers. For example, any requests for contract employees had to be first submitted to the cabinet for approval by the minister who had responsibility for the government agency in question. The need for contract employees had to be justified. The minister was required to bring to the cabinet the job specification and description for the contract position in question and was required to identify funds to meet the expenses for filling that position. Only after cabinet approval had been received could a request be made to the chief personnel officer—the public official with responsibility for developing the terms and conditions of service for public employees. Typically, while contract employees' vacation leave entitlements were less than similar regular positions, their salaries could be twice as much.

Contract employment brought an additional responsibility to bear upon traditional public service because some workers who took contract positions in the TT public service were required to obtain work permits. Trinidad and Tobago's Ministry of National Security was responsible for issuing permits to foreign nationals who had skills or competencies not found in TT. The increase in the issuance of work permits required additional staff to complete the process. It also required personnel skilled in drafting the relevant documents for submission to the permanent secretary and thereafter to the cabinet for final approval.

There has been a steady increase in the distribution of work permits to foreign contract workers. Employees recruited from abroad included skilled engineers, welders, and electronic technicians who were employed in the ministries of Works and Transport, Energy and Energy Related Industries, and Trade and Industry. For example, 3,234 work permits were granted to foreigners in 2002. By 2005, that figure had increased to 4,444 workers—an increase of 27% in three years. A recent publication from the Trinidad and Tobago *Guardian* newspaper stated that, according to an official at the National Security Ministry, about 6,791 applications for work permits had been submitted. However, only 4,311 work permits were processed in 2010, indicating a slight decrease from previous years' figures.

The short supply of such skills in the TT public service is because the nation's education curriculum has offered few courses in the scientific and technological fields. This deficiency is being addressed by the TT governments (past and current), who see education and training of nationals as a strategic priority and policy mandate. Under programs such as Government Assistance for Tuition Expenses (GATE) and Higher Education Loan Program (HELP), TT nationals can obtain funding or qualify for free tuition to further their educational training. The objective is to develop and train TT nationals to fill these skill gaps in the labor force.

Contract employment therefore expanded the public service structure and inadvertently affected the culture of public service. The resulting problems also required tenured HR practitioners to obtain skills in diversity management to address the needs of expatriates. Two separate agencies were given responsibility for handling the affairs of contract employees based on their country of origin: The Ministry of Foreign Affairs was responsible for addressing the needs of citizens from other Caribbean countries, while the Ministry of National Security issued work permits to other international employees. This arrangement often led to overlapping functions and additional expenditure by TT government ministries.

Use of contract labor led to increased expenditure for advertising positions and assigning personnel to provide staff functions such as screening and selecting the right person to fill the vacancy. An additional cost was incurred for travel and accommodation when international and regional recruits were brought in for interviews.

It was costlier in the short run to recruit and employ expatriates because foreigners required salaries comparable to those of their peers in their home country. In addition, there were allowances, such as relocation and foreign service premiums, that were not paid to locals. It was therefore imperative that the TT government—based on its 2020 Vision—embark on outreach programs, projects, and workshops targeting secondary- and tertiary-level students. The goal was to inform them of the need for expertise in specific areas such as ICT, medicine, and entrepreneurship and to make them aware that public service could be seen as a desirable option for employment. Many highly skilled nationals preferred either to seek employment in the private sector or to emigrate.

Employee Morale

The morale of TT public employees was adversely affected by contract employment of non-nationals and other private sector employees. Many of these tenured public service workers had to train the new employees and orient them to the public service. More specifically, the supposed superiority of contract workers, hoarding of technical information, and contract workers' ignorance of public service rules and procedures all had a negative impact on the morale of permanent employees. Some contract workers became managers or heads of departments. In other cases, permanent employees were required to teach contract workers about work protocols, job requirements, procedures, rules, culture, and many other areas.

On the other hand, the TT government was encouraging public employees to be more client focused, customer driven, and goal oriented, all hallmarks of NPM principles. However, the introduction of contract and contingency labor was sending a negative message to tenured workers regarding their performance and competence levels. One of the government's strategic priorities was an educated workforce to enhance delivery of its goods and services. But its decision to introduce contract employment was perceived as a direct attack on the professionalism of public employees, which seriously impeded their productivity and performance.

This impact is still being felt as contract workers continue to be employed in the TT public service. Similar results have been reported elsewhere in the research literature (Chen and Brudney 2009; Pearce 1993).

Performance Management

The TT government placed tremendous importance on the performance management function in the public service, which had been redesigned in 2001 for tenured public employees. The new system was implemented to support and enhance employee development and performance toward the achievement of public service goals (Cooper 2010). Other requirements of the new employee performance and management system included (1) annual meetings of employees and supervisors to identify and agree on employees' duties, performance targets, and goals; (2) quarterly meetings to determine whether an employee was on target to achieving identified goals; and (3) agreement on training and development programs to reduce the gap between required and actual performance (Government of Trinidad and Tobago Ministry of Public Administration and Information 1995).

Public employees' pay, promotion, and long-term development were contingent on the quality of their performance. Each government agency was responsible for monitoring the performance of its contract employees; however, there was no established system to provide feedback on their performance. In spite of their ignorance of public service policies and procedures, these employees often had their contracts renewed with enhanced pay and benefits.

Contract employment afforded management in the central HR agencies the flexibility to hire and discipline workers as the need arose. But the discipline option was rarely used because politicians might have been responsible for the hiring of some individuals (Cooper 2010). This practice is supported by Mills' (1992) argument about "the nonsense of neutrality" in small nation states. Public employees, although required to serve whichever government was in power, have political party preferences and derive personal benefits from political patronage.

Loyalty and Commitment of Contract Workers

There is a perception that tenured public employees are more committed to the socioeconomic development of TT but lack the necessary competencies to lead the transformation process. However, while contract employees could assist in the transformation process, they could not take the lead because they were neither loyal nor fully committed to the public service organization. Most contracted employees have remained on the job because of the attractive reward packages. But there were some in very strategic positions who opted to leave for a new job with longevity and tenure.

This practice had a very negative impact on the government's socioeconomic development plan. It engaged the attention of and unions, which were opposed to contract employment in positions that might have been filled by tenured employees. Such a result is one of the risks or downsides in using contract employment. The nonpermanent status of such employment leads to less commitment to the organization with negative outcomes on employment relationships both for regular and contract employees. These outcomes are linked in the research literature to perceived psychological contract breaches and social exclusion (Chen and Brudney 2009; Pearce 1993).

The Industrial Relations Climate

Trinidad and Tobago had always prided itself on the outcomes of negotiations with employee representative associations and on its relatively stable industrial relations climate. However, contract employment has been a point of contention for most employee representative associations. From the union and HR points of view, contract employment in TT was abused and exploitative because there were no protection and benefits for contract employees.

Additionally, contract employment prevented some eligible tenured employees from attaining the highest ranks of their career tracks. The motivational effect of potential upward mobility was lost. At best, contract employment should be used only as a short-term measure. While there were critical areas such as ICT positions for which using the contract approach was an appropriate strategy, contract workers began to be used in noncritical areas.

In cases where both tenured and contract employment fail to meet the country's development goals, the government can resort to private sector management consultants, which is in effect another form of contract employment. Management consultants such as PricewaterhouseCoopers and KPMG Peat Marwick and Associates have provided services in the areas of strategic planning, succession planning, and general HRM to the TT government. However, these consultants were not held accountable for their performance. Trinidad and Tobago's government and senior public officials should have tried to place accountability measures in the consultant contracts but failed to do so. The lapses in accountability—both for contract workers and consultants—and the concerns of regular employees led to a deterioration in the industrial relations climate.

Implications of Contract Employment for TT Government's Strategic Priorities

By the year 2000, the government of TT had formulated its Vision 2020 strategic plan to upgrade the country to developed nation status by

2020. Embedded in this macro-socioeconomic development plan were strategies to position the TT economy to compete effectively in the global market. Also included was the goal of providing all citizens with a better quality of life, including health care services, education, recreation, and a cleaner environment.

The Vision 2020 strategic plan had five development pillars: (1) developing innovative people, (2) nurturing a caring society, (3) enabling competitive business, (4) investing in sound infrastructure, and (5) promoting effective government. Each development pillar had a series of objectives, goals, and targets, which were to be achieved through the support of a capable public service staffed by knowledgeable and competent employees. The government's strategic intent to train all public employees was never fully realized; therefore, the demand for trained workers far outweighed the supply and led to the continuous need for and use of contract labor.

The objective of achieving developed country status by the year 2020 included creation of a number of public service positions on a continuum ranging from professional to manual jobs. These positions included such diverse occupations as doctors, IT specialists, communication specialists, HR managers, teachers, nurses, office assistants, cleaning personnel, and messenger-drivers. The government's aim was to train young students to think innovatively and to retrain and develop public servants to increase their productivity levels while delivering quality goods and services. In spite of this goal, there was a continuous increase in the number of contract employees in all job categories under the former PNM government. Hence, contingent employees in the short- to medium-term levels helped to increase knowledge management and knowledge within the TT public service (Matusik and Hill 1998). But in the longer term, the goals went unfulfilled.

The People's Partnership Government, May 2010 to Present

In May 2010, a new People's Partnership (PP) government took office. In reviewing its introduction of new policies and policy guidelines to manage the public service, one can see common threads of policy. Indeed, the new government was committed, or perhaps more committed, to training and developing new or highly skilled employees. However, it has been applying its own systems to assess contract employment before continuing or renewing the policy of contracting inherited from the previous regime.

The PP government's manifesto emphasized that human capital should be efficiently allocated to enhance productivity and economic growth through the creation of jobs ("Prosperity for All" 2010). However, many employees who held contract positions under the previous PNM government have lost their jobs. The PP government has an unwritten policy that all contract positions must be re-advertised and all current incumbents, if interested in being retained, must present themselves for interviews along with other applicants.

This policy decision led to a reduction of workers previously employed by the former PNM government. However, there has been a gradual recruitment of new contract employees under the PP government. To date, it is too early to assess the impact of the new TT government's policy decisions on contract employment. Currently, the perception is that nothing has really changed from the previous regime.

Lessons Learned

Four important lessons can be learned from TT's experience with contract employment:

- Contract employment can be used as a strategic organizational tool to assist in national development.

- Contract employment can be a mechanism for the transfer of KSAAs to the public service workforce.

- Contract employment can be used as a cost-containment mechanism.

- Contract employment can be a mixed bag of both positive and negative results, so careful planning needs to be executed when introducing this alternative recruitment technique.

Strategic Organizational Tool

Contract employment was established as a strategically sound employment policy and was, in theory, in line with the TT government's socioeconomic development plans. Contract employment of non-nationals was used as a strategic organizational tool to assist the government with on-time delivery of goods and services and in achieving its development goals. It was felt that traditional public employees did not quite understand the urgency of the government's business plans.

Governments in the Caribbean are elected every five years, and this is a very short time to prove worthiness for re-election. There were programs, plans, and policies that needed implementation, some of which required expertise that the traditional public service employee did not possess. Since governments normally have a say in the recruitment of contract workers, these employees in most cases worked along with the politicians to get the jobs completed. Trinidad and Tobago's use of contract workers can therefore be emulated by other governments who are interested in the timely delivery of goods and services.

However, careful planning and close monitoring are needed. An absence of those actions can lead to problems in accountability, transparency, abuses of power, conflict of interest, increased expenditures, and other problems. For these reasons, when contract employment is introduced, governments need to design systems, structures, and processes to track performance.

Mechanism for the Transfer of KSAAs

The system of contract employment can be used to enhance the knowledge base and productivity levels of tenured public employees. Contract employees can be used to coach; transfer knowledge, skills, and abilities; and encourage tenured public employees to adopt the right attitudes. This strategy needs the support of politicians and senior public officials to be successful. Maintaining contract employees for an indefinite period on the payroll will incur an expenditure that a government can ill afford. Arrangements must be put in place to create accountability measures in order to be responsible to taxpayers.

For example, governments can gain from the knowledge management and knowledge creation that highly skilled contingent workers can transfer to organizations. However, this transfer is not automatic. Hence, contingent employees can benefit organizations by bringing new KSAAs and, when possible, sharing them throughout public bureaucracies (Matusik and Hill 1998).

Cost-Containment Measures Relative to the Duration of Implementation

Contract employment in Trinidad and Tobago increased expenditures in the short term. The initial period of employment of contract workers ranged from one to three years, with salaries equivalent to those paid in the private sector or in industrialized countries. When contracting was used, the TT government, of necessity, provided compensation packages that were superior to those paid in the public service. The higher pay was needed to attract foreign employees to work in a developing country whose system of governance was still evolving but which required skills and knowledge comparable to those needed in developed countries.

In the short term, an additional cost was incurred for the payment of allowances, such as housing, utilities, and entertainment, which were superior to those paid to tenured workers. A 20% gratuity at the end of each contracted period was another cost. However, the government realized some savings in the long term because the costs incurred for the payment of pensions of regular workers (especially to employees in professional and technical positions) were higher than for the payment of short-term contract gratuities. But exact calculations of the costs and benefits were not made. Close monitoring and financial reporting could help to alleviate any unnecessary costs in times of economic constraints.

When a contract worker went on vacation, no replacement or leave relief was provided. Therefore, no additional cost was incurred in the short term. However, when a tenured public servant went on paid vacation leave, an additional cost was incurred for the payment of salaries to a worker performing the duties of the employee on leave. It is unclear whether money is saved if contract workers' duties remain undone during their leave. Governments need to exercise caution in hiring contract employees, and they need to analyze the costs and benefits.

Adverse Effect on Public Employee Morale

Contract employment has had a negative impact on the morale and subsequent performance of TT's tenured public employees. They are paid less than contract workers but are expected to be loyal and committed to public service. In most cases, tenured public employees are required to train and familiarize contract workers to the rules, regulations, procedures, guidelines, and protocols of public service.

Yet contract workers' pay packages can be double or more those of tenured public employees, creating potential tensions. Governments worldwide must be cognizant of this challenge posed by contract employment and put systems in place to cope with potential negative psychological and social impacts on employee relations. They should identify and develop monetary and nonmonetary reward packages for employees who cooperate with contract workers to complete tasks.

Conclusion

Public sector organizations worldwide have used contract employment as a cost containment strategy to fill the gap between existing and required competencies necessary for achieving policy goals. They have embraced this approach as part of NPM administrative reform initiatives to make governments and their public sector organizations more efficient and operate on a more businesslike basis. The intent is to transform old bureaucracies into new ones that can be competitive, resilient, and dynamic.

While the use of contract labor has provided the TT's public service organizations with various opportunities to satisfy the needs of internal and external customers, some challenges exist in the areas of organizational strategy, economic feasibility, and organizational impacts. The TT government has benefited in three key areas from the use of contract workers:

- Contract employment provided support that ranged from ICT competencies to manual labor for various projects and programs required for achieving socioeconomic development.

- Contract employment enhanced the provision of quality of goods and services. It increased the provision of service delivery to the citizenry at large, especially in modern health care and educational services. Also enhanced were processing and distribution of important personal and legal documents, such as property, death, and birth certificates.

- Trinidad and Tobago benefited and continues to benefit from the transfer of KSAAs to nationals employed in fields such as ICT, customer service, security, and HRM.

The TT government claimed that contract labor contained long-term costs incurred for the payment of salaries, wages, benefits, and allowances to tenured public sector employees. However, there was no empirical evidence to support this assertion and no mechanism to gather the needed information. Governments of developing countries need to track actual outcomes of contract employment if it is to enhance their national development objectives.

References

Ban, C. 1999. "The Contingent Workforce in the US Federal Government: A Different Approach." *International Review of Administrative Science*, Vol. 65, pp. 41–54.

Bissessar, A. 2007. "New Public Sector Reform in Trinidad and Tobago." In Ann Marie Bissessar, ed., *Rethinking the Reform Question*. Newcastle, UK: Cambridge Scholars, pp. 131–33.

Chen, C.A., and J.L. Brudney. 2009. "A Cross-Sector Comparison of Using Nonstandard Workers: Explaining Use and Impacts on the Employment Relationship." *Administration & Society*, Vol. 41, pp. 313–39.

Cooper, G. 2010. *Capacity Building in Caribbean Bureaucracies: Structural and Human Resource Management Changes*. The University of the West Indies, St. Augustine Campus, St. Augustine, Trinidad.

Garson, G.D., and E.S. Overman. 1983. *Public Management Research in the United States*. New York: Praeger.

Government of Trinidad and Tobago Ministry of Health. No date. *About Ministry of Health*. <http://www.health.gov.tt/sitepages>. [August 21, 2011].

Government of Trinidad and Tobago Ministry of Public Administration and Information. 1995. *Shaping Performance: A Manual for Performance Management in the Public Service*. Government of the Republic of Trinidad and Tobago, Office of the Prime Minister, Ministry of Public Administration, Trinidad.

Hernes, T. 2005. "Four Ideal-Type Organizational Responses to New Public Management Reforms and Some Consequences." *International Review of Administrative Sciences*, Vol. 71, pp. 5–17.

Hood, C. 1991. "A Public Management for All Seasons?" *Public Administration*, Vol. 69 (Winter), pp. 3–19.

Hood, C. 1998. "Individualized Contacts for Top Public Servants: Copying Business, Path-Dependent Political Re-Engineering—or Trobriand Cricket?" *Governance: An International Journal of Policy and Administration*, Vol. 11, no. 4, pp. 443–62.

Khademian, A.M. 1998. "What Do We Want Public Managers to Be? Comparing Reforms." *Public Administration Review*, Vol. 58, pp. 269–73.

Leland, S., and O. Smirnova. 2009. "Reassessing Privatization Strategies 25 Years Later: Revisiting Perry and Babitsky's Comparative Performance Study of Urban Bus Transit Services." *Public Administration Review*, September/October, pp. 855–67.

Lynn, L.E. 1998. "Public Management: How to Transform a Theme into a Legacy." *Public Administration Review*, Vol. 58, pp. 231–37.

Lynn, L. 1999. "The New Public Management." *Government Finance Review*, Vol. 15, pp. 15–8.

Marchack, S. No date. *Alternative Recruitment Strategies Case Study on Contract Employment in the Public Service of Trinidad and Tobago*. <http://unpan1.un.org/intradoc/groups/public/documents/UN/UNPAN021826.pdf>. [September 30, 2011].

Matusik, S.F., and C.W.L. Hill. 1998. "The Utilization of Contingent Work, Knowledge Creation, and Competitive Advantage." *Academy of Management Review*, Vol. 23, pp. 680–97.

Mills, G.E. 1992. "Caribbean Public Administration." In S. Ryan and D. Brown, eds., *Neutrality and Commitment: Issues and Problems*. St. Augustine, Trinidad: Institute of Social and Economic Research, University of the West Indies.

Osborne, D., and T. Gaebler. 1992. *Reinventing Government: How the Entrepreneurial Spirit Is Transforming the Public Sector*. Reading, MA: Addison-Wesley.

Pearce, J.L. 1993. "Toward an Organizational Behavior of Contract Laborers: Their Psychological Involvement and Effects on Employee Co-Workers." *Academy of Management Journal*, Vol. 36, pp. 1082–96.

Prosperity for All Manifesto. 2010. People's Partnership Government.

Roget, A. 2011. Address to OWTU Trade Union Members on Government's Wage Strategy. Port of Spain, Trinidad.

Trinidad and Tobago Civil Service Regulations. 1967. Port of Spain: Government Printer.

Trinidad and Tobago Government Portal. *Vision 2020 Operational Plan 2007–2010*. November 2006.

Vigoda-Gadot, E., and S. Meiri. 2008. "New Public Management Values and Person–Organization Fit: A Socio-Psychological Approach and Empirical Examination Among Public Sector Personnel." *Public Administration*, Vol. 86, no. 1, pp. 111–31.

Weikart, L.A. 2001. "The Giuliani Administration and the New Public Management in New York City." *Urban Affairs Review*, Vol. 36, pp. 359–81.

ABOUT THE CONTRIBUTORS

Keith A. Bender is a professor in the Department of Economics and the graduate program in Human Resources and Labor Relations at the University of Wisconsin–Milwaukee. Since graduating with his Ph.D. in economics from Duke University, he has held positions at the University of Aberdeen, Louisiana State University, and the Social Security Administration. He has also held visiting positions at the University of Flinders and Giessen University. His research interests are public sector labor markets, the economics of aging, compensating differentials, and the economics of subjective well-being.

Ilana Boivie is a research economist for the Communications Workers of America, where she serves as the Research Department's subject-matter expert on pensions and retirement policy. Before joining the CWA, she was director of programs for the National Institute on Retirement Security, where she conducted original research and analysis of U.S. retirement issues, frequently spoke on retirement and economic matters, and testified before policy makers about her research. She holds an M.A. in economics from New Mexico State University and a B.A. in English from Binghamton University, where she graduated magna cum laude.

Ellen Dannin is the Fannie Weiss Distinguished Faculty Scholar and Professor of Law at Pennsylvania State University. She is the author of *Taking Back the Workers' Law—How to Fight the Assault on Labor Rights* and is currently working on another book, *Thinking About Privatization? Who Does the Work and Why It Matters*. Dannin joined the Penn State Dickinson School of Law faculty in 2006 after teaching at Wayne State University Law School and in San Diego at California Western School of Law. She writes primarily in the areas of collective bargaining, privatization, New Zealand labor law, and legal education. Before entering teaching, Dannin was a trial attorney with the National Labor Relations Board. She regularly teaches courses in labor law and employment law and has taught various labor law seminars and public sector labor law.

Gloria Davis-Cooper is an assistant lecturer in the Management Studies Department at The University of West Indies. She has a B.S. in sociology with government, an M.S. in government, and an M.Ph. in governance from The University of West Indies, St. Augustine/Mona campuses. She has lectured for more than a decade in the Faculty of Social Sciences. Her research and teaching interests are in the areas of organizational behavior/ studies, public management, human resource management/development, and public policy analysis. She has more than 30 years of experience in public management and administration in Trinidad and Tobago's public services.

Sabina Dewan is the director of globalization and international employment at the Center for American Progress. She conducts research and analysis on the impact of globalization, especially trade, on international labor markets. Dewan also directs the Just Jobs Network, an international alliance of institutions that carries out joint research and advocacy to improve the quantity and quality of jobs to boost aggregate demand, create a fairer competitive playing field, and promote more inclusive economic growth. Dewan's past experience includes working at the International Labour Organization, the European Commission, and the United Nations Girls' Education Initiative. She has an advanced master's degree in quantitative studies from the Catholic University of Brussels and a second master's degree in public policy from the University of California, Los Angeles.

John S. Heywood is Distinguished Professor of Economics and director of the graduate program in Human Resources and Labor Relations at the University of Wisconsin–Milwaukee. An expert in compensation and the economics of personnel, he has held appointments in the United Kingdom, Germany, Hong Kong, and Australia. His research examines performance pay, earnings discrimination by race and gender, the determinants and consequences of family-friendly firm practices, public sector labor markets, and the economics of trade unions.

David Lewin is the Neil H. Jacoby Professor of Management, Human Resources and Organizational Behavior at the UCLA Anderson School of Management and formerly served as director of the UCLA Institute for Research on Labor and Employment. He has published widely on such topics as employment dispute resolution, wage determination, regulation of the employment relationship, and human resources and business performance. Before joining UCLA, he served as professor, director of the Ph.D. program, and director of the Human Resources Research Center at the Columbia University Graduate School of Business. Lewin is president of LERA.

Daniel J.B. Mitchell is a professor emeritus at the UCLA Anderson School of Management and the UCLA Luskin School of Public Affairs. Since retiring, he continues to teach a course on California policy issues and edits *California Policy Options*. His chapter on the California state budget appears in that annual volume. Mitchell is senior academic editor for the Employment Policy Research Network and handles the daily blogging for the UCLA Faculty Association. He received LERA's Excellence in Education award in 2007 and its Susan C. Eaton Outstanding Scholar-Practitioner Award in 2011.

Charlene M.L. Roach is a former Fulbright scholar and is a lecturer in the Department of Behavioral Sciences, The University of The West Indies, St. Augustine Campus, where she earned her undergraduate degree. She obtained her M.P.A. and Ph.D. in public administration from Arizona State University. Her areas of research and teaching are in public management/ public human resource management, organizational behavior/studies for the public sector, and e-government. She is a foreign correspondent for an international teaching and learning journal, *The Journal of Public Affairs Education*, and a reviewer for a Caribbean teaching and learning journal.

William M. Rodgers III is a professor of public policy and chief economist at the Heldrich Center for Workforce Development at the Bloustein School of Planning and Public Policy, Rutgers University. He is also a member of the graduate faculty of Rutgers School of Management and Labor Relations and a senior research affiliate of the National Poverty Center, University of Michigan. Rodgers is a member of the National Academy of Social Insurance and serves on its board of directors. In 2000, Rodgers served as chief economist at the U.S. Department of Labor, appointed by Alexis Herman, U.S. Secretary of Labor.

Mildred E. Warner is a professor of city and regional planning at Cornell University. Her research focuses on devolution and privatization and new models of service delivery among U.S. local governments. She has consulted widely with local government associations, including the International City/County Management Association, and with public sector unions such as AFSCME, AFT, CUPE, and PSI.

Christian E. Weller is a professor of public policy at the University of Massachusetts–Boston and a Senior Fellow at the Center for American Progress. He specializes in retirement income security, wealth inequality and risk exposure, and international financial instability. He has published more than 100 academic works in journals such as the *Cambridge Journal of Economics*, the *Journal of Policy Analysis and Management*, the *Journal of International Business Studies*, and the *Journal of Aging and Social Policy* and in more than 300 popular publications. His work is frequently cited in the press. Weller holds a Ph.D. in economics from the University of Massachusetts–Amherst.